THAT SPLENDID LITTLE WAR

A Comprehensive Guide to Spanish-American War Research

Including the Boxer Rebellion and the Philippine Insurrection

Michael L. Strauss, AG®

Heritage Books
2025

HERITAGE BOOKS

AN IMPRINT OF HERITAGE BOOKS, INC.

Books, CDs, and more—Worldwide

For our listing of thousands of titles see our website
at
www.HeritageBooks.com

Published 2025 by
HERITAGE BOOKS, INC.
Publishing Division
5810 Ruatan Street
Berwyn Heights, MD 20740

Front Cover—Lieutenant Colonel John Jacob Astor, Inspector General of United States Volunteers with the 5th Army Corps, pictured with his staff in 1898 in Cuba.

Back Cover (top right)—Three soldiers of Company K of the 30th United States Volunteer Infantry were taken in the Philippines in 1901. One is identified and pictured on the left: Private John M. Bicknell.

Back Cover (lower left)—Photo of the author.

All three photographs are courtesy of Michael L. Strauss

International Standard Book Number
Paperbound: 978-0-7884-4731-0

Dedication

To my wife Diane and each of my children, Christine, Stephanie, Levi, Jacob, Katarina, Elijah, and Helena. Their encouragement and support have been vital to the writing of this book.

Acknowledgment

With all research and writing projects, any author owes a debt of gratitude to persons and institutions that made their work possible. First, thanks are due to Ralph C. Tobias, who spent countless hours reading, editing, and proofing the original manuscript for final publication. Special thanks are also owed to Jeanette Juryea, who helped me understand how to print and edit written material for publication.

Several key research institutions and archives were consulted, including the National Archives and the Library of Congress in Washington, DC; United States Army Heritage and Education Center in Carlisle, Pennsylvania; United States Coast Guard Historian's Office in Washington, DC; United States Navy History and Heritage Command Center in Washington, DC; National Museum and Marine Corps History Division Archives in Quantico, Virginia; and the Church of Jesus Christ of Latter-day Saints Family History Library in Salt Lake City, Utah. All of these facilities and their dedicated staff offered invaluable research assistance.

Michael L. Strauss, AG®

Table of Contents

Introduction

The end of the nineteenth century witnessed the transformation of the United States from a developing nation into a global power. Historical and genealogical records document the lives of participants who fought in this war and later in the Boxer Rebellion and Philippine Insurrection.

Spanish-American War

The history of the conflict dates to the late 19th century, involving a complex web of politics, economics, and social factors. Spain's gradual decline as a world power and the United States' growing imperialistic ambitions set the stage for conflict between both countries. Events would unfold in Cuba generated by simmering discontent among the native population seeking their independence from Spain in 1895. Fueled by economic hardship, discontent turned quickly to violence, with Spain employing brutal tactics to suppress the local populace from thoughts of revolution. Spain dispatched military General Valeriano Weyler y Nicolau (1838-1930) to Cuba, where concentration camps were built in which thousands died of disease and starvation. The ruthless treatment of innocent noncombatants garnered international criticism, drawing the attention of the United States and other world powers.[1]

Figure 1: Courtesy of Library of Congress

The United States during this period experienced rapid economic growth and plotted territorial expansion amid the growing sympathy and demands for intervention. The United States Navy in January 1898, ordered the battleship USS *Maine* (pictured on the left) to Cuba to safeguard the lives of American citizens and financial interests should tensions escalate between the countries.

The warship's presence was intended to serve as a deterrent against further Spanish aggression in Cuba. Upon the warship's arrival in February 1898, tensions between the United States and Spain reached a boiling point with the explosion of the USS *Maine*, the pride of the Navy, in Havana Harbor on the evening of February 15, 1898, with a loss of 260 men onboard.[2]

---

[1] David F. Trask, *The War with Spain in 1898* (Lincoln: University of Nebraska Press, 1981), 8-9.

[2] Paul H. Silverstone, *The New Navy, 1883-1922* (New York: Routledge, 2006), 6-8; and Allan R. Millett and Peter Maslowski, *For the Common Defense: A Military History of the United States of America* (New York: Free Press, 1994), 284-285. Most historians accept that, out of the warship complement of 374 who served onboard the USS *Maine*, either 260 (from Silverstone) or 266 (from Millett and Maslowski) sailors died from the explosion in 1898.

The causes surrounding the explosion remain in dispute with President William McKinley urging patience while investigating the nature of the sinking of the great battleship. Other United States citizens were reluctant to accept this answer and blamed Spain for the incident. Sensationalist American newspapers, including William Randolph Hearst's publication in the *New York Journal* and Joseph Pulitzer's newspapers in the *New York World*, seized upon the moment to fuel public sentiment, arguing for a formal declaration of war against Spain. The newspaper rallying cry of *Remember the Maine, To Hell with Spain* appeared as headlines were used to fuel the emblematic war fever gripping the nation.[3]

Under pressure from public opinion and elected members of the United States Congress, President William McKinley grudgingly declared war on Spain on April 25, 1898. The war quickly spread across the Caribbean and the Pacific theater. One of the first major war campaigns was the Battle of Manila Bay, in the Philippines, fought on May 1, 1898, with United States naval forces under the command of Commodore George Dewey. The Navy fleet Asiatic Squadron decisively overwhelmed the Spanish Pacific Squadron, efficiently safeguarding American control over the Philippines Islands. The naval victory at Manila Bay paved the way for United States ground forces to occupy Manila. Concerned over having insufficient men to mount an attack, Army personnel were dispatched to the Philippines, where resistance leader General Emilio Aguinaldo aided the men. On August 13, 1898, the final assault on Manila began with a bombardment of Spanish defenses, leading to surrender, which resulted in the Philippine populace believing the United States would help them gain their independence. Among other supporters, expansionists in the United States had other ideas, leading to hostilities in 1899 during the Philippine Insurrection.[4]

The victory highlighted the strength of the United States Navy as a formidable sea power, spelling the end of Spanish domination in the region. Closer to our boundaries, a joint military operation between the United States Army contingent in command of Major General William R. Shafter defeated the Spanish military defenders at the Battle of Santiago de Cuba on 1 July 1898. The attacks climax and victory fought at San Juan Hill led by Lieutenant Colonel Theodore Roosevelt of the 1st United States Volunteer Cavalry, known as the *Rough Riders* for the background of the soldiers, preserved their place in the annals of military history. Fighting to support the land operations, the United States naval forces, commanded by Admiral William T. Sampson and Commodore Winfield Scott Schley, effectively destroyed the Spanish Caribbean Squadron, thus paving the way to final victory for the United States.[5] Following this victory, one final military operation shifted to Puerto Rico, which began on 25 July 1898, when United States military forces engaged the Spanish defenders at Guanica, Puerto Rico. Over several weeks, the fighting continued with skirmishes across the island until the Spanish garrisons surrendered in Puerto Rico on 13 August 1898, ending their control of the region.[6]

---

[3] Ivan Musicant, *Empire by Default: The Spanish-American War and the Dawn of the American Century* (New York: Henry Holt and Company, 1998), 143-147.

[4] Ibid., 213-223, 572-582.

[5] Stan Cohen, *Images of the Spanish-American War, April-August 1898* (Missoula: Pictorial Histories Publishing Company, 1997), 123-125. Colonel Leonard Wood commanded the 1st United States Volunteer Cavalry (in command of the 2nd Brigade, Cavalry Division), with Roosevelt second in command and leading the regiment at the battle on 1 July 1898. His men fought on Kettle Hill before ascending San Juan Hill (or Heights) and defeating the Spanish defenders. The battle of Santiago de Cuba also took other actions at El Cancy.

[6] Musicant, *Empire by Default*, 520-533.

The end of the war came to a swift conclusion with the Spanish meeting at the negotiation table and signing of the Treaty of Paris (in the drawing below) on 10 December 1898. The provisions of the treaty would cede control of Puerto Rico, Guam, and the Philippines to the United States, and recognizing the independence of Cuba.

THE SPANISH-AMERICAN TREATY OF PEACE, PARIS DEC 10 1898.

Figure 2: Courtesy of Library of Congress

The United States also acquired the Philippines from the Spanish, where independence was not immediate, which the following year would bring our country into conflict again. The acquisition of new territories marked a significant expansion of influence in the Caribbean and Pacific, fortifying the United States status as a global power. The war also raised questions about our role as an imperialistic nation that sparked debate about the moral obligations to our newly acquired territories.[7]

Boxer Rebellion

The beginning of the 20th century found China in a state of internal confusion; and wrought with external pressures from foreign powers. The seat of government of the Qing Dynasty was weakened in China by corruption and the inability to control the population in its vast territories.

---

[7] Trask, *The War with Spain in 1898,* 445-482, 484.

Outsider Western nations attempted to influence China through industrialization, imperialism, and market forces by exploiting the local populace for personal financial gains. At the core of the internal problems in China, a militant crusade led by members of the Society of Righteous and Harmonious Fists, known as the Boxers, gained support among the rural peasantry and urban poor to expel Westerners from the country and were viewed as champions against malevolent western influences.[8]

Violence erupted in mainland China during the Spring of 1900 when the Boxers moved in force to besiege the ancient city of Peking, where a Western force of men defended the legations. On May 30, 1900, the defenders sent an urgent plea for help for soldiers to aid the beleaguered foreign missionaries, Christians, and other business interests holed up in the legations.

Figure 3: Courtesy of National Archives

The

The United States and seven other countries responded by dispatching hundreds of sailors and marines (the group pictured in Figure 3 sent in relief of the siege of Peking) to the city defenses who arrived by June 4, 1900. Afterward, the Boxers began their deadly assault on the foreigners

---

[8] Mitchell G. Klingenberg, *Lessons in Coalition Warfighting from the Boxer Uprising* (Carlisle: United States Army War College Press, 2023), 19-26.

dcfcnding within the walls of the legation. The image on the left page shows a small detachment of United States Marines defending the legations.[9]

Word was transmitted outside the legations to relieve the defenders at Peking before they were overwhelmed and defeated. On June 9, 1900, the first coalition forces left Tientsin, China, with 2,100 men from the United States, England, Germany, Russia, France, Japan, Italy, and Austria to send aid to the legation garrison. Strong Boxer opposition forced the relief column to return to Tientsin in another attempt to break the siege. On August 5, 1900, the Allied forces mounted another relief expedition of between 18,000 to 20,000 men who managed to break through the encircled lines of the legation defenders after fighting two battles against the Boxers and their supporters. The larger expeditionary forces reached the foreign legations and relieved the defenders on August 14, 1900, after a period of 55 days under siege. Veterans of the United States Regular Army and the Navy and Marine Corps participated in defeating the Boxers. Volunteer militia and soldiers were not recruited for the fighting in China.[10]

The Boxers' defeat and the westerner's relief had long-term consequences for China and their international relations. In the aftermath of internal fighting, the Qing Dynasty was further weakened, which hastened its eventual takeover for establishing the Republic of China in 1912. The Boxer Rebellion made visible the susceptibilities of China's traditional military and social structures in the face of modern military practices and the use of weaponry. The failure to banish foreigners and restore Chinese sovereignty made China embark on modernization and reform to compete economically and politically with the Western powers.[11]

Philippine Insurrection

Following the end of the Spanish-American War in 1898, this struggle would arise due to the tumultuous relationship between the United States and the Philippines. The conflict was deeply rooted in aspirations for Philippine independence. Filipino nationalists allied themselves with the United States and sought to revolt against Spain in 1898 with the support of the United States. With the defeat of Spain, many Filipinos anticipated their independence, which quickly turned to opposition under the leadership of General Emilio Aguinaldo, a prominent leader in the revolution against Spain, now emerged as a central figure in this resistance, leading the local populace in opposition to American occupation. The conflict came to be known as the Philippine Insurrection or the Philippine-American War.[12]

---

[9] Paul A. Cohen, *History in Three Keys: The Boxers as Event, Experience and Myth* (New York: Columbia University Press, 1997), 3-14. The ancient city of Peking, also called Pekin, is now known as Beijing.
[10] Diana Preston, *The Boxer Rebellion: The Dramatic Story of China's War on Foreigners that Shook the World in the Summer of 1900* (New York: Berkley Books, 2000), 89-105, 213-233.
[11] Ibid., 320-361.
[12] Brian McAllister Linn, *The Philippine War, 1899–1902* (Lawrence: University Press of Kansas, 2000), 3-41.

Using unrestricted guerrilla warfare tactics, Filipino insurgents led by Aguinaldo and other leaders used hit-and-run attacks, traps, and acts of sabotage against a numerically superior military force of men from the United States Army. Fighting between both factions broke out on February 4, 1899, in what was the Battle of Manila.[13] The officers and men of the American Army struggled to acclimate to the strange topography and the radical warfare tactics employed by the insurgents, which led to brutal fighting characterized by widespread violence and killings by the military forces on both sides. To combat the stiff resistance of Filipino insurgents' American military forces waged a war of attrition aimed at depriving the enemy of support by destroying their lines of supplies, villages, and means to prolong their fight. Pictured below is the village of Pasig burning with members of the Hawthorne Artillery Battery in the foreground.[14]

Figure 4: Courtesy of Library of Congress

Gradually, the fighting during the Philippine Insurrection reached a turning point following the capture of General Aguinaldo on March 23, 1901, by American soldiers of the United States Army in the command of Colonel Frederick Funston. Aguinaldo's capture significantly affected

[13] Ibid., 42-64.
[14] John Morgan Gates, "The Nature of the Anti-American Resistance Movement in the Philippines, 1899-1901." *The Journal of Asian Studies* 59:3 (2000): 619–640.

the insurgents and the Filipino resistance movement. After his capture, fighting continued for more than a year until hostilities ceased between each side, and the United States officially declared an end on July 2, 1902, to the fighting. Despite the declaration, some Filipino insurgents continued to resist for several more years.[15] The Philippine Insurrection was costly for both sides, with American military casualties of 4,234 soldiers killed and thousands more wounded. For the Filipino population, civilian deaths ranged in the tens of thousands shamelessly killed.[16]

The Philippine Insurrection had profound and enduring significance in the relationship between the United States and the Philippines. The islands experienced American colonial rule with a legacy of resentment in the beginning, leading in 1934 to the United States Congress passage of the Tydings-McDuffie Act (helping their people adopt a formal Constitution), which in turn led them to gain their independence in 1946. For the United States, the insurrection provoked some debate on the morality and worth of imperialist endeavors, which helped to shape the United States' foreign policy decisions and discernments over the use of American power. The historical background shared in the introduction of all three conflicts aids in understanding the different records created during and after the end of the fighting. Using service records, pensions, and other appropriate genealogical material provides answers to questions about veterans who served in any of the wars found in the chapters of this monograph.[17]

GENEALOGY CLUE: When viewing the alphabetical indexes for pensions covering from 1861-1934, the words *"War with Spain"* will help distinguish this conflict from the Civil War. Regiment designations were repeated in each of the war periods. Knowing the war will help eliminate needless time wasted.

---

[15] Stuart Creighton Miller, *Benevolent Assimilation: The American Conquest of the Philippines, 1899–1903* (Westford: Yale University Press, 1982), 168-170, 250.
[16] Michael Clodfelter, *Warfare and Armed Conflicts: A Statistical Encyclopedia of Casualty and Other Figures, 1492-2015* (Jefferson: McFarland & Company, 2017), 240-241. The number of Filipinos killed was at least 16,000, with another 200,000 civilians who died from diseases and starvation.
[17] Miller, *Benevolent Assimilation*, 253-267.

Compiled Military Service Records

Compiled Military Service Records is one of the first records to study to document Spanish-American War and Philippine Insurrection veterans. Commonly abbreviated as CMSR, the records cover soldiers in volunteer military organizations. The records were first indexed and organized under the direction of General Fred C. Ainsworth to gain more permanent access. Genealogists owe much to Ainsworth and his team of clerks for the records he provided. A native of Vermont, Ainsworth joined the United States Army in 1874 and later was appointed head of the Records & Pension (called the R&P) Office in 1886. By 1889, this office was called the Records & Pension Division of the Surgeon General Office.

The work of the pension office during the late nineteenth century required veterans who applied for their pensions or other benefits to be painstakingly researched to validate their claims of service. This process was time-consuming and labor-intensive. General Ainsworth suggested that the United States War Department index and catalog all volunteer soldiers and military units from the Revolutionary War through the Philippine Insurrection. By late 1894, the Mexican War, Civil War, and Indian Wars were complete, and carding of the prior War of 1812 and the Revolutionary War was begun. The older wars used Treasury, Interior, and State Department records to replace information lost in a disastrous fire on November 8, 1800.[18]

Figure 5: Courtesy of National Archives

On May 15, 1894, at the direction of Secretary of War Daniel S. Lamont, a decision was made that would impact the CMSRs and the way they were cataloged with the R&P Office in charge of all volunteer enlistments. The Spanish-American War and the Philippine Insurrection soldiers were indexed and cataloged in real time, often as the events occurred to the soldiers in the field. The original muster rolls and other documents were quickly turned over to Ainsworth. This would change by 1907. Beginning in 1904, the War Department began a restructuring as the R&P Office was merged with the AGO office. In turn, Ainsworth would have control over the records of both the Regular and Volunteer Armies. This change came too late to affect the Regular Army documents because Ainsworth's clerks were still working on recording all of the information from the Confederates during the late Civil War. Therefore, the Regular Army was never card-indexed or cataloged by Ainsworth. The Adjutant General Office would have that responsibility. Ainsworth served as the Adjutant General of the United States Army from 1904

---

[18] Claire Prechtel-Kluskens, "Thank You General Fred C. Ainsworth" *NGS Magazine* 37: 4 (October-December 2011), 54-57; and Siert F. Riepma "A Soldier Archivist and His Records: Major General Fred C. Ainsworth" *American Archivist* 4: 3 (July, 1941), 178-187.

until 1912, when he resigned from his position. The reason for his resignation was rather complicated, but the Secretary of War Henry Stimson proposed the reorganization of the Army Staff, thereby having each of the Department Heads report to the Chief of Staff and not to the United States Congress. Ainsworth opposed this viewpoint and, in turn, resigned from his office. Returning to civilian life, he lived until June 5, 1934, when he died in Washington, DC.[19]

Spanish-American War

The general index for soldiers during the Spanish-American War is found in M871 (Microfilm Series 871) at the National Archives in Washington, DC, covering all volunteer soldiers who fought in the War with Spain. The names are arranged alphabetically.

General Index to Compiled Service Records of Volunteer Soldiers During the War with Spain on *Fold3* at: https://www.fold3.com/title/879/spanish-american-war-service-record-index.

General Index to Compiled Service Records of Volunteer Soldiers During the War with Spain on *Ancestry* at: https://www.ancestry.com/search/collections/2400.

General Index to Compiled Service Records of Volunteer Soldiers During the War with Spain on https://www.familysearch.org/search/collection/1919583?collectionNameFilter=true

Some of the geographic states that participated in the war have separate indexes for volunteer soldiers. The names are duplicated within each index.

M240 – Index to Compiled Military Service Records of Volunteer Soldiers Who Served During the War with Spain in Organizations from the State of Louisiana. Not available online.

M413 – Index to Compiled Military Service Records of Volunteer Soldiers Who Served During the War with Spain in Organizations from the State of North Carolina. Not available online.

M1087 – Compiled Service Records of Volunteer Soldiers who Served in the Florida Infantry During the War with Spain. Arranged alphabetically by name and includes unit information at: https://www.fold3.com/title/905/spanish-american-war-service-records-florida

Boxer Rebellion

No Compiled Military Service Records are available for the Boxer Rebellion, but those for the regular army do exist. The United States military forces in China consisted of United States Regular Army, United States Marines, and detached United States Navy personnel stationed onboard warships that transported men to the combat zone. See individual chapters for the Navy and the Marine Corps detailing these records.

---

[19] Mabel E. Deutrich "Fred C. Ainsworth: The Story of a Vermont Archivist" *Vermont History* 27 (January 1959): 22-23; and *The Evening Star*, June 5, 1934.

Philippine Insurrection

The general index for soldiers during the Philippine Insurrection is found in M872 (Microfilm Series 872) at the National Archives in Washington, DC, covering all volunteer soldiers who fought against the Philippine insurgents. The names are arranged alphabetically.

General Index to Compiled Service Records of Volunteer Soldiers During the Philippine Insurrection including United States Volunteers and State organizations at *FamilySearch* at: https://www.familysearch.org/search/catalog/347273?availability=Family%20History%20Library

If the name of someone who served during the Philippine Insurrection does not appear in the above index, check the Spanish-American War index previously listed in this publication.

The CMSRs are bound together in a hard-cardboard, flip-open pouch with separate cards that detail the entire length of service for a soldier. Written on the pouch are the individual card numbers (all stamps in red ink with dates on the back of each of the cards inside the pouch), the soldier's name, unit, rank in, and rank out.

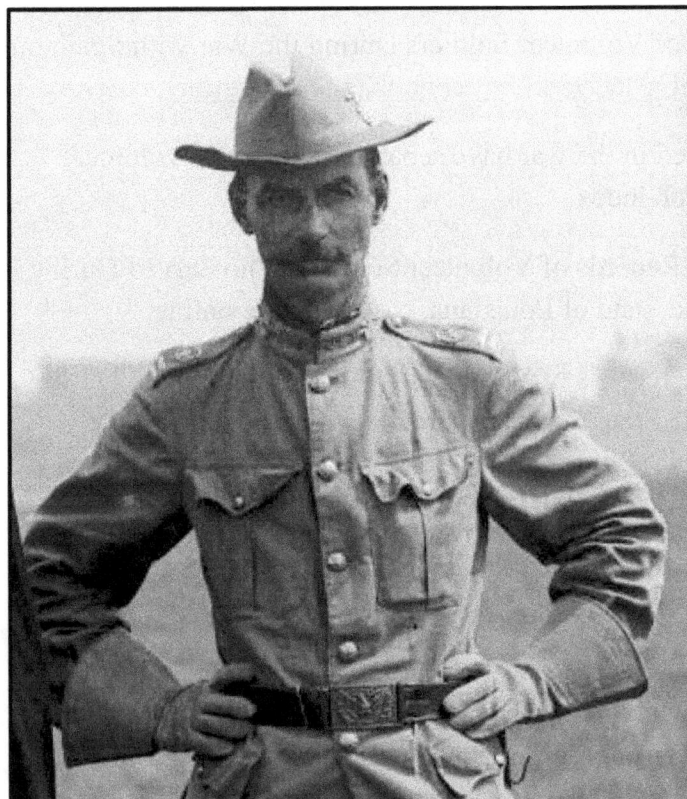

Figure 6: Courtesy of "Rough Riders" by Theodore Roosevelt, 1899.

Kane, Woodbury

Co. K, 1 U.S. Vol. Cavalry.

(Spanish War.)

Private Captain

CARD NUMBERS.

1 42347317
2 42351292
3 1378

Number of medical cards herein 0

Number of personal papers herein 4

Book Mark:

See also

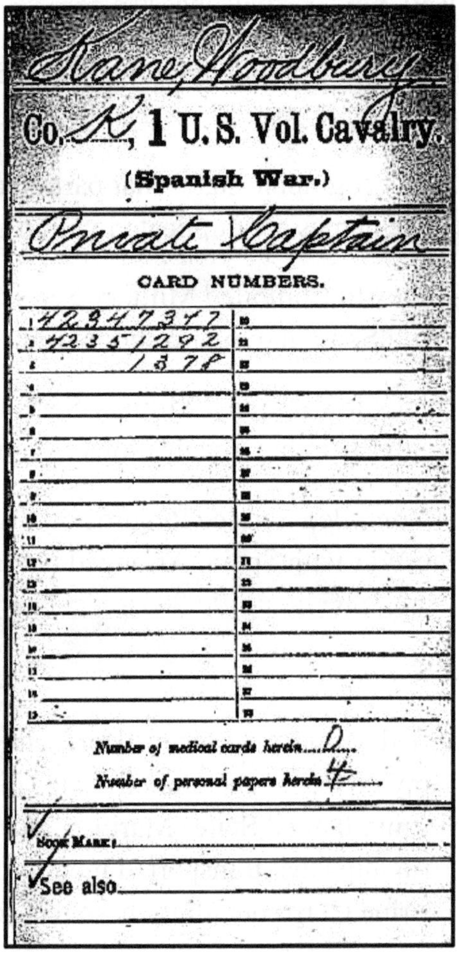

Figure 7: Courtesy of National Archives

The number of personal papers, medical cards, bookmark notation, and any alias or other name used by the soldier while in service. The image on the previous page is the Compiled Military

Service Record pouch for Captain Woodbury Kane, who served in the Spanish-American War as the commanding officer of Company K of the 1st United States Volunteer Cavalry.

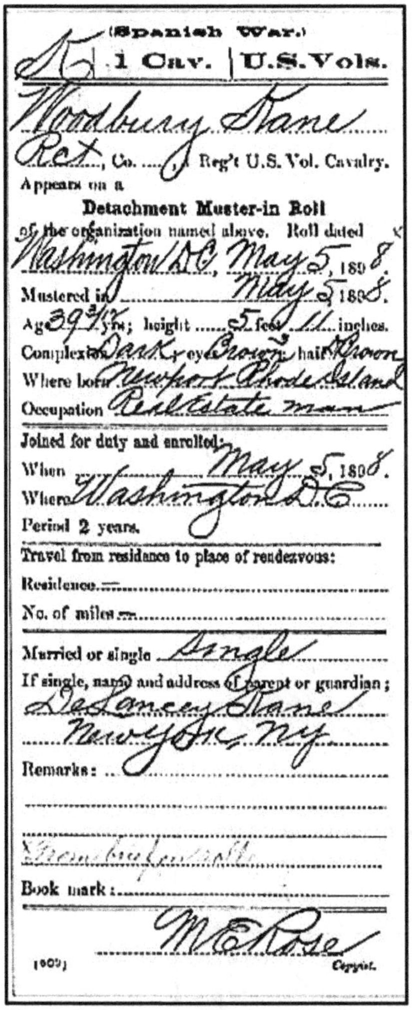
(Spanish War.)
K | 1 Cav. | U.S.Vols.
Woodbury Kane
Pvt., Co. K, 1 Reg't U.S. Vol. Cavalry.
Appears on a
Detachment Muster-in Roll
of the organization named above. Roll dated
Washington DC, May 5, 1898.
Mustered in May 5 1898.
Age 39 yrs; height 5 feet 11 inches.
Complexion Dark; eyes Brown; hair Brown
Where born Newport Rhode Island
Occupation Real Estate man
Joined for duty and enrolled:
When May 5, 1898.
Where Washington D.C.
Period 2 years.
Travel from residence to place of rendezvous:
Residence —
No. of miles —
Married or single Single
If single, name and address of parent or guardian;
DeLancey Kane
New York, NY
Remarks:
Book mark:
M. E. Rose
(909) Copyist.

Figure 8: Courtesy of National Archives

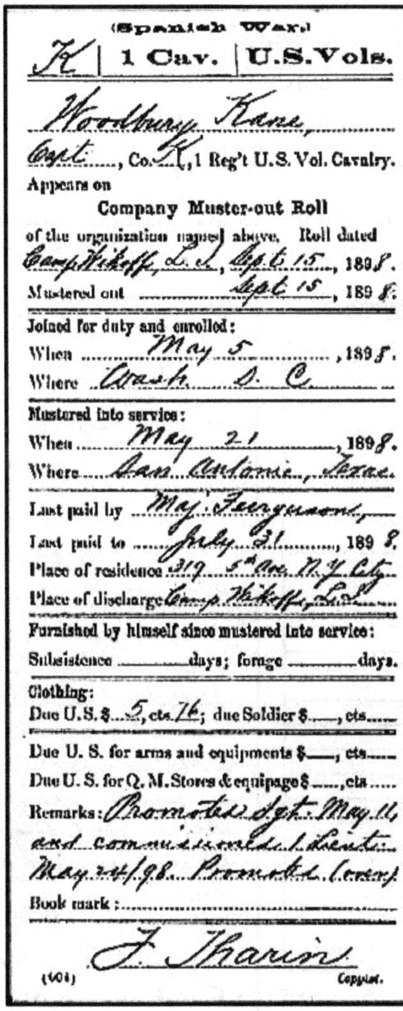
(Spanish War.)
K | 1 Cav. | U.S.Vols.
Woodbury Kane
Capt., Co. K, 1 Reg't U.S. Vol. Cavalry.
Appears on
Company Muster-out Roll
of the organization named above. Roll dated
Camp Wikoff, L. I., Sept 15, 1898.
Mustered out Sept 15, 1898.
Joined for duty and enrolled:
When May 5, 1898.
Where Wash. D. C.
Mustered into service:
When May 21, 1898.
Where San Antonio, Texas.
Last paid by Maj. Ferguson,
Last paid to July 31, 1898.
Place of residence 319 5th Ave. N.Y. City
Place of discharge Camp Wikoff, L.I.
Furnished by himself since mustered into service:
Subsistence — days; forage — days.
Clothing:
Due U.S. $5, cts. 76; due Soldier $—, cts.—
Due U. S. for arms and equipments $—, cts.—
Due U. S. for Q. M. Stores & equipage $—, cts.—
Remarks: Promoted Sgt. May 11, and commissioned 1 Lieut. May 24/98. Promoted Capt.
Book mark:
J. Tharin
(404) Copyist.

Figure 9: Courtesy of National Archives

This unit was known as the "*Rough Riders*" under the command of Colonel Theodore Roosevelt. Not to be confused with the 1st United States Regular Cavalry, which fought alongside Roosevelt at the Battle of San Juan Hill in July 1898. Other records inside the pouch included Captain Kane's muster-in and muster-out cards. The muster-in card to the left (dated May 5, 1898, in Washington, DC) indicates Private Woodbury Kane enlisted during the Spanish-American War. The card stated Kane was 39 years old, born in Newport, Rhode Island, was single, and listed his guardian or parent as DeLancy Kane of New York, NY.

Kane's muster-out card on the right recorded that he was mustered out of service on September 15, 1898, at Camp Wikoff, Long Island, New York, and that he held the rank of Captain, with the remarks section on the bottom of the card listing when he was promoted to Sergeant and when he was commissioned as an officer. In addition to the Compiled Military Service Records, other sources of new genealogical information include where an ancestor served, the strength of the military unit, and additional documents or personnel papers added to the CMSRs and later dates. Three of the added sets of records can be searched for any participant.

Record of Event Cards

These indexed cards track the military unit movements and actions while in service and are broken down to the regiment and company level. Some of these cards contain more information than others. Information on these cards varies, with some containing more details on movements, while others provide perhaps only the duty station. Each entry can be used with the CMSRs to show the activities of an ancestor. These cards are commonly called "*Record of Events*" or ROE cards. During the earlier Revolutionary War, they were called "*Caption Cards*" and provided much the same information. The ROE cards for the Spanish-American War and the Philippine Insurrection are attached at the beginning or end of the regiment's original rolls. One set that is digitized includes the 1st Florida Volunteer Infantry during the Spanish-American War.

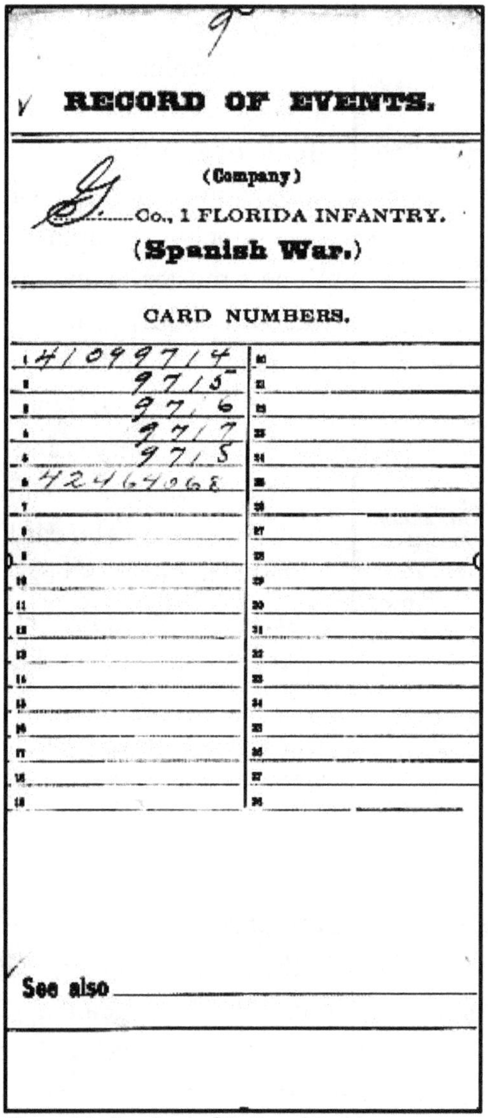

9

RECORD OF EVENTS.

G (Company) Co., 1 FLORIDA INFANTRY.

(Spanish War.)

CARD NUMBERS.

1 41099714
2 9715
3 9716
4 9717
5 9718
6 42464068

See also

Figure 10: Courtesy of National Archives

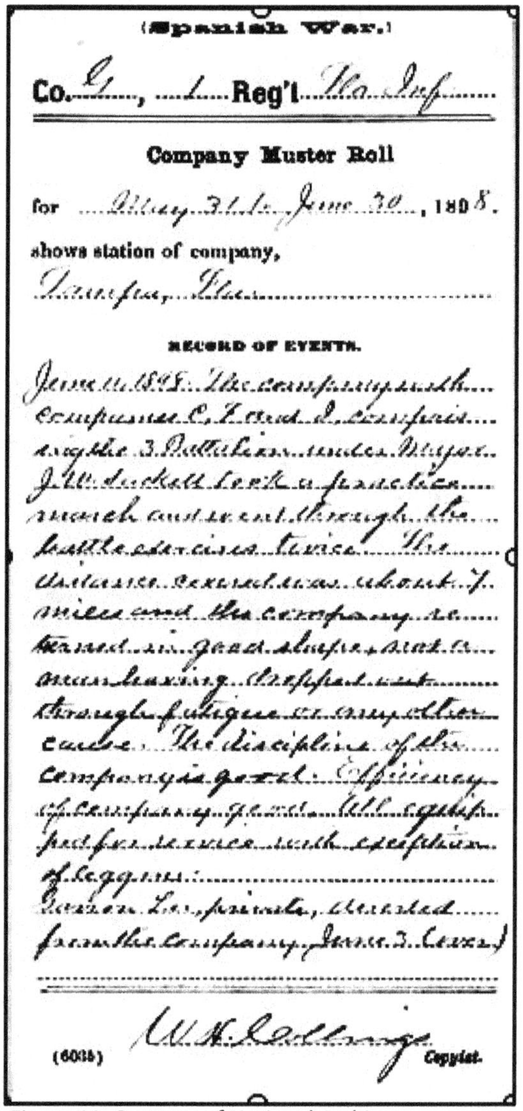

(Spanish War.)

Co. G, 1 Reg't Fla. Inf.

Company Muster Roll

for May 31 to June 30, 1898.

shows station of company,

Tampa, Fla.

RECORD OF EVENTS.

June 11, 1898. The company with companies E, F and I, comprising the 3 Battalion under Major J. W. Luckett took a practice march and went through the battle exercises twice. The distance covered was about 7 miles and the company returned in good shape, not a man having dropped out through fatigue or any other cause. The discipline of the company is good. Efficiency of company good. All equipped for service with exception of leggins.

Jason Lee, private, deserted from the company June 3. (over.)

(6036) W. H. Collings, Copyist.

Figure 11: Courtesy of National Archives

Bookmark Notation Files

When errors or changes in the original records that Ainsworth cataloged were discovered, the Adjutant General Office (AGO) created a separate record file that was attached outside of the original CMSRs, with a notation near the bottom of the hard cardboard pouch listing the file number and year of entry of the bookmark. These records can only be ordered from the military archivist at NARA in Washington, DC, and are not digitized.

Ainsworth's Lists

The United States Adjutant General Office (AGO) kept carded records of military organizations from the Revolutionary War through the Philippine Insurrection. The listing does not include the

Boxer Rebellion is limited to volunteer units that fought in all wars. The list has been commonly referred to as the "Ainsworth List," named after Colonel Fred C. Ainsworth, who cataloged and indexed the original materials.

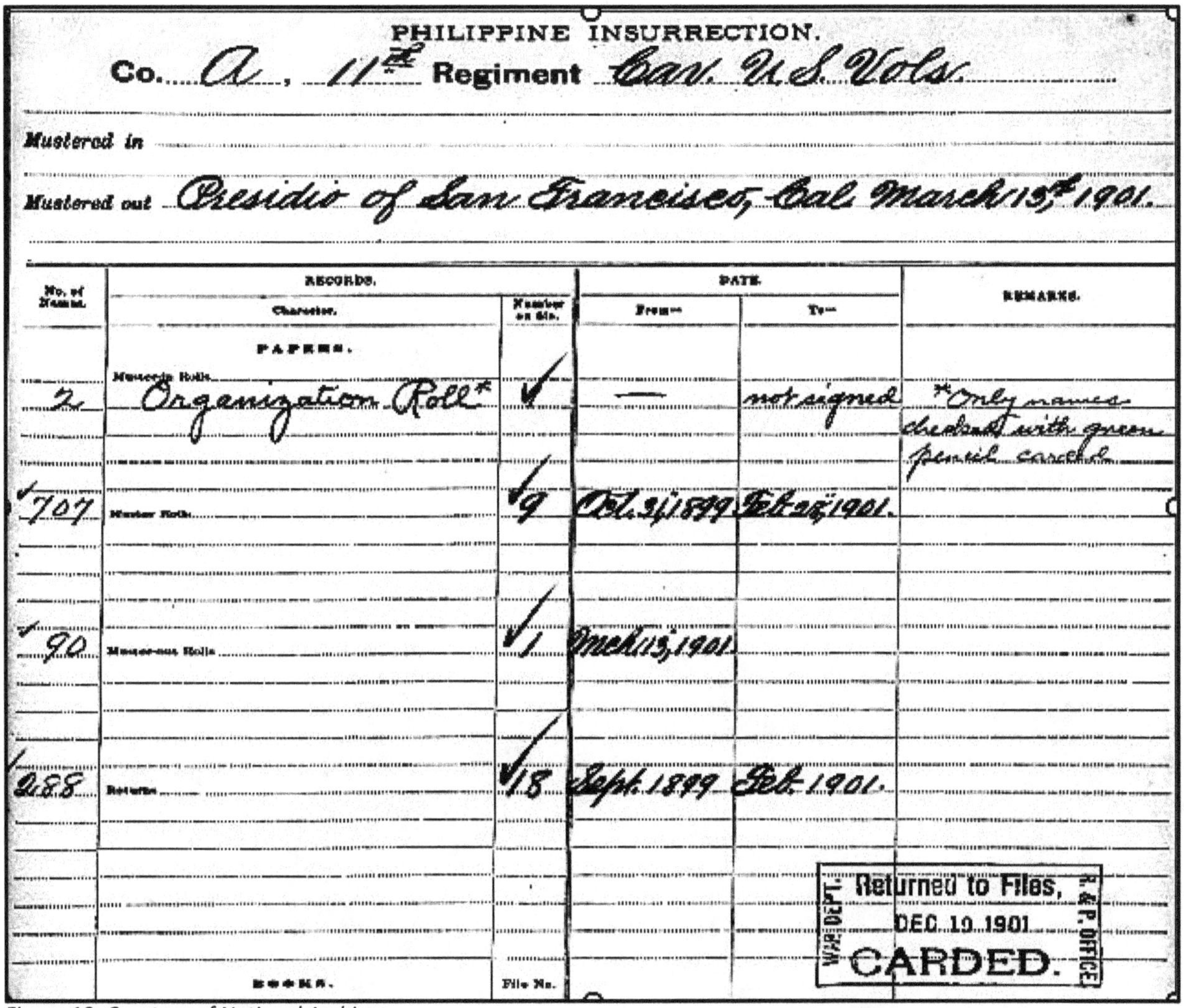

PHILIPPINE INSURRECTION.

Co. A, 11th Regiment Cav. U.S. Vols.

Mustered in

Mustered out Presidio of San Francisco, Cal. March 13th 1901.

No. of Names.	Records. Character.	Number on file.	Date. From—	To—	Remarks.
	Papers.				
2	Muster-in Rolls. Organization Roll*	✓	—	not signed	*Only names checked with green pencil circle.
707	Muster Rolls.	9	Oct. 31, 1899	Feb. 28, 1901.	
90	Muster-out Rolls.	1	Mch 13, 1901.		
288	Returns.	18	Sept. 1899	Feb. 1901.	
	Books.	File No.			

Returned to Files, DEC. 10 1901 CARDED. War Dept. R. & P. Office.

Figure 12: Courtesy of National Archives

The lists were cataloged and organized by military unit. The breakdown of each regiment's command structure starts with the Field & Staff (F&S), the regimental bands, followed alphabetically by companies A, B, and C, and continues to the end of the regiments. Each company contains mustering-in or mustering-out information (where this occurred), along with the regimental strengths and company-level status. The above example shows Company A of the 11th United States Cavalry that was mustered out of service during the Philippine Insurrection on 13 March 1901 at the Presidio in San Francisco, CA.

The original copies of the Ainsworth list are located at the National Archives in Washington, DC, and have been microfilmed (series T817), totaling 112 rolls, and digitized on *FamilySearch*.

https://www.familysearch.org/search/catalog/539623?availability=Family%20History%20Library
FamilySearch has separated them by military war periods and by state of origin.

GENEALOGY TOOL: Online research tools that can yield results to find difficult information about a Spanish-American War ancestor can be found using Archive Grid, Hathi Trust, and the National Union Catalog of Manuscript Collections.

Regular Army Records

Following the end of the Civil War in 1865, the armies in the field began to demobilize. Numbers decreased gradually, with regular army soldiers being scattered in the reconstructed south, stationed on the border as tensions with Mexico grew, or participating in the pacification of the western Indians.

The United States Army Reorganization Act, passed by Congress on July 28, 1866 (14 Stat. 332), established the official peacetime army consisting of forty-five regiments of infantry, ten regiments of cavalry, and five regiments of artillery. The act also is credited with the birth of the "Buffalo Soldiers" who served in the American west. The numbers of men overall would decrease with an act of Congress on June 16, 1874 (18 Stat. 72), making appropriations for support of the army with an authorized strength of twenty-five thousand men. Numbers would remain stable until 1898.[20]

Organizations	Enlisted	Officers	Regiments	Totals
General Officers and Staff	532	2026	0	2,558
Infantry	12,828	886	25	13,714
Cavalry	6,047	437	10	6,484
Artillery	4,486	288	7	4,774
Miscellaneous Troops	653	0	0	653
TOTALS:	26,040	2,143	42	28,183

In the weeks preceding the formal declaration of war between the United States and Spain on April 21, 1898, the United States Army aggregate number of personnel totaled 28,183 officers and enlisted, divided into forty-two regiments of infantry, cavalry, and artillery batteries. The table above provides the breakdown of each of the organizations of the regular army and respective strengths on April 1, 1898.[21]

---

[20] Leonard L. Lerwill, *The Personnel Replacement System in the United States Army* (Washington DC: United States Army Center for Military History, 1988), 128-129.

[21] Steve R. Waddell, *United States Army Logistics: From the American Revolution to 9/11* (Denver: Greenwood Publishing Group, 2011), 87; and Marvin A. Kreidberg and Merton G. Henry. *History of Military Mobilization in the United States Army, 1775-1945,* (Washington DC: U.S. Government Printing Office, 1955), 148-150.

Most of the regiments in the regular army were scattered at more than eighty military outposts throughout the western states and territories. Very little effort was made in the years before the outbreak of the war with Spain to enlarge the numbers of the army. Enlistment in the regulars was strictly voluntary, with a small increase in recruiting stations opened between 1897 and 1898 as tensions mounted between the United States and Spain.[22]

For the purposes of organization and administrating daily activities of the U.S. Army during the Spanish-American War, General Order No. 7 (dated March 11, 1898) was used to divide the country geographically into eight separate military departments, each with a regional

headquarters designed to keep records. The map above shows the department boundaries and each of the headquarters' cities listed for each area from coast to coast. The records of the regular army are detailed and contain valuable historical information.[23]

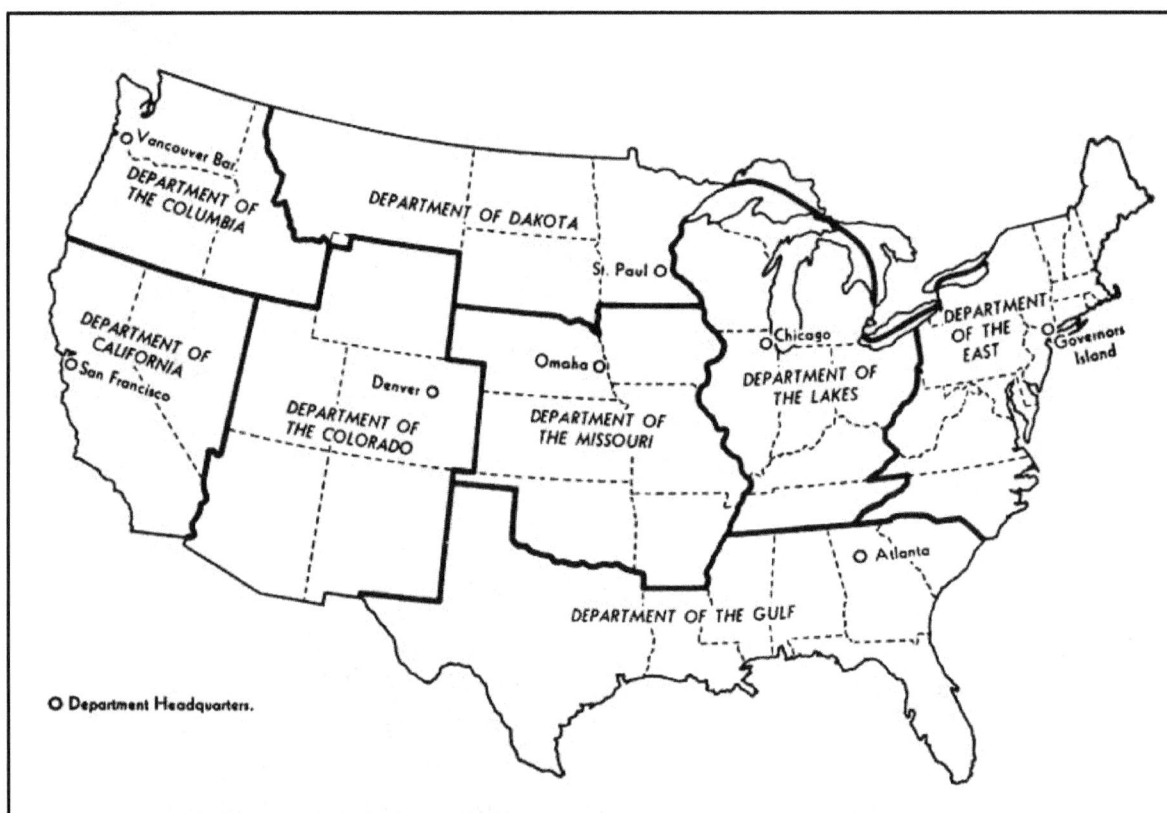

Figure 13: Courtesy of United States Army Center of Military History

---

[22] Ibid, 150.

[23] General Orders: War Department, Adjutant General's Office, (Washington, DC: U.S. Government Printing Office, 1898), 21-22; Kreidberg and Henry, *History of Military Mobilization in the United States Army, 1775-1945,* 150-151.

Register of Enlistments:

The regular army registers of enlistments are the equivalent of the volunteer's compiled military service records. Colonel Fred C. Ainsworth and his clerks never indexed or cataloged these documents. These records, covering the infantry, cavalry (formally called dragoons), artillery, and the Corps of Engineers, are in the custody of the National Archives in Washington, DC. Furthermore, the records cover 1798-1914 and are in Record Group 94 of the Adjutant General Office. They cover through the Philippine Insurrection.

The regular army register of enlistments is available online on *FamilySearch* and *Ancestry*.

https://www.familysearch.org/search/collection/1880762 indexed by the name of the soldiers.

https://www.ancestry.com/search/collections/1198, with full scanned copies of the original ledger entries on two pages. Details on the enlistment include the name of the soldier, age at the time of enlistment, birthplace, date of enlistment, and assigned unit, along with remarks about the soldier's military service.

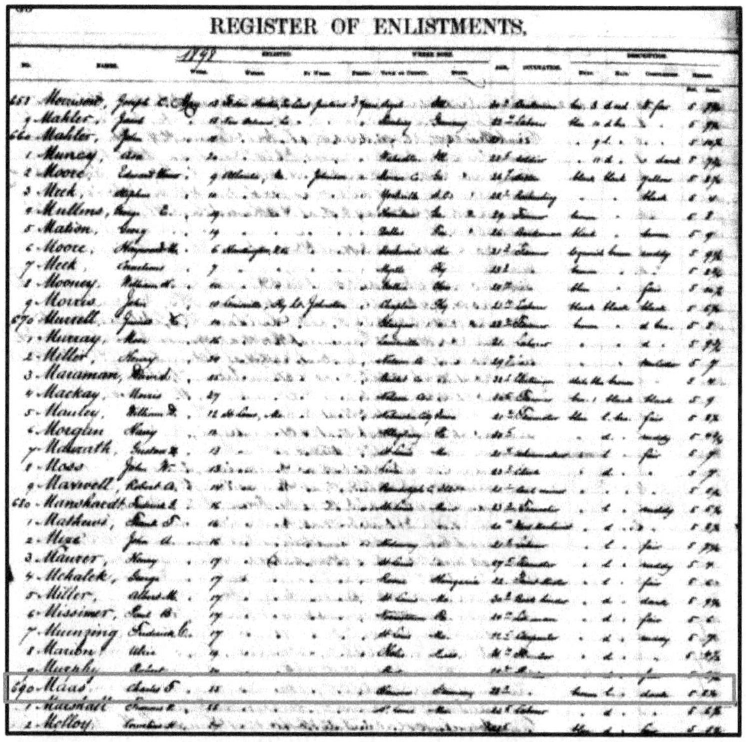

Figure 14: Courtesy of National Archives

Figure 15: Courtesy of Michael L. Strauss

The image above shows page 1 of 2 of the registers of enlistments for men in May 1898. Charles F. Maas, a native of Hanover, Germany, enlisted in the United States Army on May 26, 1898, in St. Louis, Missouri, and was assigned to Company E of the 15th United States Infantry. Maas was discharged on January 19, 1899, per General Order No. 40 at Camp Albert G. Forse in Huntsville, Alabama. His military service as a Private was with good conduct.

Regular Army Returns:

The United States Army recorded monthly reports of unit strengths, locations, and the names of commanders of each of the regiments stationed with the army. The records cover from 1821 to 1916 and are in the custody of the National Archives in Washington, DC., in Record Group 94. Individual muster rolls with company commanders are often provided, along with the names, ranks, locations, and duties or causes of men present, absent, or discharged from duty. The rolls also provide aggregate numbers of enlisted and officers.

The army returns are divided between infantry and non-infantry (including cavalry and artillery) and are digitized on *Ancestry.*

https://www.ancestry.com/search/collections/2229/ indexed for infantry regiments by the name of the soldiers and browsable by the military unit and sub-grouped by dates.

https://www.ancestry.com/search/collections/1225/ indexed (for non-infantry) by the soldiers' names, browsable by the military unit, and sub-grouped by dates.

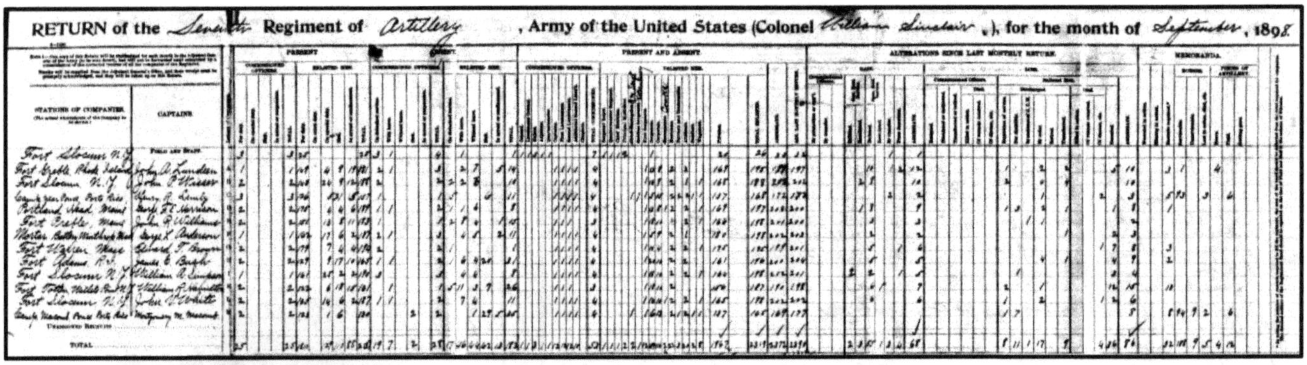
RETURN of the Seventh Regiment of Artillery, Army of the United States (Colonel William Sinclair), for the month of September, 1898.

Figure 16: Courtesy of National Archives

The above regular army return dated September 1898 shows the full roster of the 7th United States Artillery under the command of Colonel William Sinclair, with each battery numbered A through M, with each commander's name and duty station listing the aggregate totals of servicemen.

Returns from Military Posts:

The United States Army has records of returns from military posts where individual units were stationed. The collection is in the National Archives in Washington, DC custody and is in record group 94, dated between 1806 and 1916, with some dated into 1917.

The returns were completed monthly and sent to the United States War Department Adjutant General Office. Some of the information included the unit at each post, aggregate strengths of the units, commanding officers, and records of events. Posts outside the United States are also included, with locations where fighting occurred in Puerto Rico, Cuba, the Philippines, and China.

The collection is available online at https://www.ancestry.com/search/collections/1571/ indexed by name and military post location, then by post name, and sub-grouped by dates of returns.

Camp Merritt near San Francisco, California, dated May 13, 1898, showed infantry stationed at the camp during the Spanish-American War. The military post return dated July 20, 1898, for Camp Merritt in San Francisco, California, shows the aggregate total number of men stationed at the camp in the 3rd Battalion of the 18th United States Infantry under the command of Major Charles R. Paul.

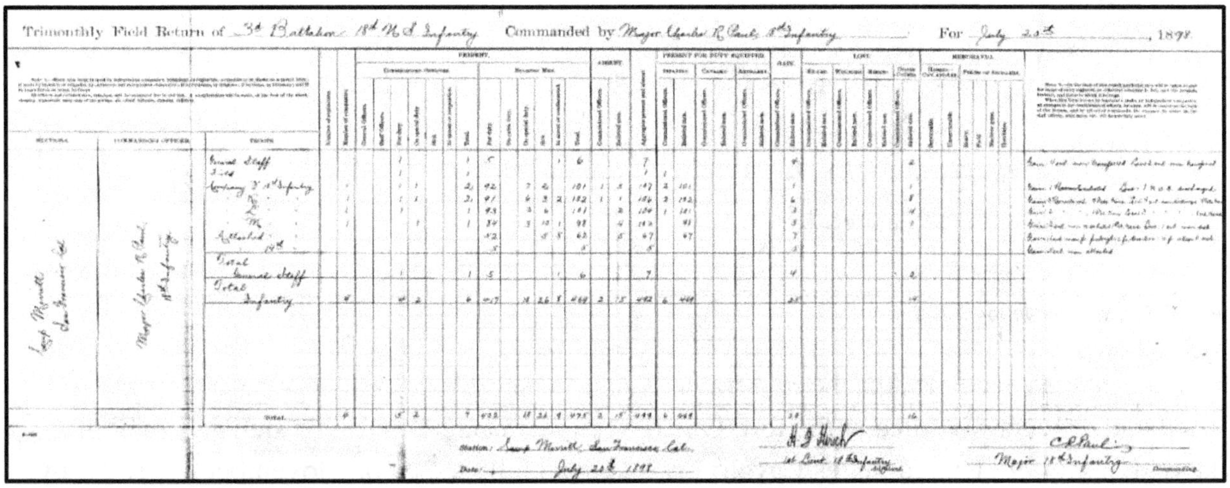

Trimonthly Field Return of 3d Battalion 18th U.S. Infantry Commanded by Major Charles R. Paul 18th Infantry For July 20th, 1898.

Station: Camp Merritt, San Francisco, Cal.

Date: July 20th 1898

C.R. Paul, Major 18th Infantry, Commanding.

Figure 17: Courtesy of National Archives

Register of Deaths:

The United States Army recorded military burials. The collection, covering 1768-1921, is in the custody of the National Archives in Washington, DC, in record group 92 for the quartermaster general. The returns provide the name, rank, military unit, date of death, and other remarks for regular army personnel.

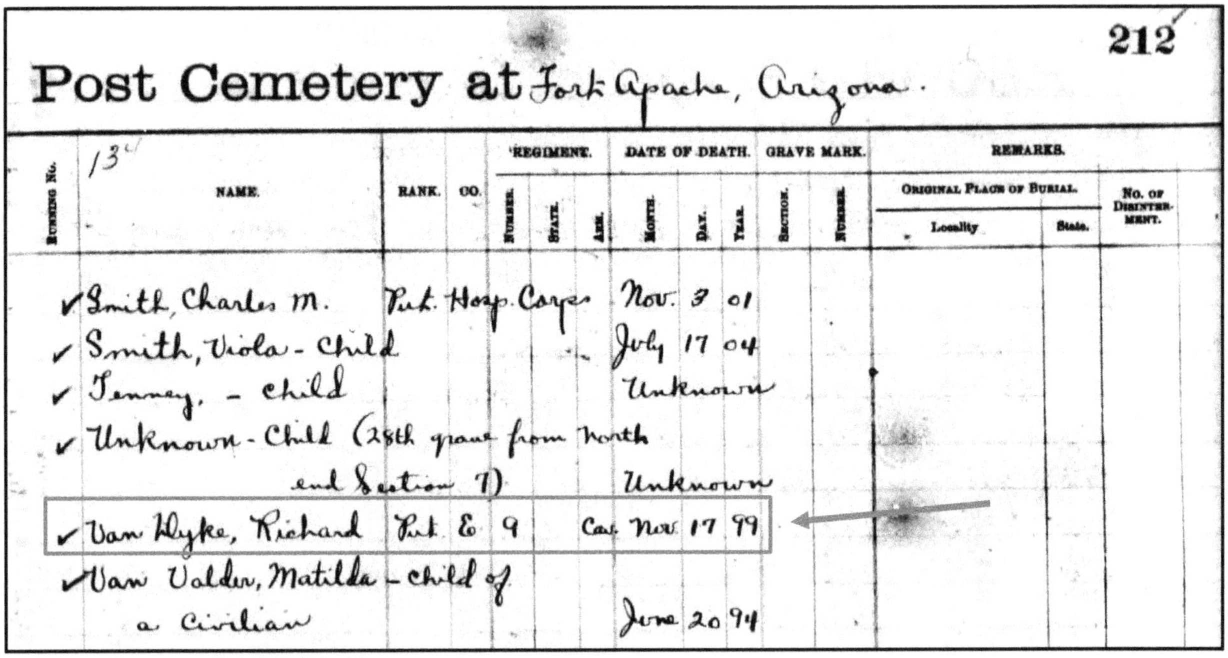

Post Cemetery at Fort Apache, Arizona.

212

13

Running No.	Name	Rank	Co.	Regiment: Number	Regiment: State	Regiment: Arm	Date of Death: Month	Day	Year	Grave Mark: Section	Grave Mark: Number	Remarks: Original Place of Burial: Locality	State	No. of Disinterment
	✓ Smith, Charles M.	Pvt. Hosp. Corps					Nov.	3	01					
	✓ Smith, Viola - Child						July	17	04					
	✓ Tenney, - child						Unknown							
	✓ Unknown - Child (28th grave from north end Section 7)						Unknown							
	✓ Van Dyke, Richard	Pvt.	E	9		Cav.	Nov.	17	99					
	✓ Van Valder, Matilda - child of a Civilian						June	20	94					

Figure 18: Courtesy of National Archives

The post cemetery for Fort Apache in Arizona Territory shows the deaths of regular army enlisted and officers who died at the fort. One of the individuals listed, Private Richard Van Dyke of Troop E. 9th United States Cavalry, was accidentally killed on November 17, 1899, by Private Daniel J. Murdock from the same regiment.[24]

GENEALOGY TIP Search in all related military documents such as the compiled military service records, muster rolls, pensions, and other records such as census to find commonly used abbreviations during the wars.

[24] *Arizona Republic*, November 24, 1899.

Military Pension Records

Pension records can provide details about a veteran's military service and rich genealogical information on family members. The original records are found in Record Group 15 of the National Archives in Washington, DC. Later pensions are at the National Personnel Record Center in St. Louis, MO. To understand pensions, researchers need to become familiar with the various pension laws to know how the veteran, widow, or other dependent was eligible and how they came to apply for a government pension.

A complete listing of pension laws covering multiple war periods from 26 August 1776 (found in the Journals of the Continental Congress) to the pension act passed on 28 June 1934 is at *Genealogy Quest,* where links to the laws passed by Congress can be found.[25] Each link provides the congressional statute at large reference with the translated documents. Another excellent reference source covering pensions acts is found in a book entitled *"Federal Military Pensions in the United States"* written by William H. Glasson. It is available for free download on *Hathi Trust* online.[26]

Pension Indexes:

Indexes for veterans of the Spanish-American War, Boxer Rebellion, and the later Philippine Insurrection are available online at multiple locations. The first index is alphabetically listed by the veteran, widow, or guardians and at two online locations:

United States, Civil War Pension Index: General Index to Pension Files, 1861-1934 found on *Ancestry* at: https://www.ancestry.com/search/collections/4654

United States General Index to Pension Files, 1861-1934 found online at *FamilySearch* at: https://www.familysearch.org/search/collection/1919699

Besides the above-referenced wars, the indexes also include men who served during the Civil War and post-war years covering the Indian war periods and the regular army. The card index also considers those men who served in volunteer regiments during the Spanish-American War and the later Philippine Insurrection. The general indexes include cards that cover veterans who served in the United States Navy and the Revenue Cutter Service. The cards can always be distinguished by their much darker card stock.

Another index is cataloged by unit organization. This index covers the period from 1861 to 1900 and the same wars. The unit information should be known and can be browsed online by regiment type. Remember that unit designations were used again between the Civil War and the

---

[25] Pension Acts. Accessed 13 June 2020. http://genealogy-quest.com/military-pensions/pension-acts

[26] William H. Glasson, Federal Military Pension in the United States. Accessed 13 June 2020. https://catalog.hathitrust.org/Record/001153790.

later Spanish-American War. When looking for pensioners from the Spanish-American war, take note of the words "War with Spain" stamped onto the index cards to help separate military service from the Civil War or any other war periods (including the Boxer Rebellion or Philippine-Insurrection).

Pension applications for service in the US Army between 1861 and 1900 are available on *Fold3* at https://www.fold3.com/title/57/civil-war-pensions-index.

In 1921, the United States Congress organized the Veterans Bureau. On July 21, 1930, by Executive Order No. 5398, President Hoover combined the Veterans Bureau with the Bureau of Pensions and Home for Disabled Veterans to form a single office called the Veterans Administration (now called Veterans Affairs), an independent executive agency.

Spanish-American War Pensioner Example from National Archives:

James S. Carnahan was born November 2, 1870, in Keyser, West Virginia. He was the son of James S. and Margaret Monaghan. His father worked for the Pennsylvania Railroad as an engineer and died on 25 November 1905 in Lancaster, Pennsylvania.[27] In 1898, Carnahan lived at 304 S. 4th Street in Columbia, Pennsylvania, and, like his father, had worked for the railroad.[28]

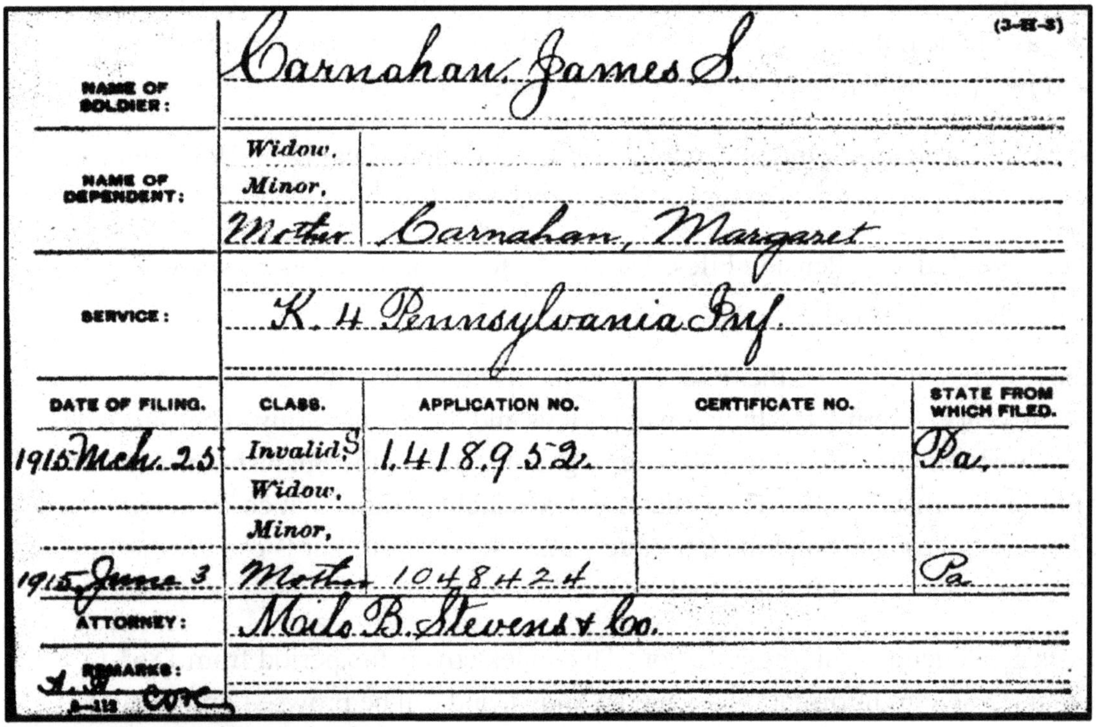
(3-II-3)

NAME OF SOLDIER: Carnahan, James S.

NAME OF DEPENDENT: Widow, Minor, Mother Carnahan, Margaret

SERVICE: K. 4 Pennsylvania Inf.

DATE OF FILING.	CLASS.	APPLICATION NO.	CERTIFICATE NO.	STATE FROM WHICH FILED.
1915 Mch. 25	Invalid, S	1.418.952		Pa.
	Widow,			
	Minor,			
1915 June 3	Mother	1048424		Pa.

ATTORNEY: Milo B. Stevens & Co.

REMARKS: A. H. Corc.

Figure 19: Courtesy of National Archives

---

[27] Pennsylvania Death Certificates, 1906-1967. Pennsylvania Department of Health, RG11. Assessed 16 September 2020 at: https://www.ancestry.com/imageviewer/collections/5164/images/41381_2421401574_0580-03196?pId=2429738; and *Lancaster New Era*. November 25, 1905.

[28] Ralph L. Polk. *Lancaster City and County Directory for 1898*. (Philadelphia: R.L. Polk & Company Publishers, 1898), 625.

The previous image shows the *Ancestry* indexed card for the pension for James S. Carnahan, who served in Company K. 4th Pennsylvania Infantry during the Spanish-American War. Carnahan joined the regiment on June 29, 1898, and was mustered in on July 1, 1898, at Mt. Gretna, PA. Later, he was promoted to corporal on July 11, 1898, and mustered count with his company on November 16, 1898, in Philadelphia, Pennsylvania.[29]

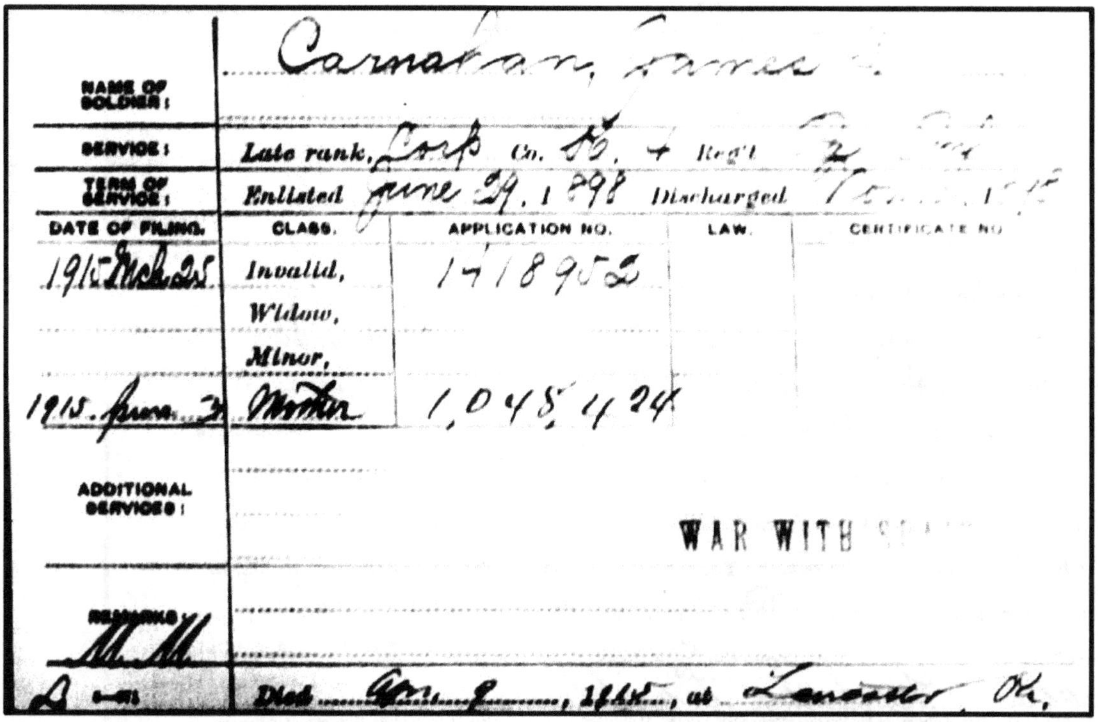
NAME OF SOLDIER: Carnahan, James

SERVICE: Late rank, Corp Co. K, 4 Reg't

TERM OF SERVICE: Enlisted June 29, 1898 Discharged

DATE OF FILING.	CLASS.	APPLICATION NO.	LAW.	CERTIFICATE NO.
1915 Mch 25	Invalid,	1418952		
	Widow,			
	Minor,			
1915 June 3	Mother	1,048,424		

ADDITIONAL SERVICES:

WAR WITH

REMARKS:

Died Apr. 8, 1915, at Lancaster, Pa.

Figure 20: Courtesy of National Archives

The above image shows the index card available on *Fold3*. This series of indexes is by organization and often includes the enlistment and discharge dates and the date and place of death provided. The "War with Spain" stamp for soldiers in this war is recorded.

In both cards, the mother of the soldier requested the veteran benefits after the death of the veteran on April 8, 1915, in Lancaster, Pennsylvania. The soldier was never married, and his mother, Margaret Carnahan, who was widowed, requested his pension payments. The mother died on January 13, 1920, in Lancaster, PA.[30] The pension index cards include a series of file numbers, the first of which are the application numbers and the certificate numbers, in addition to the state of filing, pension law, and the dates.

The original pension for James S. Carnahan, with all of the filed documents, is in the custody of the National Archives in Washington, DC. This is the central repository of all the older early

[29] Thomas J. Stewart. *Record of Pennsylvania Volunteers in the Spanish-American War, 1898*. (Harrisburg: William Stanley Ray, 1901), 157-159, 166.
[30] *Lancaster New Era*. April 9, 1915; and *Lancaster Examiner*, January 17, 1920.

twentieth-century pensions looking backward through previous war periods. When reading the original pension, Margaret Carnahan's claim was disapproved for the payments for her son, as his illness (claimed during the war) that caused his death was not contracted while in service.

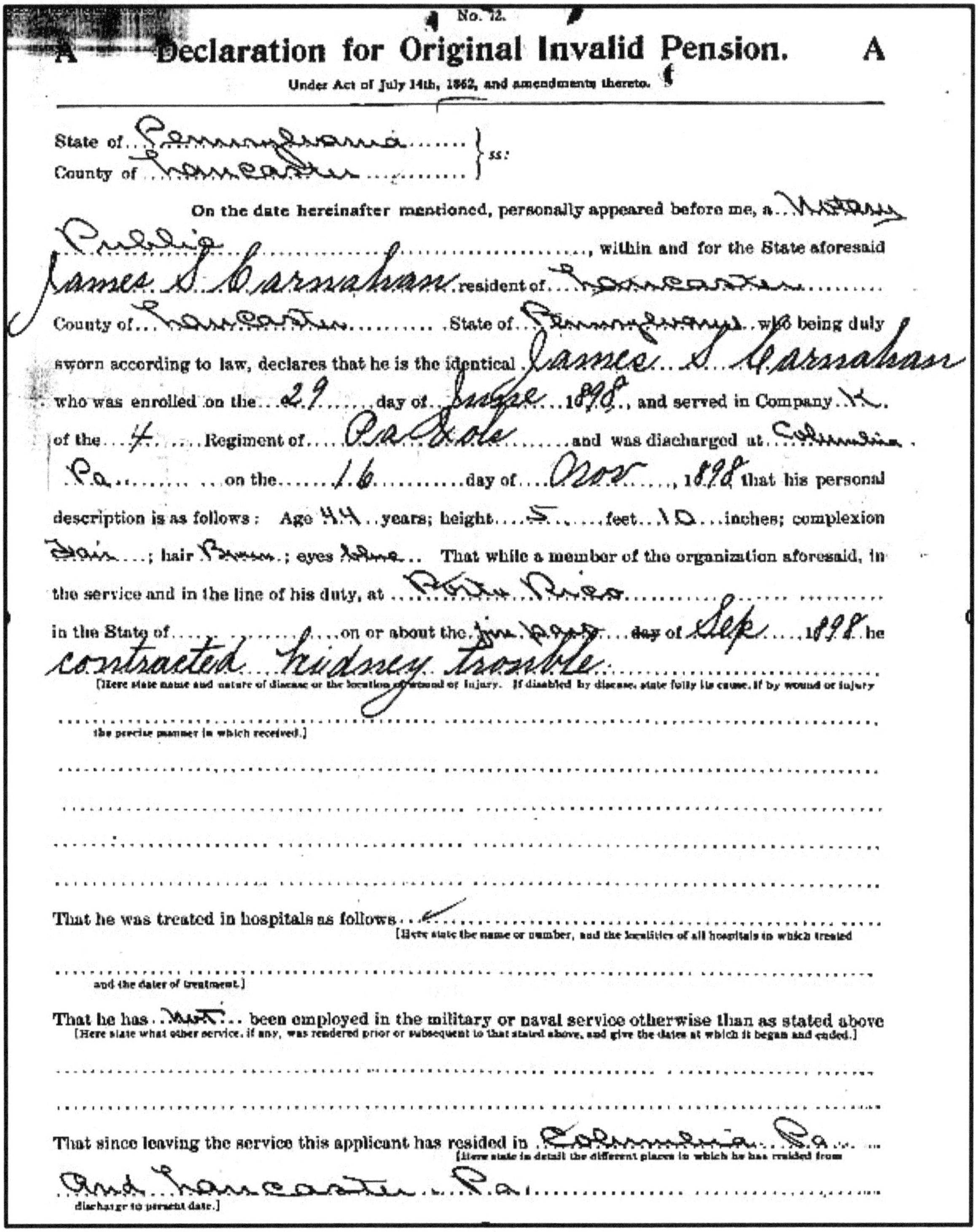

No. 12.

Declaration for Original Invalid Pension.

A   A

Under Act of July 14th, 1862, and amendments thereto.

State of _Pennsylvania_
County of _Lancaster_   } ss:

On the date hereinafter mentioned, personally appeared before me, a _Notary Public_, within and for the State aforesaid _James S. Carnahan_ resident of _Lancaster_ County of _Lancaster_ State of _Pennsylvania_ who being duly sworn according to law, declares that he is the identical _James S. Carnahan_ who was enrolled on the _29_ day of _June_ 1898, and served in Company _K_ of the _4_ Regiment of _Pa Vols_ and was discharged at _Columbia, Pa_ on the _16_ day of _Nov_, 1898 that his personal description is as follows: Age _44_ years; height _5_ feet _10_ inches; complexion _fair_; hair _brown_; eyes _blue_. That while a member of the organization aforesaid, in the service and in the line of his duty, at _Porto Rico_ in the State of _____ on or about the _____ day of _Sep_ 1898 he _contracted kidney trouble_.

[Here state name and nature of disease or the location of wound or injury. If disabled by disease, state fully its cause. If by wound or injury, the precise manner in which received.]

That he was treated in hospitals as follows _____
[Here state the name or number, and the localities of all hospitals in which treated and the dates of treatment.]

That he has _not_ been employed in the military or naval service otherwise than as stated above
[Here state what other service, if any, was rendered prior or subsequent to that stated above, and give the dates at which it began and ended.]

That since leaving the service this applicant has resided in _Columbia, Pa_ _and Lancaster, Pa_
[Here state in detail the different places in which he has resided from discharge to present date.]

Figure 21: Courtesy of National Archives

24

The mother filled out the Declaration for Original Invalid Pension form requesting the approval of the pension, which was denied. Less than a week after the death of her son, the Bureau of Pension on August 12, 1915, sent a letter denying her original claim. The image below from the original pension for Margaret Carnahan shows the pension being denied because the soldier's death was not due to his previous military service in 1898.[31]

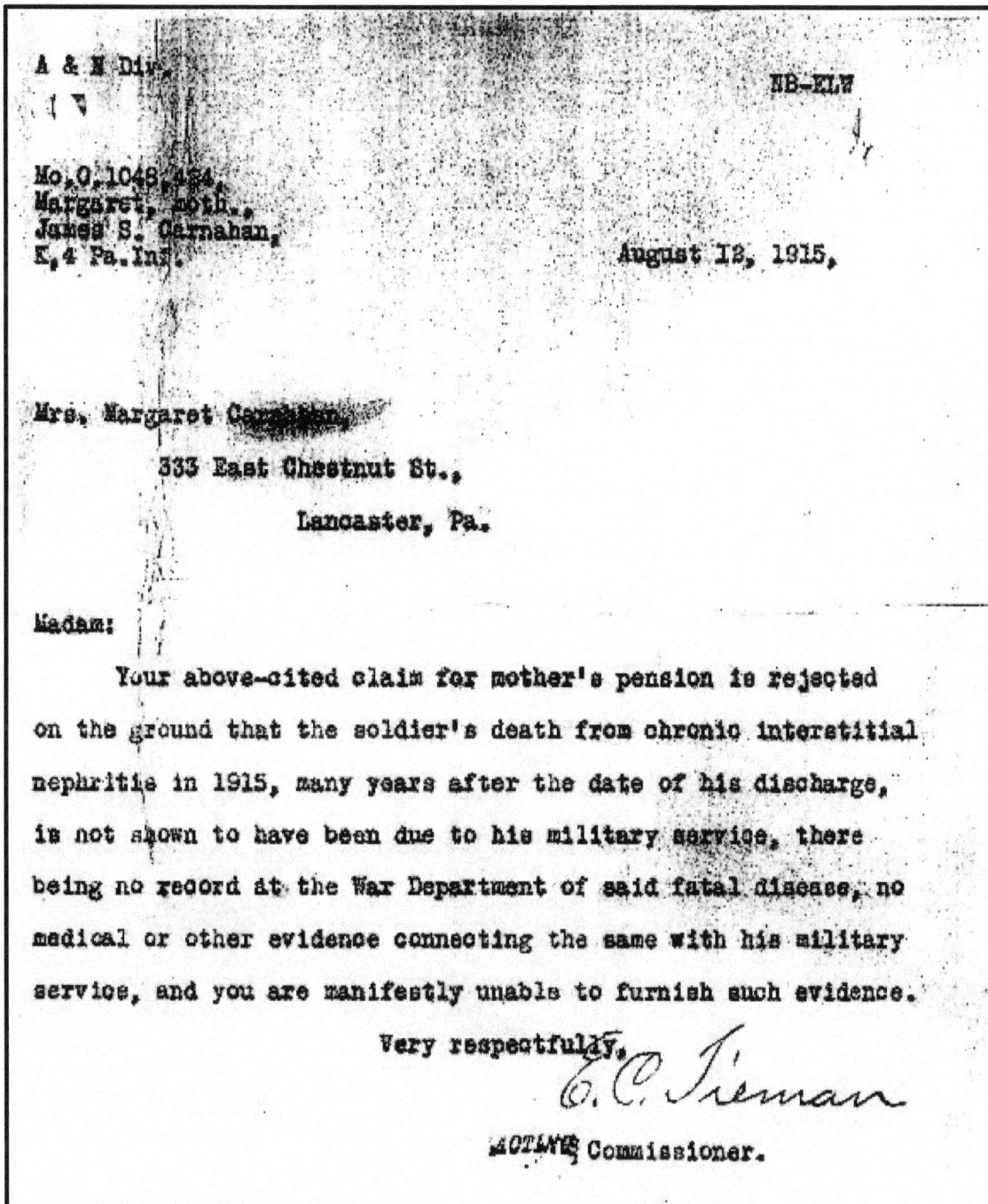

A & N Div.

NB-KLW

Mo.O.1048.424.
Margaret, moth.,
James S. Carnahan,
K, 4 Pa.Inf.

August 12, 1915,

Mrs. Margaret Carnahan,

333 East Chestnut St.,

Lancaster, Pa.

Madam:

Your above-cited claim for mother's pension is rejected on the ground that the soldier's death from chronic interstitial nephritis in 1915, many years after the date of his discharge, is not shown to have been due to his military service, there being no record at the War Department of said fatal disease, no medical or other evidence connecting the same with his military service, and you are manifestly unable to furnish such evidence.

Very respectfully,

C. C. Tieman

Acting Commissioner.

Figure 22: Courtesy of National Archives

---

[31] Margaret Carnahan. Spanish-American War pension for son James S. Carnahan of Co. K. 4th Pennsylvania Infantry. RG15 National Archives. Application No. 1048424.

Pensions indexes and original files are not all located onsite at the National Archives in the Washington, DC, office. About 1,926 pensions for older veterans of the Civil War, Indian wars, the Spanish-American War, Boxer Rebellion, and the Philippine Insurrection, some of which can be in the custody of the Veteran Affairs office, have been slowly acquisition to the National Personnel Record Center in St. Louis, Missouri. The records are still cataloged in the archives under RG15 and available upon request by the public. An online index that covers 1917-1940 also includes men who served during the Mexican Punitive Expedition of 1916 and later during World War I.

United States, Veteran Administration Master Index, 1917-1940, located online at *FamilySearch* at: https://www.familysearch.org/search/collection/2968245

The files have two numbering designations in the upper right corner to indicate who applied for the pension. If the veteran's file number is preceded by "C," this indicates the veteran was requesting his own benefits. If the veteran was deceased or someone other than the veteran applied for the benefits, the card file number will be preceded by an "XC" and often a date of application. Remember to check the National Archives first, then the National Personnel Record Center, and finally, with the local Veteran Affairs office.

Spanish-American War Pensioner Example from National Personnel Record Center:

John B. Schneller was born on December 5, 1876, in Morrison, Brown, Wisconsin, the son of the late Rev. Jacob Schneller, who served as a pastor in numerous towns in the state. He joined the state national guard on March 13, 1892, eventually obtaining the rank of 1st Lieutenant in Company L. of the 3rd Wisconsin Regiment. Most of the men were recruited from Sparta, Wisconsin, where the men enlisted on May 11, 1898, in Milwaukee, Wisconsin, to fight in Puerto Rico during the Spanish-American War. At the war's end, the men were sent back home and discharged on September 18, 1898, in Milwaukee, Wisconsin.[32]

---

[32] *The Oshkosh Northwestern*. December 21, 1961; and the Roster of the 3rd Wisconsin Volunteer Infantry by Mike Phillips and Patrick McSherry assessed 17 September 2020 at: https://www.spanamwar.com/3rdwischistory.htm.

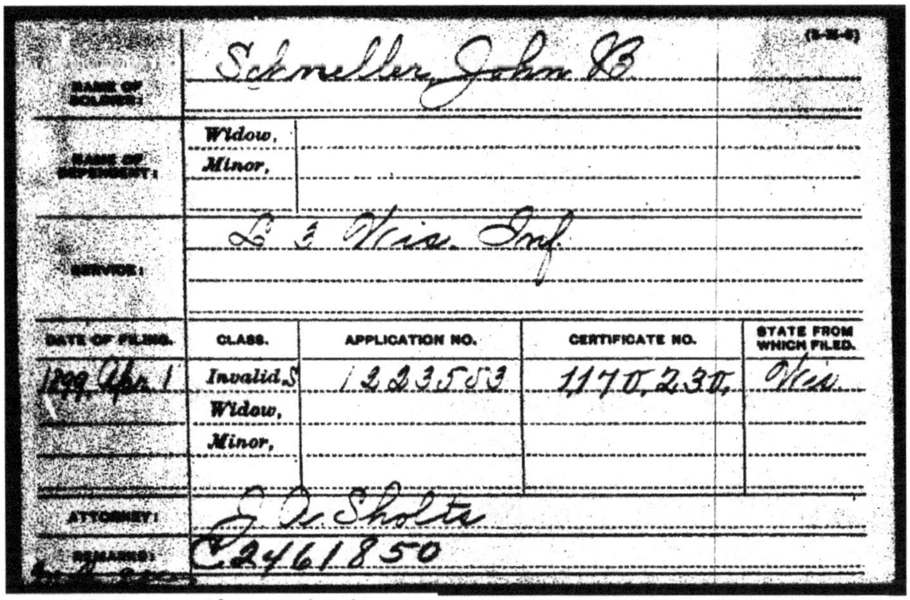

Name of soldier: Schneller, John B.
Name of dependent: Widow, Minor,
Service: K 3 Wis. Inf.

Date of filing.	Class.	Application No.	Certificate No.	State from which filed.
1899 Apr 1	Invalid, S	1223553	1170230	Wis.
	Widow,			
	Minor,			

Attorney: J. W. Sholtz
Remarks: C2461850

Figure 23: Courtesy of National Archives

The previous page image comes from the general pension index on Ancestry. John B. Schneller served with Co. K. 3rd Wisconsin Infantry. Schneller served again years later during the Mexican Punitive Expedition in 1916 and later enlisted on July 15, 1917 (after the start of World War I) to serve as a Lt. Colonel of the 128th United States Infantry. After being wounded, he transferred to the 57th Depot Brigade and was discharged on June 10, 1920. After his discharge, Schneller served as Postmaster and died on December 20, 1961, in Neenah, Wisconsin.[33]

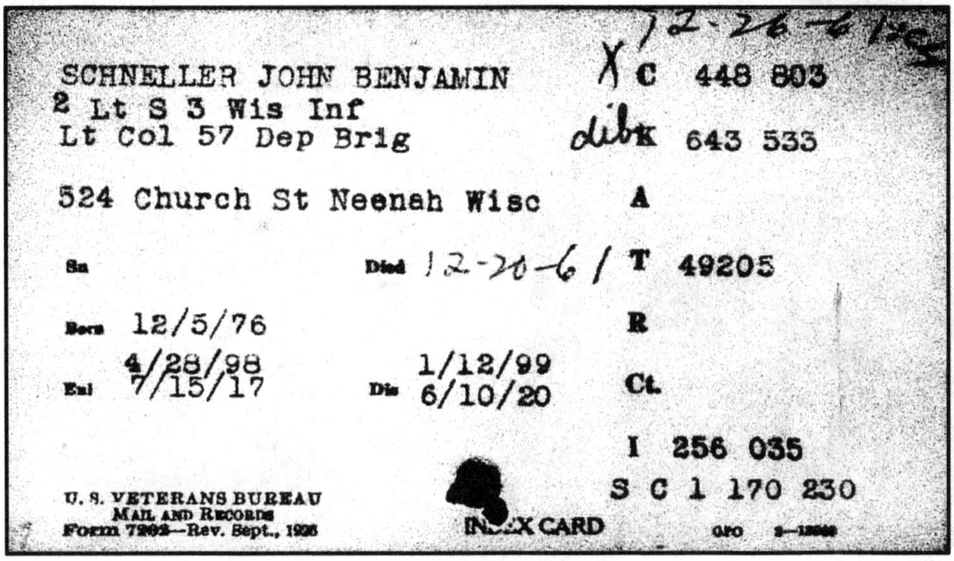

12-26-61
SCHNELLER JOHN BENJAMIN X C 448 803
2 Lt S 3 Wis Inf
Lt Col 57 Dep Brig dibK 643 533
524 Church St Neenah Wisc A
Sn Died 12-20-61 T 49205
Born 12/5/76 R
Enl 4/28/98 7/15/17 Dis 1/12/99 6/10/20 Ct.
I 256 035
S C 1 170 230
U. S. VETERANS BUREAU
MAIL AND RECORDS
Form 7202—Rev. Sept., 1926
INDEX CARD

Figure 24: Courtesy of National Personnel Record Center

[33] *The Oshkosh Northwestern.* December 21, 1961.

The later index cards contain additional military service files preceded by alphabet letters. Older war periods (before World War I), in the custody of the National Personnel Record Center, usually include the following:[34]

"SO" indicates when the soldier would apply for his own original benefits (also called "Survivor Original" file).

"SC" indicates when the soldier was approved after applying for original benefits (also called the "Survivor Certificate" file).

"WO" indicates when a widow applied for the original benefits after the death of her husband where the assigned number of the file is called the "Widows Original" file.

"WC" indicates the file after the widow applied for benefits and the applicant granted the pension. The file would be designated "Widows Certificate" for the file being approved.

The image below on the left shows John B. Schneller during the Spanish-American War in 1898. On the right is him during World War I in 1917.

Figure 25: Courtesy of Michael L. Strauss

Figure 26: Courtesy of National Archives

---

[34] VA Master Index Card File. Key to Codes and Prefixes. National Personnel Record Center. RG15. Assessed 17 September 2020. https://www.archives.gov/files/calendar/genealogy-fair/2018/6-csar-handout3.pdf, where the file is available for free download. The other codes indicate service during World War I and later wars.

Navy and Marine Corps Pensions:

Pensions for Navy and Marine Corps personnel should be checked first in the general index for pensions (1861-1934). Remember that these cards have a darker shade. If the veteran cannot be located, consider searching the U.S. Navy Veteran Pensions (1861-1910). These will be discussed in greater detail later in the section on the United States Navy.

Pension Payment Cards:

In 1907, the pension department changed to recording payments on cards. This required the transfer of information from the pension payment books. Some overlap existed, as the old books were still used until 1909 to record payments. The new cards were 5" x 8" and alphabetically by the name of the pensioner or widow. The collection consists of nearly two million cards.

The cards are divided into four separate classes of records: Army Invalid and Army Widow (including volunteers, National Guard, and regulars) and Navy Invalid and Navy Widow (which includes the United States Navy, Marine Corps, and Revenue Cutter Service). The name of the veteran or widow indexes all. Two additional classes were added including Army Minor and Navy Minor, detailing the veteran's minor children in cases of the widows.

A major change in the form of the card occurred in 1923 when payments were changed to monthly instead of quarterly. The original cards are in the custody of the National Archives in RG15 at the Washington, DC, office for the Records of the Veterans Administration. These documents have been microfilmed and later digitized online. The collection is found on M850, covering 1907-1933 in 2,539 rolls of microfilm except for veterans of World War I.

https://www.familysearch.org/search/collection/1832324 indexed by name of veteran or widow. The front and back of the cards are scanned.

https://www.fold3.com/title/964/us-veterans-administration-pension-payment-cards indexed by name of veteran or widow. The front and back of the cards are scanned.

https://archive.org/details/veteransadminpensionpaymentcards?&sort=-downloads&page=2 This is a free website interface but less practical to use and browsable.

Figure 27: Courtesy of Michael L. Strauss

William T. Parsons was born on August 29, 1851, in Buffalo, New York. He was the son of John H. Parsons and Anna M. Hutton (originally from Geneva, NY).[35] He joined the New York National Guard on June 25, 1879, in Company F, 65th Regiment. Later promoted to Captain on January 7, 1880, and Major on October 27, 1887, Parsons was active in the guard until the Spanish-American War.[36] Parsons' regiment was called up by executive order from President William McKinley in 1898. He was transferred to the 202nd NY Infantry on July 1, 1898, in Buffalo, New York, and served on the F&S (Field & Staff) with the rank of 1st Lieutenant and served as the regimental quartermaster. During the Spanish-American War, Parsons became ill and was absent at Havana, Cuba, and later discharged on April 15, 1899, at Savannah, GA.[37] William T. Parsons returned to Buffalo, NY, and died on October 13, 1901.[38]

___

[35] Henry Parsons, *Parsons Family: Descendants of Cornet Joseph Parson, 1636-1655*, (New York: Frank Allaben Genealogical Company, 1912), 300.
[36] *Annual Report of the Adjutant General of the States of New York for the Year 1897* (Albany: New York State Printers, 1897), 119.
[37] New York, Spanish American War Military and Naval Service Records, 1898-1902, *Ancestry*. Accessed on 17 September 2020 at: https://www.ancestry.com/search/collections/5351.
[38] *The Buffalo Times*, October 14, 1901.

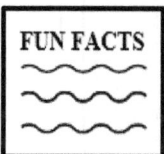

NAME: *Matilda C. Parsons*				5822			Certificate No. *58/206*																
Last paid to:				**Date:** *17 25*				**Remarks:**															
Yr.	Qr.	Day.	Amount.	Yr.	Qr.	Day.	Amount.	Yr.	Qr.	Day.	Amount.	Yr.	Qr.	Day.	Amount.	Yr.	Qr.	Day.	Amount.	Yr.	Qr.	Day.	Amount.
1907.	1			1911.	1			1915.	1	4	54	1919.	1	4	76		9	4	50	1927.	1		
	2				2	APR 1911			2	4	51		2	4	75		0	4	25		2		
	3				3	7 A B W			3	4	51		3	4	75		11	4	25		3		
	4				4	4 N D B			4	4	51		4	4	75		12	4			4		
1908.	1			1912.	1	4 A B W		1916.	1	4	51	1920.	1	4	75		1	4		1928.	1		
	2				2	5 NT			2	4	51		2	4	75		2	4			2		Trans. to Hq.
	3				3	6 N D B			3	4	51		3	4	75		3				3		Payment Card.
	4				4	12			4	4	51		4	4	75		4				4		
1909.	1			1913.	1	4 NDB		1917.	1	4	51	1921.	1	4	75	1925.	1			1929.	1		
	2				2	4 51			2	4	51		2	4	75		2				2		
	3				3	4			3	4	51		3	4	75		3				3		
	4				4	4			4	4	51		4	4	75		4				4		
1910.	1			1914.	1	4 51		1918.	1	4	74 47	1922.	1	4	75	1926.	1			1930.	1		
	2				2	4 51			2	4	75		2	4	75		2				2		
	3				3	4 51			3	4	75		3	4	75		3				3		
	4				4	4 54			4	4	76		4	GROUP 1 PAID TO JULY 4, 1923			4				4		

Figure 28: Images Courtesy of National Archives

The card indexes above (both front and back) are the pension payment cards for the widow of William T. Parsons. His wife, Matilda C. Parsons, was paid on July 4, 1923.

> **FUN FACTS**
>
> **DID YOU KNOW** the Spanish-American War cost the United States about 250 million dollars and 3,000 lives? Only about ten percent of the deaths were from the battlefield, with the rest due to transmittable diseases and other causes.

United States Census Records

The United States Census (first recorded in 1790) was a decennial census mandated through Article 1, Section 2 of the United States Constitution. It stated that "*Representatives and direct Taxes shall be apportioned among the several States ... according to their respective Numbers*". The first enumeration occurred within three years of the ratification of the Constitution and was taken thereafter every ten years.[39]

Several federal census schedules have recorded information on persons who served during the Spanish-American War, the Boxer Rebellion, and the Philippine Insurrection. The census years containing this information include 1900, 1930, 1940, and 1950.

1900 United States Census

The 1900 United States Census enumerated military personnel who were on active duty. All persons in the military, naval, or marine service of the United States were enumerated. This included civilians who were connected as employees of the federal government. The census forms would enumerate active-duty personnel and the families of officers and enlisted men in the military service stationed overseas.[40]

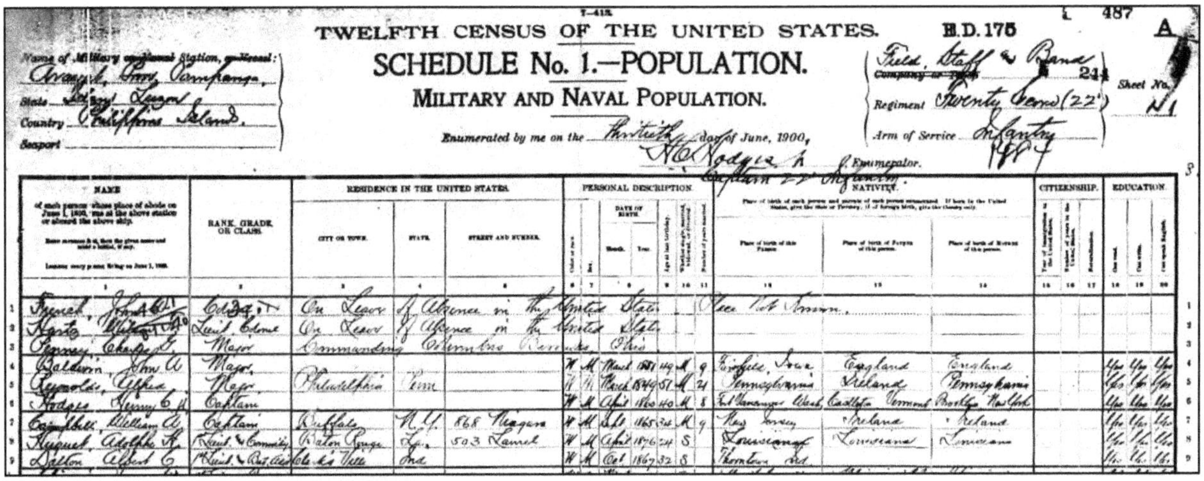
TWELFTH CENSUS OF THE UNITED STATES.

SCHEDULE No. 1.—POPULATION.

MILITARY AND NAVAL POPULATION.

E.D. 175

Enumerated by me on the Thirtieth day of June, 1900,

Figure 29: Courtesy of the National Archives

The Bureau of the Census cooperated with the Department of War and the Department of the Navy to complete the census information on two forms:

- Form 7-413-Schedule No. 1 of military and naval population

[39] *Two Hundred Years of U.S. Census Taking: Population and Housing Questions, 1790-1990* (Washington, DC: U.S. Government Printing Office, 1989), 1.

[40] *Twelfth Census of the United States: Instructions to Enumerators* (Washington, DC: U.S. Government Printing Office, 1900), 9.

- Form 7-224- Schedule No. 1 of civilians of the U.S. at military or naval stations.[41]

VETERANS	
Whether a veteran of the U.S. military or naval forces mobilized for any war or expedition	
Yes or No	What war or expedition
30	31

Figure 30: Courtesy of Bureau of the U.S. Census

This census targeted regional areas of China, Cuba, Guam, Philippines, Puerto Rico, and Tutuila (American Samoa), where, at the end of the Spanish-American War, these areas were under United States control. The census enumerator required the name of the military station, state, country, or (if applicable) the seaport. Also recorded was the company or troop, regiment, and arm of service. The general questions asked each person included:

- Name of each person on 1 June 1900 at the station or aboard ship
- Person's rank, grade, or class
- Residence in the United States for each person; city or town, state, and street number
- Personal description of each person, gender, date of birth, age, marital status including widowed persons and number of years married
- Nativity of each person-birthplace of person, father, and their mother
- Citizenship status of immigration, number of years in the United States, and whether naturalized. This only applies to foreign-born people.
- Educational status-whether the person could read, write, or speak English.

The 1900 census is available online on *FamilySearch*, and *Ancestry*.

https://www.familysearch.org/search/collection/ 1325221 *FamilySearch* has a menu under Armed Forces-Foreign Counties for listings.

https://www.ancestry.com/search/collections/7602 *Ancestry* has a dropdown menu for Military and Naval Forces.

1930 United States Census

The 1930 United States Census also required answers to questions regarding veterans and their service. This included any veteran alive from any previous war or expedition.

All persons enumerated over 21 years of age were asked about their veteran status.

---

[41] Karen M. Mills, *Americans Overseas in U.S. Censuses* (Washington, DC: U.S. Government Printing Office, 1993), 8.

Question 30 – Whether any person was an ex-service Army, Navy, or Marine Corps member. The Coast Guard and the prior Revenue Cutter Service were omitted. The person had to respond "Yes" or "No".

Question 31 – This question is directed at any veteran. Which war or expedition served would be listed for each war period abbreviations (see below listing) of those used.

The abbreviations used for question 31 include:[42]

- Spanish-American War to be abbreviated as "SP"
- Philippine Insurrection to be abbreviated as "PHIL"
- Boxer Rebellion to be abbreviated as "BOX"

The 1930 census is available online on *FamilySearch*, and *Ancestry*.

https://www.familysearch.org/search/collection/1810731 With *FamilySearch*, names can be searched or browsed by geographic areas of the United States.

https://www.ancestry.com/search/collections/6224 With *Ancestry*, names can be searched individually or browsed by areas of the United States.

https://www.fold3.com/publication/20/us-census-federal-1930 With Fold3, names can be searched or browsed by areas of the United States.

1940 United States Census

The 1940 census also asked questions of veterans. These only applied to about 5% of persons enumerated overall for the United States population. Any person enumerated who has their information listed on lines numbers 14, 29, 55, and 68 was to receive supplemental questions at the bottom of each form and fill in question numbers 39-41 requesting veteran status.

All persons enumerated on 14, 29, 55, and 68 were asked if they or their spouse, widow or child (under age 18) was a veteran.

Question 39 – If any of the above applied to answer "Yes,"

Question 40 – This question was directed to the child of a veteran and asked whether dead. An enumerated person must answer "Yes" or "No"

Question 41 – Question directed at any veteran. Which war or military service was rendered? Enumerated would list for each war period abbreviations (see below listing).

---

[42] *Fifteenth Census: Instructions to Enumerators, Population and Agriculture* (Washington, DC: U.S. Government Printing Office, 1930), 237-241.

VETERANS			
Is this person a veteran of the United States military forces; or the wife, widow, or under 18-year-old child of a veteran?			
If so, enter "Yes"	If child, is veteran-father dead? (Yes or No)	War or military service	CODE (Leave blank)
39	40	41	I

Figure 31: Courtesy of Bureau of the U.S. Census

The coded column was left blank intentionally.

The code column was not to be filled out by the enumerator. This was to be used by the United States Census Bureau staff for internal statistics.

The abbreviations used for question 41 include.[43]

Spanish-American War, Philippine Insurrection or Boxer Rebellion- Code "S"

Both Spanish-American War and World War I- Code "SW"

Regulars (including Army, Navy, or Marine Corps) during peacetime only -Code "R"

The 1940 census is available online on *FamilySearch*, and *Ancestry*.

https://www.familysearch.org/1940census With *FamilySearch*, individual names can be searched, and this allows users to browse by geographic region of the United States.

https://www.ancestry.com/search/collections/2442 With *Ancestry,* names can be searched, or the geographic areas of the United States can be browsed.

1950 United States Census

On October 5, 1978, the United States government passed Public Law 95-416, which restricted access to the U.S. Census for 72 years after being enumerated. The "72-Year Rule" will be released to the public on April 1, 2022.[44]

The 1950 census also asked questions of veterans. These applied to a small portion of the overall population. Any person enumerated who has their information listed on lines numbers 4, 9, 14, 19, and 24 was to receive supplemental questions at the bottom of each form and fill in question numbers 33a, 33b, and 33c requesting veteran status.[45]

---

[43] *Sixteenth Decennial Census of the United States: Instructions to Enumerators* (Washington, DC: Department of Commerce-Bureau of the Census, 1940), 76-77.
[44] Public Law 95-416. Accessed 13 June 2020. https://www.census.gov/history/pdf/NARA_Legislation.pdf.
[45] 1950 Enumerators Manual. Accessed 13 June 2020. https://www.census.gov/content/dam/Census/programs-surveys/decennial/technical-documentation/questionnaires/1950instructions.pdf.

Questions 33a and 33b – Whether any persons served in World War I or II. Answer to be given as "Yes" or "No".

Question 33c – Whether any other time in military service or another war period to be answered "Yes" or "No."

If Male— (Ask each question) Did he ever serve in the U. S. Armed Forces during—		
World War II	World War I	Any other time, including present service
33a	33b	33c
☐ Yes ☐ No	☐ Yes ☐ No	☐ Yes ☐ No
☐ Yes ☐ No	☐ Yes ☐ No	☐ Yes ☐ No

Figure 32: Courtesy of Bureau of U.S. Census

These questions only applied to men over 14 and were not asked of women. Any veterans who served during the Spanish-American War, Boxer Rebellion, or Philippine Insurrection would be in their late 60s or older and could have responded with an answer to the affirmative that they served in an earlier war period.

GENEALOGY TOOL Research help can be found using Wikipedia pages from the website for FamilySearch titled United States Military Records where patrons can search military conflicts from the Colonial Wars to the Vietnam War. Wiki pages cover resources to locate persons who served in each of the military period and not weapons, battles, or tactics.

State Census Records

The taking of state census often follows the pattern of in-between the decennial years of the United States Federal Census. Some states recorded information during less common time periods (like New York in 1892). Unfortunately, not all state census returns have survived, and some are only partially available to researchers. The enumeration of military information and questions is found in more than one state's returns. Iowa [1915, 1925], Minnesota [1905], and South Dakota [1915, 1925, 1935, and 1945] all asked questions of residents who fought in the Spanish-American War.[46]

Iowa State Census

1905 Census – The information requested for military service asked whether the enumerated served in the Civil War, the Mexican War, or the Spanish-American War. Also asked were the company, regiment, state, type of service, date of enlistment, and discharge.

https://www.familysearch.org/search/collection/2126961 With *FamilySearch*, individual names can be searched for or browsed by the counties in the state.

1915 Census – The information requested for military service asked whether the enumerated served in the Civil War, Mexican War, or the Spanish-American War. Also asked was the company, regiment, state, and the type of service-infantry, cavalry, or artillery, or the Navy.

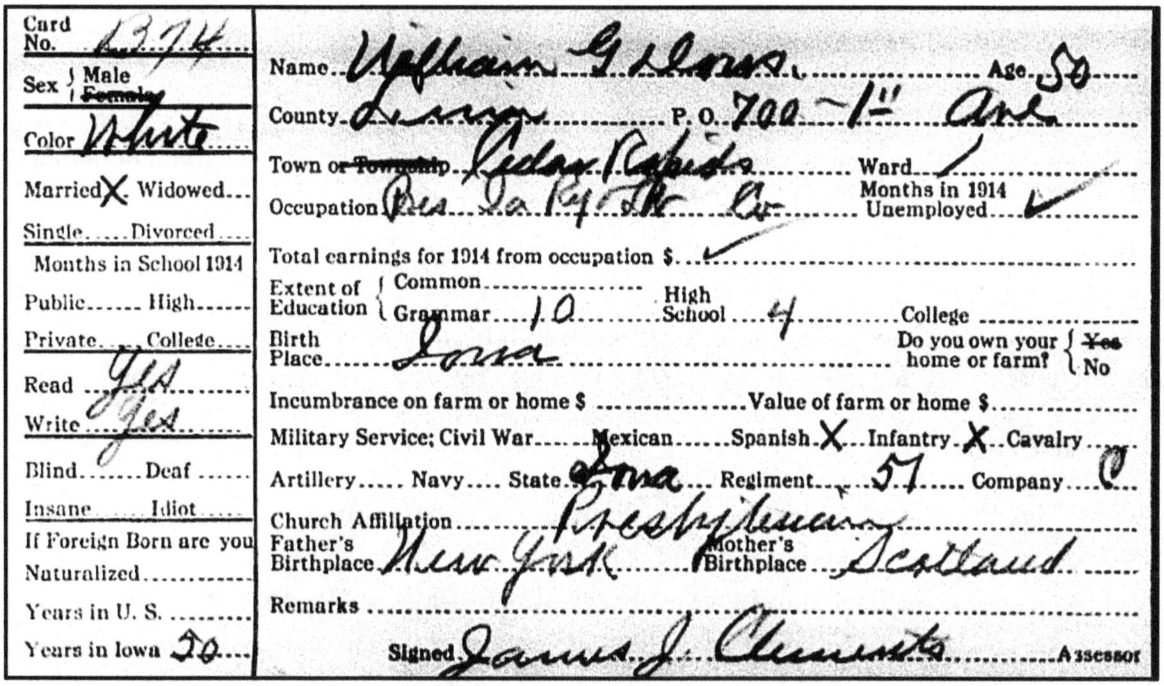
Card No. 1374
Sex Male ~~Female~~
Color White
Married X Widowed
Single Divorced
Months in School 1914
Public High
Private College
Read Yes
Write Yes
Blind Deaf
Insane Idiot
If Foreign Born are you Naturalized
Years in U. S.
Years in Iowa 50

Name William G. [illegible] Age 50
County Linn P. O. 700 – 1st Ave.
Town or ~~Township~~ Cedar Rapids Ward 1
Occupation Pres. Ia. Ry. & Lt. Co. Months in 1914 Unemployed ✓
Total earnings for 1914 from occupation $ ✓
Extent of Education: Common; Grammar 10; High School 4; College
Birth Place Iowa
Do you own your home or farm? ~~Yes~~ No
Incumbrance on farm or home $ Value of farm or home $
Military Service; Civil War Mexican Spanish X Infantry X Cavalry
Artillery Navy State Iowa Regiment 51 Company C
Church Affiliation Presbyterian
Father's Birthplace New York Mother's Birthplace Scotland
Remarks
Signed James J. Clements Assessor

Figure 33: Courtesy of Iowa State Historical Department-Des Moines, IA

46 Loretto Dennis Szucs, *The Source: A Guidebook to American Genealogy* (Salt Lake City: Ancestry, 2006), 204-206 and Ann S. Lainhart, *State Census Records* (Baltimore: Genealogical Publishing Company, 1992), 9-11.

On the previous page is the 1915 Iowa State Census sheet enumerated for William G. Dows (pictured on the left), who resided at 700 1ˢᵗ Avenue in Cedar Rapids, IA. He was appointed Colonel of the 49ᵗʰ Iowa Infantry on April 26, 1898, at Camp McKinley in Des Moines, IA, and mustered out on May 13, 1899, in Savannah, GA, with his regiment that served in Cuba.

On December 19, 1898, Dow and his unit were ordered to board transport ships bound for Cuba. Upon arrival two days later, the regiment marched to Havana, where the men would serve on garrison duty for the rest of the war. The regiment was relieved on April 4, 1899, with orders to return to the United States and, in turn, to be discharged.[47]

Figure 34: Courtesy of The Story of the Forty-Ninth Iowa, 1918

https://www.familysearch.org/search/collection/2240483 With *FamilySearch*, individual names can be searched for or browsed by the counties in the state.

1925 Census – The information requested for military service asked whether the enumerated served in the Civil War, Spanish-American War, or World War I. The questions asked included whether the enumerated person was the veteran, the branch of service for each war, and whether the person was enlisted or drafted into service. It should be noted that, unlike other wars, the Spanish-American War enlistees could not be drafted as no national conscription was in place.

https://www.familysearch.org/search/collection/2224537 With *FamilySearch*, individual names can be searched for or browsed by the counties in the state.

Ancestry has a nice collection of the Iowa state census online searchable between 1836-1925.

https://www.ancestry.com/search/collections/1084 With *Ancestry*, the Iowa state census collection can be searched for individual names or browsed by specific year and location.

Minnesota State Census

1905 Census – The information requested for military service was limited to the Civil War and the Spanish-American War. If service was indicated, the type of service was asked. The census at the time used the abbreviations [Civ] for Civil War, [Span] for Spanish-American War, then [Sold] for soldier, and lastly [Sail] for sailor. The military information is limited and can be found in the last two columns (on the right) on the census pages.

---

[47] *Roster and Record of Iowa Soldiers of the Mexican War, Indian Campaigns, War of the Rebellion and the Spanish-American and Philippine Wars* (Des Moines: Emory H. English State Printer, 1911), 281-283.

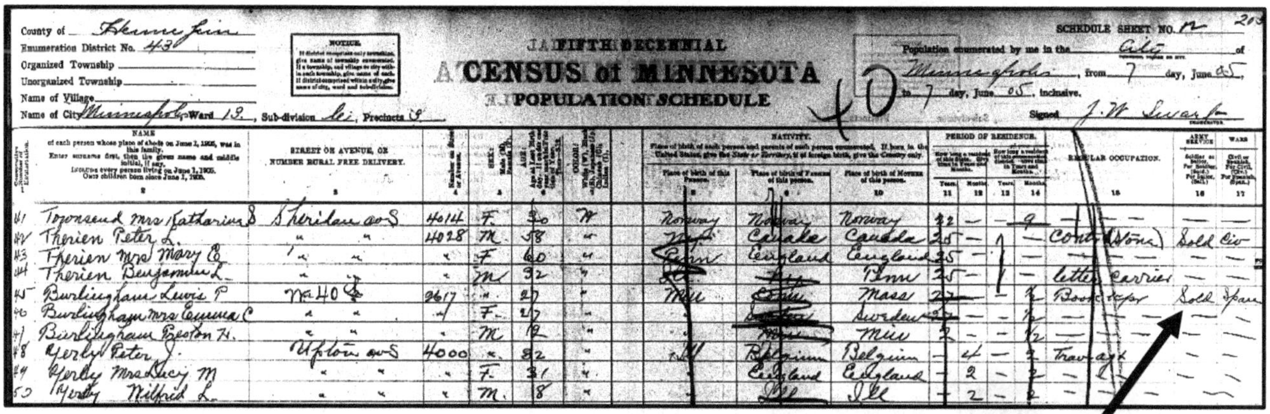

Figure 35: Courtesy of Minnesota State Library-St. Paul, MN   Military Service Columns

On the fifth line above is Lewis P. Burlingham, who served in Company K. of the 13th Minnesota Infantry. He mustered on April 29, 1898, in Stillwater, MN, and left the Presidio in San Francisco, CA, to fight in the Philippines. The regiment arrived too late to participate in the war but remained on duty for the Philippine Insurrection and participated in multiple skirmishes and engagements before being mustered out on October 3, 1899, in San Francisco, CA.[48]

https://www.familysearch.org/search/collection/1503056 With *FamilySearch*, individual names can be searched for or browsed by the counties in the state.

South Dakota State Census

1915 Census – The information requested for military service asked whether the enumerated served in the Civil War, the Mexican War, or the Spanish-American War. The census also asked for the company, regiment, and state of service.

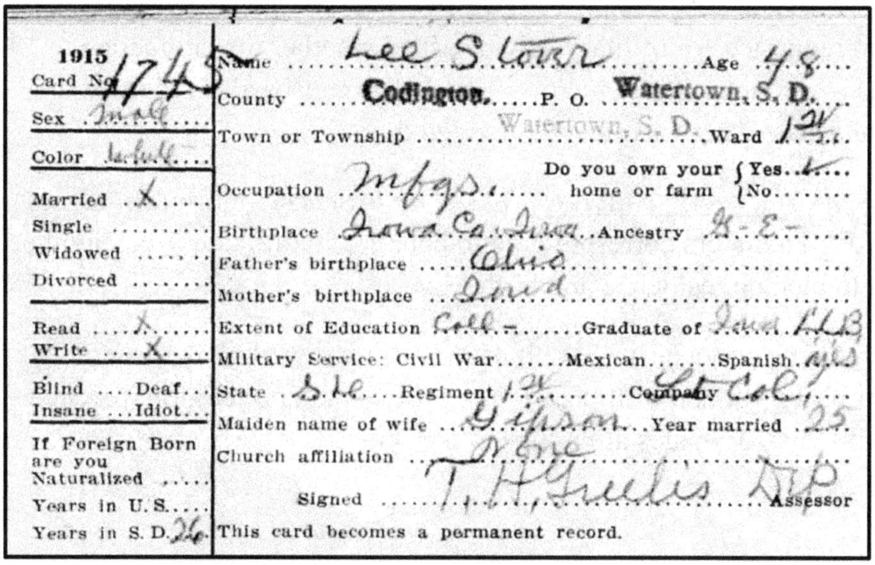

Figure 36: Courtesy of South Dakota Historical Society

---

[48] Franklin F. Holbrook, *Minnesota in the Spanish-American War and the Philippine Insurrection* (St. Paul: Minnesota War Records Commission, 1923), 219.

At the bottom of the previous page is the 1915 South Dakota State Census sheet enumerated for Lee Stover, who resided in the 1st ward of Watertown, SD, in the census year. He was appointed Lt. Colonel for the 1st South Dakota Infantry regiment on April 25, 1898, at Fort Meade in South Dakota, and served overseas in the Philippines, where he participated in the fighting with his regiment. Upon his return, he was discharged on October 5, 1899, along with the rest of the men in San Francisco, CA, where the men would return home to South Dakota to their families.

The 1st South Dakota Infantry sustained several killed and wounded during the Philippine Insurrection.[49]

Figure 37: Courtesy of A Brief History of South Dakota, 1905.

https://www.familysearch.org/search/collection/1476041 With *FamilySearch,* individual names can be searched or browsed by film numbers corresponding to counties in the state if the number is known. Filters can be added to include birthplace and birth year.

https://www.ancestry.com/search/collections/60160 With *Ancestry,* individual names can be searched using filters added for birth year and birthplace. Other filters include nationality, marriage year, race, and gender. No scanned images are online at Ancestry.

1925 Census – The information requested for military service asked whether the enumerated served in the Civil War, Spanish-American War, or World War I. The census also recorded the company, regiment, division, and state where service was rendered.

https://www.familysearch.org/search/collection/1476077 With *FamilySearch,* individual names can be searched or browsed by film numbers corresponding to counties in the state if the number is known. Filters can be added to include residence and birth years.

https://www.ancestry.com/search/collections/60161 With *Ancestry,* individual names can be searched using filters added for birth year and birthplace. Other filters include religion, parent's birthplace, race, and gender. No scanned images are online at Ancestry.

---

[49] Doane Robinson, *A Brief History of South Dakota* (New York: American Book Company, 1905), 187-193; and Doane Robinson, *History of South Dakota, vol I* (Indianapolis: B.F. Bowen & Company, 1904), 363-385, 426.

1935 Census – The information requested for military service asked whether the enumerated served in the Civil War, Spanish-American War, or World War I. The census also required the company, regiment, division, and state where service was rendered.

https://www.familysearch.org/search/collection/1614831 With *FamilySearch,* individual names can be searched or browsed by film numbers corresponding to counties in the state if the number is known. Filters can be added to include residence, birth, and marriage dates.

https://www.ancestry.com/search/collections/60162 With *Ancestry,* individual names can be searched using filters added for birth year and birthplace. Other filters include marital status, post office, naturalization status, race, and gender. No scanned images are online for this census at Ancestry.

1945 Census – The information requested for military service asked whether the enumerated served in the Spanish-American War, World War I, and World War II. The census also asked for the company, regiment, division, and state where service was rendered.

https://www.familysearch.org/search/collection/1747589 With *FamilySearch,* individual names can be searched or browsed by film numbers corresponding to counties in the state if the number is known. Filters can be added to include residence and birth year.

https://www.ancestry.com/search/collections/60163 With *Ancestry,* individual names can be searched using filters added for birth year and birthplace. Other filters include marital status, years in the United States, post office, parent's birthplace, race, and gender. No scanned images are online for this census at Ancestry.

New York State Census

1917 Census – New York passed a resolution in the assembly on March 29, 1917 (Stat. § 185. 1917) in the weeks leading up to World War I to provide for a military census. Different questionnaires were asked of males and females. Questions 26-30 asked whether the enumerated person was a veteran, organization, and dates of service, and later service information.[50]

The census covered all males between the ages of 16 to 50 years. This date range included men who served during the Spanish-American War, the Boxer Rebellion, and the Philippine Insurrection. Checking state town and city archives could turn up copies of the original census forms. Afterward, an inventory report was published showing the form and questions asking about prior service and details about the census.

---

[50] *Laws of the States of New York passed at the one hundred and fortieth session of the Legislature* (Albany: J.B. Lyon Company, 1917), 185. The session law is found in Chapter 103.

The images below show part of the form used for the 1917 New York Military Census.[51]

*THE QUESTIONNAIRE FOR MALES.

DO NOT WRITE IN THIS MARGIN

Election District.......... Subdivision_____ Town or City....................... County.......................

STATE OF NEW YORK
THE ADJUTANT GENERAL'S OFFICE
MILITARY CENSUS BUREAU
ALBANY

Census and Inventory of the Military Resources of the State under Chapter 103, Laws of 1917, and Acts Supplementary Thereto, and Enrollment of Persons Liable to Service in the Militia under Chapter 41, Laws of 1909, and Acts Amendatory Thereof (Military Law) by Order and Direction of the Governor

Form for Males 16 to 50 Years of Age Inclusive. Use Pen and Ink. Sign Personally. Do Not Fold

Figure 38: Courtesy of New York State Military Census and Inventory

26. Have you ever been in the military or naval service, or had military or naval training at school, college, camp or cruise?...

(a) In what organizations?	(b) Date of enlistment?	(c) Date of discharge?	(d) In what grade?

Figure 39: Courtesy of New York State Military Census and Inventory

GENEALOGY CLUE State census questionnaires did not ask about those veterans who served in the Boxer Rebellion or the Philippine Insurrection. Those listed as Spanish-American war veterans could have all served in the other two conflicts.

---

[51] Ibid., the questions for numbers 27-30 were additional questions outside prior military or National Guard service. At the time of the census enumeration, the Selective Service Act of 1917 had not passed Congress, which would otherwise make this census unnecessary.

United States Navy

In the last two decades of the twentieth century, the Navy perceived a transformation as the service looked to rebuild and retire larger numbers of aged warships that had fought in the late Civil War. Led by Secretary of the Navy William H. Hunt in 1883, Congress appropriated funds to construct several armored cruisers, following in 1885 with the building and launching of our first two battleships (including the USS *Maine*) beginning in 1886.[52]

The passage of the Navy Act of 1890 further strengthened the service, with several more capital ships completed or under construction joining the fleet. This brought about a change, with the United States Navy taking shape among the strongest navies in the world.[53]

In the opening months of 1898, tensions between Spain and the United States began to escalate, with the Navy dispatching the USS *Maine* to the Spanish colony in Cuba both as a show of force and to protect the interests of our citizens. At 9:40 PM on the night of February 15, 1898, the force of an explosion blew apart the warship with the loss of 260 officers and men onboard. This event would lead to President William McKinley declaring war on Spain in April 1898.

Figure 40: Courtesy of Library of Congress

Figure 41: Courtesy of Naval History and Heritage Command

The Secretary of the Navy was John D. Long (above on left), with the Assistant Secretary of the Navy Theodore Roosevelt (on the right) in charge of Navy operations. Earlier on February 26, 1898, Commodore George Dewey received a cable from Roosevelt to be ready in the event of war so that the Spanish squadron would not go on the offensive in the Philippine Islands.[54]

---

[52] Nathan Miller, *The U.S. Navy a History, 3rd Edition*, (Annapolis: Naval Institute Press, 1997), 149-155.

[53] Ibid., 155. The United States Navy in 1870 was in twelfth place among the world powers, and by the mid-1890s, had moved to fifth place compared to other world navies.

[54] Ronald H. Spector, *Admiral of the New Empire: The Life and Career of George Dewey*, (Baton Rouge: Louisiana State University Press, 1974), 44.

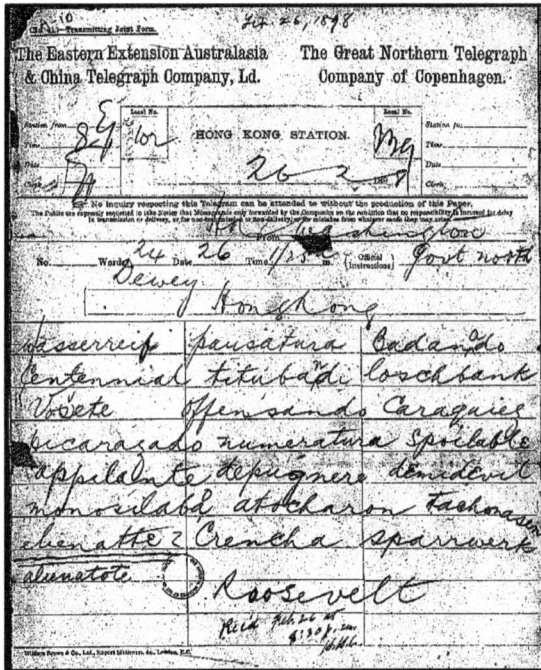

Figure 42: Courtesy of National Archives (RG45)

The cable (written in code) authorized Dewey to engage the enemy. War was declared in April 1898 without the knowledge of Secretary Long. The Asiatic fleet set sail for Manilla Bay with eight warships and a collier. On the morning of 1 May 1898, they attacked and soundly defeated the Spanish fleet guarding the harbor.

The United States Navy played an important role in winning the Spanish-American War and contributed to the victories in the Boxer Rebellion and the later Philippine Insurrection. Acting to block the harbors and riverways of the enemy, keeping the Spanish from either reinforcing their positions or receiving needed supplies, the United States Navy performed honorably.

The United States' victories by the end of 1902 ushered in a new era of naval history by bringing about a modern Navy. This new fleet would stand as sentinels to guide the United States into the entry of World War I on 6 April 1917.

RG24 in the National Archives in Washington, DC, contains records of officers and enlisted personnel during the Spanish-American War, Boxer Rebellion, and the Philippine Insurrection.[55]

Officers

Entry 139. *Register of Applications, 1897-1917*. A three-volume set of registers containing applications for commissions. The indexes are arranged alphabetically by name of the applicant and include detailed information on both military and civilian life

Entry 143. *Applications for Appointment, 1875-1878, 1886-1917*. Records of applications for appointment as officers in the Navy. The series is sub-grouped into sixteen types of officer positions, including commissioned and warrant status.

Entry 145. *Letters offering Services in the Event of War with Spain, 1898*. This set of records for officers is unique to the Spanish-American War and contains letters of application requesting to be commissioned in the Navy. Each of the files are arranged by the name of the applicant.

---

[55] Virgil E. Baugh. *Preliminary Inventories of the National Archives of the United States*. Records of the Bureau of Naval Personnel. No. 123. In Record Group 24, (Washington, DC: National Archives and Records Administration, 1960), 46-71.

Entry 149: *List of Applicants for Voluntary Retirement, 1899-1915*. The listing of officers is indexed alphabetically by surname and arranged by date. Volumes are labeled *"Partial Key"* based on those officers who requested retirement from the Navy.

Entry 165: *Commissions Issued to Officer, 1844-1936*. Indexed and arranged alphabetically by the first letter of the name of the officer, recording on printed forms their date of appointment when commissioned in the United States Navy.

Entry 166: *Warrants Issued to Officers, 1846-1925*. Within the military rank structure between enlisted and commissioned officers in the United States Navy were Warrants who were military occupational specialists, the highest grade of enlisted petty officers not commissioned.

Entry 185: *Lists of Officers, 1878-1909*. This series of records is divided into three separate lists:

1) List of officers on ships recorded quarterly from 1878-1905
2) List of officers on shore duty recorded quarterly from 1895-1909
3) List of officers on short stations, no at sea, recorded quarterly from 1907-1909

The listed are arranged and indexed by year, then sub-grouped by ship (or short station), and then alphabetically by the officer's name.

Enlisted Men

Entry 204: *Records Relating to Enlisted men who served in the Navy between 1842 and 1885*. This set of records consists of folded papers placed into envelopes and commonly referred to as Navy *"Jackets"* for each enlisted sailor. This collection is especially helpful if the sailor served multiple enlistments through the Spanish-American War. Documents and correspondence can include records from 1885 to 1941 for sailors making claims, applying for pensions, and seeking to be admitted to an aged home for sailors.

Entry 205: *Correspondence Jackets on Enlisted Men, 1904-1943*. This record set continues with previous entry no. 204, and includes letters, enclosures, affidavits, and other legal documents for sailors in the United States Navy.

Entry 210: *Record Cards for Recipients of Medals, Badges, Bars, and Pins issued by the Navy Department, 1899-1910*. Indexed records are arranged alphabetically by the recipient's name and include the type of award received, the date, and the certificate number.

Entry 219: *Weekly Returns of Enlistments at Naval Rendezvous, 1855-1891*. This is especially helpful in locating a career Navy sailor who enlisted before the Spanish-American War but would continue in service. It is very similar to the Army CMSRs that record name, age, birthplace, residence, occupation, physical description, and any prior service. Arranged by dates of enlistment and by port of rendezvous. This series of original weekly returns is available online at *Fold3*: https://www.fold3.com/title/777/naval-enlistment-weekly-returns-1855-1891

Entry 222: *Weekly Returns of Recruits on Receiving Ships, 1855-1902.* Arranged by weekly rendezvous for enlisting sailors. Receiving ships were training vessels where newly recruited men would receive rudimentary training before assignment.

Entry 224: *Keys to and Registers of Enlistment Returns, 1846-1902.* The largest collection of Navy records pertinent to service during the Spanish-American War and the Philippine Insurrection called "Key to Enlistment Returns," records the name, enlistment dates, and a summary of the sailor's military service.

Entry 238: *Record of Certificates of Discharge Issued under Act of Congress Approved 14 August 1888, covering 1889-1901.* Certificates are arranged alphabetically by the first letter of the sailor's name. This includes the name, date, and a brief service record review.

Entry 240. *Descriptive Lists of Deserters, 1902-1911.* The Set of records at the end of the Philippine Insurrection includes sailors who have enlisted previously. Arranged by the first letter of the name, each entry contained a detailed description of the deserter.

The National Personnel Record Center in St. Louis, MO, also has copies of service files for sailors in their custody. For enlisted discharged, deceased, or who retired from 1886-1994, and for officers from 1903-1994, requests should also be sent using Standard Form 180 downloaded: https://www.archives.gov/files/sf180-request-pertaining-to-military-records-exp-april2018-1.pdf

Muster Rolls

Found in Entry 132, 133, and 134 are Muster Rolls of Ships (1860-1900), Muster Rolls of Stations and Shipping Articles (1891-1900), and Muster Rolls of Ship and Shore Establishments (1898-1939). Entries include the name, rank, or rate of the sailor.

Ship Logs

Log books were recorded daily for vessels of the United States Navy. Entries usually included the ship's name, list of the officers, and compliment of the enlisted crew, including petty officers, seaman, ordinary seaman, landsman, boys, and number of marines onboard. The opening page also contained the service dates, the captain's name, and ports where stationed.

During the Spanish-American War, the United States Navy used a classification system for rating ships. This new system replaced an older archaic classification based on the number of guns and decks on warships. Now, the Navy would rate vessels by tonnage.[56]

LOG BOOK

OF THE

U. S. S Vicksburg

3rd Rate,

Main Battery 6
of Secondary Battery 6 Guns,

COMMANDED BY

Commander A. B. H. Lillie, U. S. Navy,

Attached to Squadron.

Commencing April 21st, 1898,

at Norfolk, Virginia,

and ending October 15th, 1898,

at Norfolk, Virginia

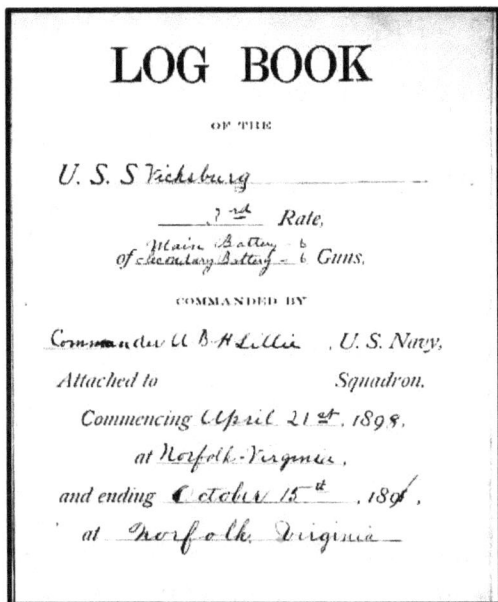

Figure 43: Courtesy of National Archives

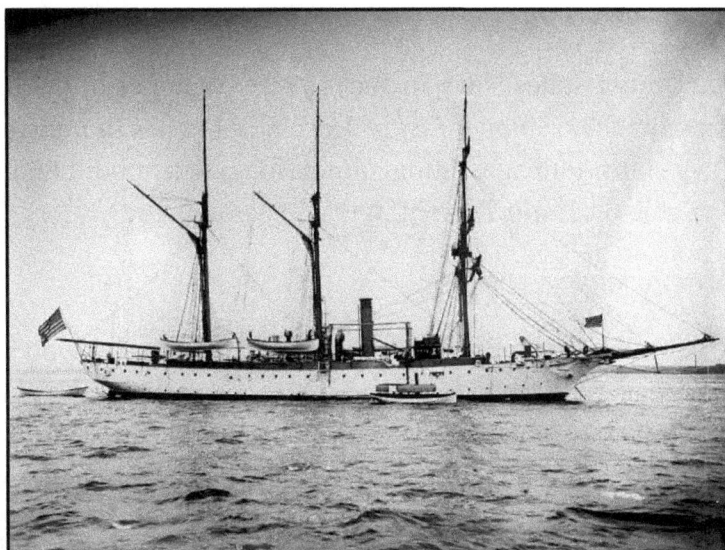

Figure 44: Courtesy of Naval History and Heritage Command

The above warship USS *Vicksburg* was a composite (iron keel and wooden planking) gunboat of United States Navy design laid down and launched on December 5, 1896, from the Bath Iron Works in Maine. With an armament of 6-4 inch, 4-six pounders, 2-1pounders she was classified as 3rd Rate by Navy tonnage.

LIST OF OFFICERS

Attached to and on board of the U. S. Steamer Vicksburg. 3rd Rate, commanded by Commander A. B. H. Lillie, U. S. N., during the period covered by this Log Book, from April 21st, 1898, to , 18 .

NAME.	RANK.	NAME.	RANK.
Lillie, A. B. H.	Commander		
Bresap, James C.	Lieutenant		
Carter, Fidelio S.	Lieutenant		
Marvell, George A.	Ensign		
Barnes, Cassius B.	Ensign		
Schenck, Robt C.	Asst Paymaster		
Johnson, Moulton K.	" Surgeon		
Price, Claud	" Engineer		
Stewart, John W.	Lieutenant		
Senn, T. J.	Ensign		
Baldwin, C.	Ensign		
Blish, J B	Lieutenant		
Hewell, J. R.	Ensign		
Ellis, M St C.	Ensign		
Grove, W. B.	Assistant Surgeon		
Harrison, M. K.	Ensign		
Roper, W. G.	Naval Cadet		

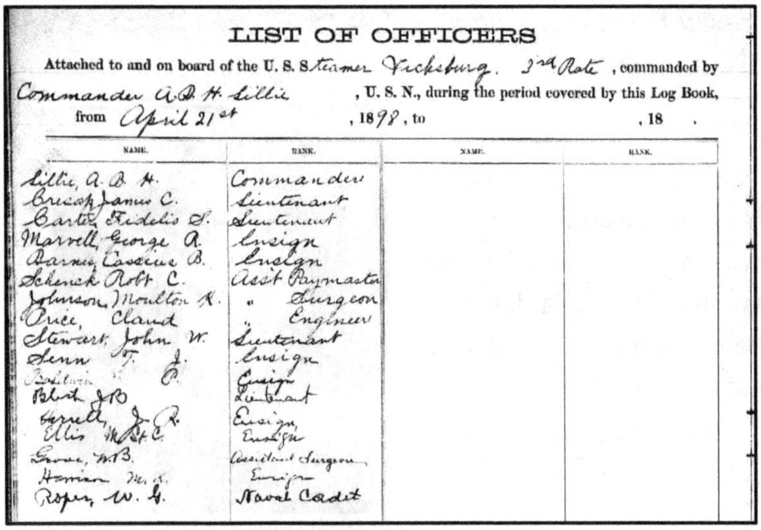

Figure 45: Courtesy of National Archives

Service included the Spanish-American War, where attached to the North Atlantic Squadron, the USS Vicksburg patrolled near Cuba, where between May 5, 1898, and June 24, 1898, she captured three Spanish blockade runners. Later service included patrolling near Luzon during the Philippine Insurrection with the Asiatic Squadron. After World War I, the vessel was transferred to the United States Coast Guard on 2 May 1921

[56] H.T. Peck, PhD. *The International Cyclopedia*, (New York: Dodd, Mead and Company, 1899), 437. The new rating system classed warships: 1st Rate-4,000 tons or more, 2nd Rate-2,000-4,000 tons, 3rd Rate-1,000-2,000 tons, and 4th Rate-under 1,000 tons. Warships of different rates were commanded by officers in the chain of command.

and renamed USCGC *Alexander Hamilton*.[57] The previous page logs book entries contained the list of commissioned officers onboard. The log above dates from April 21, 1898, with the warship under Commander Abraham Bruyn Hasbrouck Lillie.[58]

List of Navy Ships

The United States Navy includes yearly volumes of published lists of merchant vessels and warships titled *Annual List of Merchant Vessels of the United States* that includes the names of Navy ships, tonnage, rating, dimensions, where built and by whom, rigging, propulsion, and draft available on *Hathi Trust* at: https://catalog.hathitrust.org/Record/008420432.

Navy Pensions

Pension indexes for officers and enlisted personnel who served in the Navy during the Spanish-American War can be searched in the general index to pensions from 1861-1934. If not located, search in the United States Navy pension indexes, 1861-1910, divided into four subseries of records. See abbreviations in the chapter on *Military Pension Records*.

M1274 (Microfilm)-*Case Files of Disapproved Pension Applications of Widows and Other Dependents of Civil War and later Navy Veterans* (widow original-abbreviation WO)

M1279 (Microfilm)-*Case Files of Approved Pension Applications of Widows and Other Dependents of Civil War and later Navy Veterans* (widow certificates-abbreviation WC)

M1408 (Microfilm)-*Case Files of Disapproved Pension Applications of Civil War and Later Navy Veterans* (invalid survivor original-abbreviation SO)

M1469 (Microfilm)- *Case Files of Approved Pension Applications of Civil War and Later Navy Veterans* (invalid survivor certificate-abbreviation SC)

The image on the right shows Chief Yeoman George H. Ellis who was killed on July 3, 1898, at the battle of Santiago, Cuba. The report of death shared grisly details on the circumstances of how the deceased died in action. Ellis was the only United States Navy casualty during the battle and was buried in Cuba, later disinterred, repatriated, and buried at the Evergreens Cemetery in Brooklyn, NY. His former shipmates and officers attended the memorial service on October 2, 1898, with an opening address by Lt. Governor Timothy L. Woodruff of New York.[59]

Figure 46: Courtesy of Library of Congress

---

[57] Silverstone, *The New Navy, 1883-1922*, 70.
[58] Lewis R. Hamersly, *The Records of Living Officers of the U.S. Navy and Marine Corps*, (New York: L.R. Hamersly and Company, 1898), 104.
[59] *Evening Star*, July 4, 1898; and The *Brooklyn Daily Eagle*, October 1, 1898.

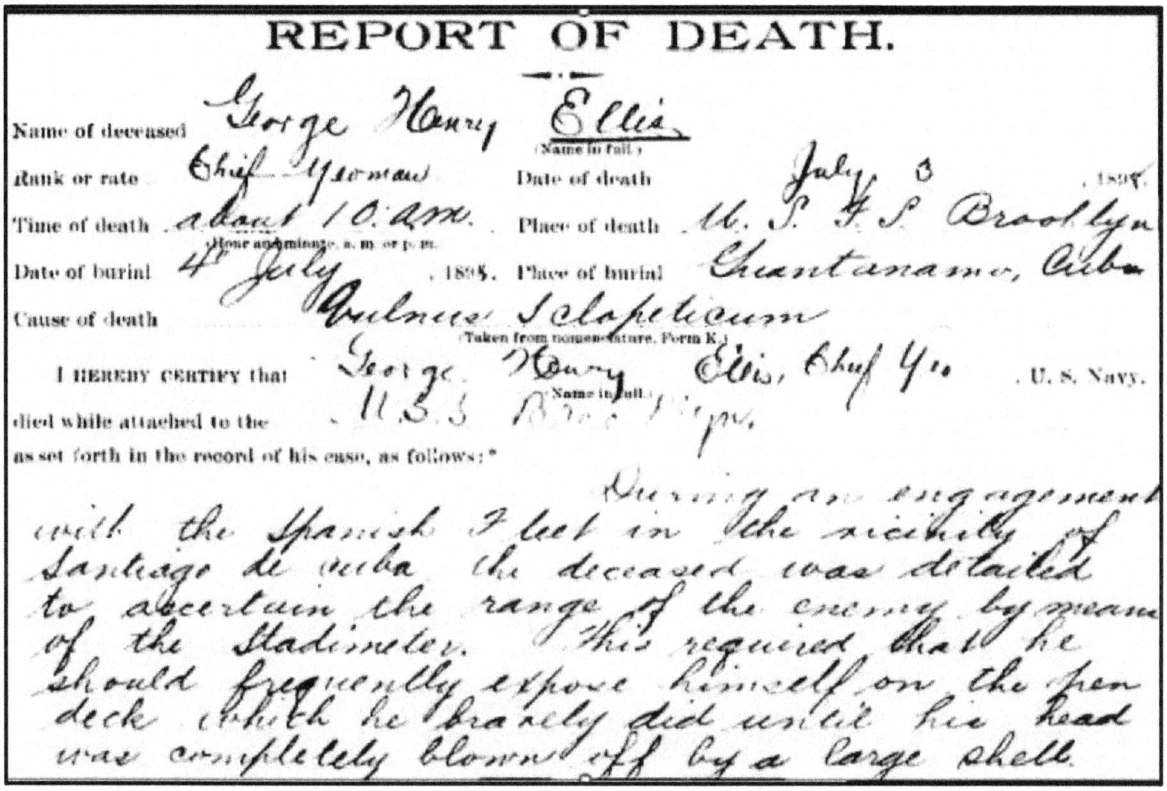

REPORT OF DEATH.

Name of deceased *George Henry Ellis*
(Name in full.)

Rank or rate *Chief Yeoman* Date of death *July 3*, 1898.

Time of death *about 10 a.m.* Place of death *U. S. F. S. Brooklyn*
(Hour and minute, a. m. or p. m.)

Date of burial *4th July*, 1898. Place of burial *Guantanamo, Cuba*

Cause of death *Vulnus Sclapeticum*
(Taken from nomenclature, Form K.)

I HEREBY CERTIFY that *George Henry Ellis, Chief Y°*, U. S. Navy.
(Name in full.)

died while attached to the *U. S. S. Brooklyn*,

as set forth in the record of his case, as follows:*

During an engagement with the Spanish Fleet in the vicinity of Santiago de Cuba the deceased was detailed to ascertain the range of the enemy by means of the Stadimeter. This required that he should frequently expose himself on the upper deck which he bravely did until his head was completely blown off by a large shell.

Figure 47: Courtesy of National Archives

The widow, Sadie Ellis, formally Simonson, married George H. Ellis (Navy pension on the next page) on 19 June 1896 in Brooklyn, NY. After his death, she remarried John L. Sweeney on March 18, 1911, in Brooklyn, NY, and divorced him on July 5, 1932, in San Diego, CA. Sadie, after her divorce, resumed her former married name and died on July 14, 1936, in San Diego, CA, and was buried next to her husband in the Evergreens Cemetery in Brooklyn, NY.[60]

The United States Navy pension indexes are searchable online on three separate databases. The first is available online at *Ancestry* at: https://www.ancestry.com/search/collections/1357

Another option to find the United States Navy pensions is to search online at *FamilySearch*: https://www.familysearch.org/search/collection/1852605

[60] Sarah M. Sweeney Declaration of Remarried Widow's Pension, RG 15 National Archives; and *Brooklyn Times Union*, July 17, 1936.

DECLARATION FOR REMARRIED WIDOW'S PENSION
ACT OF MAY 1, 1926
WAR WITH SPAIN, PHILIPPINE INSURRECTION, AND CHINESE BOXER REBELLION

State of .....**CALIFORNIA**...................., County of ....**SAN DIEGO**..........................., ss:

On this .....**5th**..... day of .....**July**......., 19..**32** before me, the undersigned, personally appeared ——— **SADIE M. SWEENEY** ———————————, who makes the following declaration as an application for pension under the provisions of the Act of Congress approved May 1, 1926.

That she is .....**55**..... years of age, that she was born on ....**April 23rd**........,**1876** at ....**Brooklyn, New York.**...

That she was formerly the widow of ....**GEO. H. ELLIS**...................................., who ENLISTED on ...., 1........., at ....**New York City**..................., under the name of ....**George H. Ellis**....................... in .... **U. S. Navy, and was killed in** ....

(If in the Army; or vessel, if in the Navy)

................**July 3rd**........., 1..**898**......, having served ninety days or more, or died in service, or was discharged for a disability incurred in service and line of duty in the Army, Navy, or Marine Corps of the United States during the War with Spain, the Chinese Boxer Rebellion, or the Philippine Insurrection, between April 21, 1898, and July 4, 1902, and who DIED ......**July 3rd**........, 1..**898**..., at .**the Battle of Santiago, Cuba.**..........

That he also served in ....

(Here give a complete statement of all other military,

naval, or Marine Corps service, if any, at whatever time rendered)

and that, except as herein stated, said soldier (sailor or marine) was .**not.** employed in the military or naval service of the United States:

THAT SHE WAS MARRIED to said soldier (sailor or marine) on ....**June 19th.**..., 1..**896**...., under the name of ....**Sadie M. Simonson**.................., by .....**Reverend Dickson (A. C.)**...................... at ....**Brooklyn, N.Y.**...; that she had ..**not**.. been previously married, that he had ....**not**.. been previously married.

That she was NOT divorced from the soldier (sailor or marine); that after his death she REMARRIED to .....**John L. Sweeney**.................... at .....**New York, N.Y.**.......

.... or that she was divorced from him on ..**July 5, 1932.**...., at .**San Diego, Calif.**; on the grounds of .**incompatibility** that he did .———.. serve in the Army, Navy, or Marine Corps of the United States, **Enlisted U. S. Navy Sept.**

(If said husband rendered service, here describe

6, 1893; Retired March 14, 1930;Service No.40469;Retirement No.1744905;

same and give number of any pension claim based thereon)

That she did .**not**... marry again after the death of the soldier (sailor or marine), except to ...**said Sweeney.**.....

....................................., named above. ....

(If claimant contracted any other marriage after the death of the soldier (sailor or marine).

Figure 48: Courtesy of National Archives

The same set of records is grouped individually (not unlike *Ancestry* and *FamilySearch*), where they are grouped together. *Fold3* has opted to separate the four titles:

Navy Widows Originals (Disapproved) pensions, 1861-1910 are browsable online on *Fold3* at: https://www.fold3.com/title/783/navy-widows-originals-disapproved

Navy Widows Certificates pensions covering 1861-1910 are browsable online on *Fold3* at: https://www.fold3.com/title/121/navy-widows-certificates

Navy Survivor Originals (Disapproved) pensions, 1861-1910 are browsable online on *Fold3* at: https://www.fold3.com/title/780/navy-survivors-originals-disapproved

Navy Survivors Certificates pensions, 1861-1910 are browsable online on *Fold3* at: https://www.fold3.com/title/120/navy-survivors-certificates

Additional Resources

For officers, one of the best-published sources for commissioned officers in the Navy and the Marine Corps is published by Edward W. Callahan and available on Google Books at: https://www.google.com/books/edition/List_of_Officers_of_the_Navy_of_the_Unit/2ngtAAAAYAAJ?hl=en&gbpv=0. The reference can be downloaded for free.

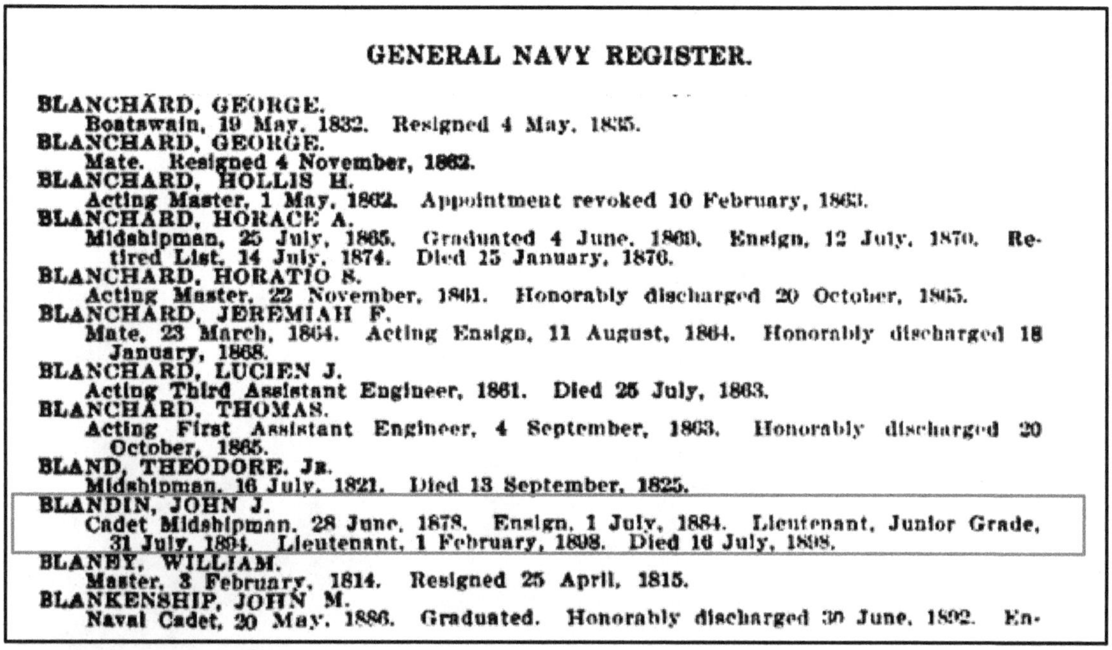

GENERAL NAVY REGISTER.

BLANCHARD, GEORGE.
    Boatswain, 19 May, 1832. Resigned 4 May, 1835.
BLANCHARD, GEORGE.
    Mate. Resigned 4 November, 1862.
BLANCHARD, HOLLIS H.
    Acting Master, 1 May, 1862. Appointment revoked 10 February, 1863.
BLANCHARD, HORACE A.
    Midshipman, 25 July, 1865. Graduated 4 June, 1869. Ensign, 12 July, 1870. Retired List, 14 July, 1874. Died 25 January, 1876.
BLANCHARD, HORATIO S.
    Acting Master, 22 November, 1861. Honorably discharged 20 October, 1865.
BLANCHARD, JEREMIAH F.
    Mate, 23 March, 1864. Acting Ensign, 11 August, 1864. Honorably discharged 18 January, 1868.
BLANCHARD, LUCIEN J.
    Acting Third Assistant Engineer, 1861. Died 25 July, 1863.
BLANCHARD, THOMAS.
    Acting First Assistant Engineer, 4 September, 1863. Honorably discharged 20 October, 1865.
BLAND, THEODORE, Jr.
    Midshipman, 16 July, 1821. Died 13 September, 1825.
BLANDIN, JOHN J.
    Cadet Midshipman, 28 June, 1878. Ensign, 1 July, 1884. Lieutenant, Junior Grade, 31 July, 1894. Lieutenant, 1 February, 1898. Died 16 July, 1898.
BLANEY, WILLIAM.
    Master, 3 February, 1814. Resigned 25 April, 1815.
BLANKENSHIP, JOHN M.
    Naval Cadet, 20 May, 1886. Graduated. Honorably discharged 30 June, 1892. En-

Figure 49: Courtesy of Google Books

Figure 50: Courtesy of The USS Maine (1899) Book

Lieutenant John Joseph Blandin, born in Selma, AL, joined the United States Navy in June 1878 as a new cadet at the academy. Commissioned an Ensign on July 1, 1884, he was transferred to sea duty, later promoted to Lieutenant Junior Grade, and ordered aboard the USS *Maine* on 20 June 1897 until the night of the explosion. After the sinking, he was ordered to Key West, FL, which led to several weeks with the naval board of inquiry until he was transferred to Washington, DC, for duty in the United States Navy War Department. Blandin died shortly after his last transfer on July 16, 1898, in Baltimore, MD, which brought on the stress and shock of the previous attack, and was buried with honors at the United States Naval Academy cemetery in Annapolis, MD.[61]

[61] *The Baltimore Sun*, July 18, 1898.

The United States Navy and Marine Corps (including the reserves) kept active registers of officers published nearly every year (since 1825), available online for free on *Hathi Trust* at: https://catalog.hathitrust.org/Record/000523460. This list records active duty, reservists, cadets, and other personnel with their names, ranks, present stations, and dates of service.

GENEALOGY TIP For records of the United States Navy not in the National Archives, research can be conducted at the United States Naval Institute located in Annapolis, Maryland, where access to finding aids and digital images.

United States Marine Corps

In the months leading up to the Spanish-American War, marines served onboard navy warships as marine detachments or gun crews. On the night of February 15, 1898, the USS *Maine* exploded in Havana harbor with a huge loss of lives, including twenty-eight marines. With the war's end later in the year, the Marine Corps would be called again into action during the Boxer Rebellion in 1900 and during the Philippine Insurrection from 1899-1902.

The explosion of the USS *Maine* eventually led the United States Congress to declare war against Spain on April 25, 1898. On the eve of the war, the Marine Corps numbered about 3,500 officers and men and immediately sought to mobilize. Commandant Colonel Charles Heywood distributed new bolt action rifles in preparation to form the Marine Expeditionary Battalions.[62]

Lieutenant Colonel Robert W. Huntington (commissioned in 1861) was a seasoned, experienced officer ordered to command the 1st Marine Battalion. The unit was five infantry companies of 23 officers and 623 enlisted men and one artillery company of four-3-inch landing guns.[63]

The United States Marine Corps was involved in some of the heaviest fighting in Cuba, having participated in the first land battle of the war. Sailing on the USS *Panther*, the men arrived in force off Santiago, Cuba, on June 10, 1898. The marine detachment hoisted the first United States flag on Cuban soil the following day. The men, over the course of the war, the Boxer Rebellion and the Philippine Insurrection, saw sporadic fighting, some heavier than others, including the battle of Guantanamo, Cuba, between June 6-10, 1898, for which they received favorable press. The opposing Spanish forces they encountered always had them outnumbered. Still, the Marines lived up to their motto of "Semper Fidelis," or always faithful.[64]

One of the most important genealogy resources documenting military service depends on when the Marine was discharged. For members discharged before January 1, 1905, the personnel files are referred to as "Jackets" and are located onsite at the National Archives in Washington, DC.

For Marines discharged after the above date in 1905, the files are in the custody of the National Personnel Record Center (NPRC) in St. Louis, Missouri, and are under the heading of the Official Military Personnel Files or OMPF file. Marines who were not career soldiers and served during the war periods and then separated will have the personnel files at NARA. Most files contain enlistment papers, a descriptive roll, a conduct record either onboard ship or at a duty station, and a record of any awards or ribbons received. The records found at the National Archives are in RG127, and after 1895, the names are arranged alphabetically.

---

[62] *Marines in the Spanish-American War, 1895-1899: Anthology and Annotated Bibliography*, (Washington, DC: History and Museums Division, U.S. Marine Corps, 1998), 4-6.

[63] Ibid., 6.

[64] *Trevor K. Plante* "New Glory to Its Already Gallant Record: The First Marine Battalion in the Spanish-American War" *Prologue: Quarterly of the National Archives* 30:1 (Spring, 1998): 21-31.

The OMPF files at the National Personnel Record Center contain detailed files of career Marines who remained in service after 1905. Daniel J. Daly was awarded the Medal of Honor twice for military action, first on July 19, 1901, during the Boxer Rebellion, and later during the invasion and occupation of Haiti on October 24, 1915.

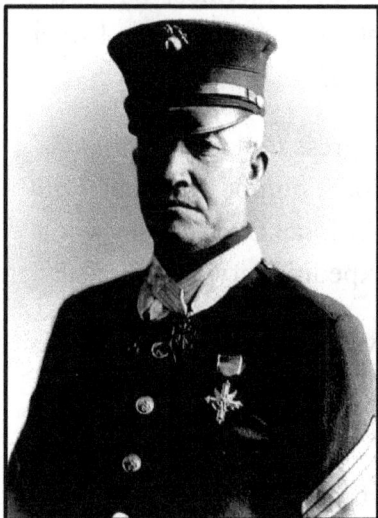

Figure 51: Courtesy of USMC Archives

Daly was born on November 11, 1873, in Glen Cove, New York, and joined the Marine Corps on January 10, 1899, at New York, NY, and served during the Philippine Insurrection and in the Boxer Rebellion during the siege on Peking, China.[65]

At the end of his enlistment in 1904, he was retained in service, reenlisting five more times until his discharge on February 6, 1929, in Philadelphia, PA. After his retirement, he lived with his sister, Mrs. Mary Loeb, and died on April 27, 1937, in Glendale, Queens, New York.[66] The record below is the first enlistment record for Private Daniel J. Daly from his Official Military Personnel File in St. Louis, MO.

The OMPF file is completely intact at the NPRC. The total number of pages in the file is 433 images. This includes his multiple enlistments, discharge papers, and medical and health records as part of the file.

This service file was not affected by the fire on July 12, 1973, at NPRC as records from the Marine Corps were not damaged.

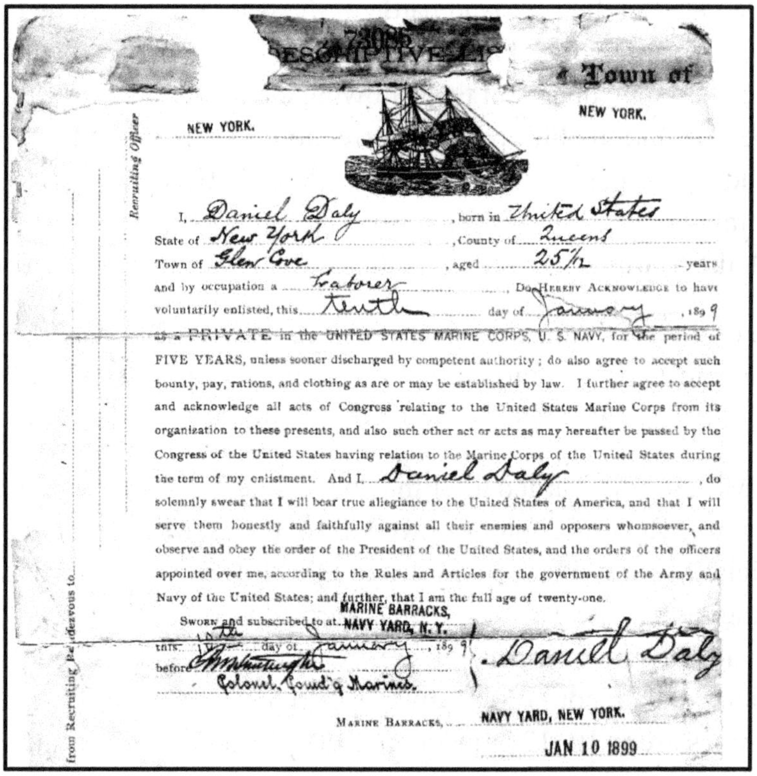

Town of

NEW YORK. NEW YORK.

Recruiting Officer

I, Daniel Daly, born in United States State of New York, County of Queens Town of Glen Cove, aged 25 1/2 years and by occupation a laborer, Do Hereby Acknowledge to have voluntarily enlisted, this tenth day of January, 1899 as a PRIVATE in the UNITED STATES MARINE CORPS, U. S. NAVY, for the period of FIVE YEARS, unless sooner discharged by competent authority; do also agree to accept such bounty, pay, rations, and clothing as are or may be established by law. I further agree to accept and acknowledge all acts of Congress relating to the United States Marine Corps from its organization to these presents, and also such other act or acts as may hereafter be passed by the Congress of the United States having relation to the Marine Corps of the United States during the term of my enlistment. And I, Daniel Daly, do solemnly swear that I will bear true allegiance to the United States of America, and that I will serve them honestly and faithfully against all their enemies and opposers whomsoever, and observe and obey the order of the President of the United States, and the orders of the officers appointed over me, according to the Rules and Articles for the government of the Army and Navy of the United States; and further, that I am the full age of twenty-one.

Sworn and subscribed to at MARINE BARRACKS, NAVY YARD, N. Y. this 10th day of January, 1899 before [illegible] Colonel Comd'g Marines. } Daniel Daly

MARINE BARRACKS, NAVY YARD, NEW YORK. JAN 10 1899

from Recruiting Rendezvous to

Figure 52: Courtesy of National Personnel Record Center-St. Louis, MO

---

[65] Abstract of Spanish-American War Military and Naval Service Records, 1898-1902. Series B0809. New York Adjutant General Office. New York State Archives in Albany, NY.

[66] *The Brooklyn Daily Eagle*, April 27, 1937; and Official Military Personnel File for Daniel Daly. RG127. National Personnel Record Center. St. Louis, MO.

The National Archives in Washington, DC, in RG127, records officers and enlisted personnel during the Spanish-American War, Boxer Rebellion, and the Philippine Insurrection.[67]

Officers:

Entry 65: *Monthly Reports of Details of Officers of the Marine Corps, 1894-1907*, indexed and separated by month, providing details of assignment to ship or shore duty stations.

Entry 67: *Record of Military Service of Marine Corps Officers, 1899-1904.* The volume is arranged by year and indexed by descending order of rank. Entries include the name, state from where appointed, and date their commission was taken under oath.

Enlisted Men:

Entry 75: *Alphabetical Card List of Enlisted Men of the Marine Corps, 1798-1941.* These cards are arranged and indexed alphabetically by the surname of the enlistee and then by first name.

Entry 77: *Size Rolls, 1798-1899, 1900-1901.* Like the CMSRs of the United States Army, these are arranged by time of enlistment and include name, rank, place of birth, age, and the physical description of the enlistee.

Entry 79: *Descriptive Lists, 1879-1903.* It is an interesting set of records very similar to the size rolls, arranged by surname, and chronologically thereafter. The lists provide descriptive data on the Marines, include some family histories, and highlight military service.

Entry 88: *Registers of Deserters, 1809-1907.* This set of registers provided detailed information on enlisted men who deserted, including whether they were apprehended or if the soldiers surrendered.

Entry 91: *Registers of Discharges, 1838-1927.* When Marines ended their term of service, each Marine would receive a discharge. The registers highlight their service time and provide the details of when, where, and what type of discharge was awarded.

Entry 97: *Death Registers of Enlisted Men, 1868-1942.* Arranged alphabetically by the first letter of the surname and then by date of death. The registers include the name of the Marine killed, their date and the location where the death occurred, and the cause of death. Often the unit organization is supplied.

Marines who enlisted in the Corps were generally recruited for periods of four years. This was very similar to the regular United States Army periods of induction, but would be different from the volunteer army during each of the above referenced wars.

---

[67] Maizie Johnson, *Records of the United States Marine Corps.* National Archives Inventory, RG127 (Washington, DC: National Archives and Records Administration, 1970), 18-23.

All previously referenced sets of records are not digitized and must be requested at the National Archives by the military archivist. One set of records not covered are digitized online are the Muster Rolls of the United States Marine Corps, 1798-1940. Found in RG127 and on microfilm publication T1118, these records have been scanned and made available online at *Ancestry*: https://www.ancestry.com/search/collections/1089.

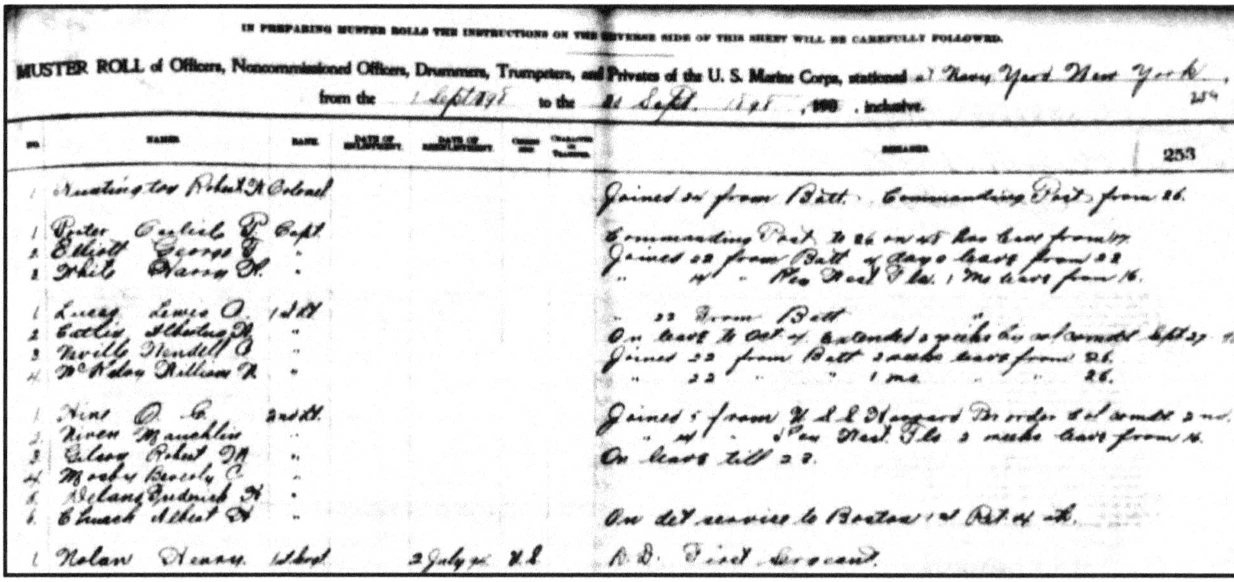
IN PREPARING MUSTER ROLLS THE INSTRUCTIONS ON THE REVERSE SIDE OF THIS SHEET WILL BE CAREFULLY FOLLOWED.

MUSTER ROLL of Officers, Noncommissioned Officers, Drummers, Trumpeters, and Privates of the U. S. Marine Corps, stationed at Navy Yard New York, from the 1 Sept 98 to the 30 Sept. 98, 189 , inclusive.

253

Figure 53: Courtesy of National Archives

The above muster roll dated between September 1, 1898, and September 30, 1898, shows some officers of what would constitute the 1st Marine Battalion during the Spanish-American War. The roll shows the Navy yard station in New York, NY, with Colonel Robert W. Huntington listed as the commanding officer at the yard.

A group of five 1st Marine Battalion officers posed at Camp Heywood, Seavey Island near Portsmouth, NH, in 1898, which would serve as a prison for the Spanish during the war. Pictured on the far left is 1st Lieutenant Lewis Lucas, stationed at the New York yard above.

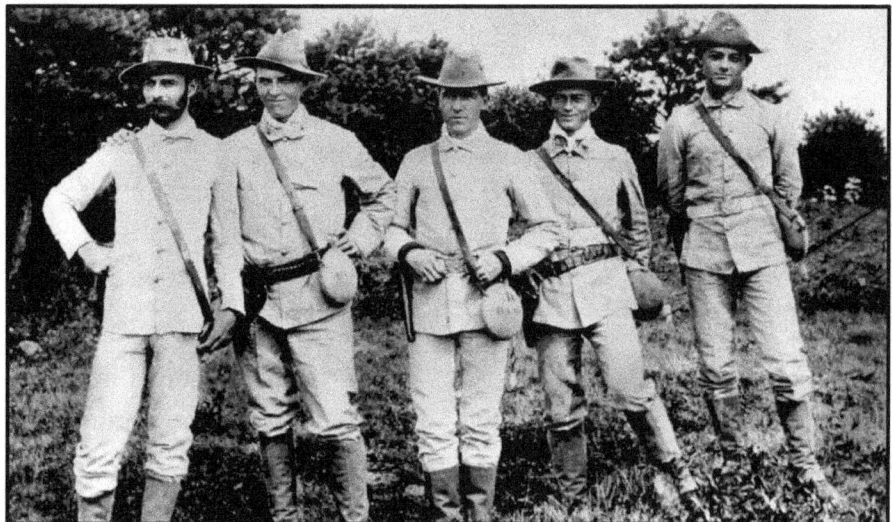

Figure 54: Courtesy of Naval History and Heritage Command

Another published source previously mentioned the Navy and Marine Corps officers who served from 1775 to 1900. Published by Edward W. Callahan and available on Google Books at: https://www.google.com/books/edition/List_of_Officers_of_the_Navy_of_the_Unit/2ngtAAAA YAAJ?hl=en&gbpv=0. The reference can be downloaded for free.

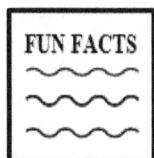

Figure 55: Courtesy of Google Books

Figure 56: Courtesy of USMC Archives

The above-highlighted entry shows Marine Corps career officer Smedley D. Butler, newly commissioned 1st Lieutenant on April 8, 1899, participated in the Philippine Insurrection, and was later promoted to Captain on July 23, 1900, during the Boxer Rebellion. Butler continued in the Marine Corps and retired following the death of Commandant General Wendell C. Neville on October 1, 1931, when, as the senior general officer, he was overlooked for promotion to the new position.[68]

FUN FACTS

DID YOU KNOW that in April 1898, the United States Congress passed a resolution on collecting an excise tax based on customers using telephones to make long-distance calls? The money collected partly was used to pay the war debt during the Spanish-American War and repealed in 1902.

---

[68] Mark Strecker, *Smedley D. Butler, USMC A Biography*, (Jefferson: McFarland and Company, 2011), 29-55.

United States Revenue Cutter Service

The United States Revenue Cutter Service traces its origins to the late eighteenth century. It was initially called the Revenue Marines when organized under an act of the United States Congress on August 4, 1790 (1 Stat. 175) under the direction of the First Secretary of Treasury Alexander Hamilton.

In 1790, the newly formed Revenue Cutter Service was outfitted with ten cutters to protect and safeguard revenue. First envisioned as a force of revenue tax collectors, over time, their ability to conduct many diverse missions, some simultaneously, during both peacetime and war, became the hallmark of the service. More organizational changes would occur after the Civil War with the formation of the Revenue Marine division in 1871, followed by an act of congress on July 31, 1894 (28 Stat. 171), formally organizing the Revenue Cutter Service.

Shortly before President William McKinley declared war on Spain on April 21, 1898, he issued an executive order (EO 05-03) that directed the temporary transfer of thirteen Revenue Cutters to the United States Navy on March 24, 1898, and another seven cutters dispatched to cooperate with the United States Army. The Revenue Service cutters transferred to the Navy included USRC *Calumet*, USRC *Commodore Perry*, USRC *Grant*, USRC *Hamilton*, USRC *Hudson*, USRC *Levi Woodbury*, USRC *Louis McLane*, USRC *Manning*, USRC *McCulloch*, USRC *Morrill*, USRC *Richard Rush*, USRC *Thomas Corwin*, and USRC *Windom*.[69] Those who cooperate with the United States Army (under Navy control) by patrolling in the minefields of several harbors and guarding the entrances included USRC *Dallas*, USRC *Dexter*, USRC *Winona*, USRC *Smith*, USRC *Galveston*, USRC *Guthrie*, and USRC *Penrose*.[70]

Revenue Cutter Service personnel transferred to the Navy were sent to Admiral Sampson's North Atlantic Squadron, Admiral Dewey's Asiatic Squadron, and Pacific Coast Squadron. Those cutters were stationed at Boston, MA; Newport, RI; Mobile Bay, AL; New Orleans, LA; Baltimore, MD; Pensacola, FL, and along the Mississippi River with the following breakdown:[71]

Attached Commands	Cutters	Guns	Officers	Enlisted
Navy-North Atlantic Squadron	8	43	58	339
Navy-Asiatic Squadron	1	6	10	95
Navy-Pacific Coast	4	12	30	128
Army-Cooperation	7	10	33	163
Totals	20	71	131	625

[69] *Record of Movements: Vessels of the United States Coast Guard 1790-December 31, 1933.* (Washington, DC: U.S. Coast Guard Headquarters, 1989), 489-494; and *CIS Index to Presidential Executive Orders & Proclamations* (Washington, DC: Congressional Information Services, Inc., 1987), 1117.
[70] Ibid., 489-494.
[71] *The United States Revenue Cutter Service in the War with Spain, 1898.* (Washington, DC; Government Printing Office, 1899), 5-8.

The Revenue Cutter Service, in combination with the Navy, had limited combat exposure against the Spanish. Two cutters, however, did see fighting in Cuba and the Philippines.

United States Revenue Cutter Hudson

The battle of Cardenas, Cuba, fought on May 11, 1898, had the Spanish armored gunboat *Antonio Lopez* and shore batteries near the harbor entrance engaged in heated action against the United States Navy torpedo boat USS *Winslow* under the command of Lieutenant John B. Bernadou, and accompanied by the gunboat USS *Wilmington*, and the USRC *Hudson*. In a short time, the USS *Winslow* was disabled and had the steering knocked out, causing the torpedo boat to drift dangerously close to shore. The commanding officer was wounded, and a well-placed shot had killed the executive officer Ensign Worth Bagley and four crewmembers.[72]

Lt. Frank H. Newcomb of the USRC *Hudson* was dispatched, under orders, to rescue and tow the distressed torpedo boat to safety and, in turn, came under fire in the early afternoon hours. By 3 PM, the cutter had secured a tow line ahead of the torpedo boat, during which the enemy kept up a constant fire. Later, with the fighting completed close to dark, the USRC *Hudson* was ordered to Key West with dispatches of the engagement, carrying the several dead and wounded from the USS *Winslow*. In his after-action report, Lt. Newcomb stated that his cutter received only slight damage, and that more than one hundred thirty shells were fired during the day's action.[73]

On June 27, 1898, President William McKinley wrote to Congress recommending that the officers and men of the *USRC Hudson* be recognized: a gold medal of honor to Lt. Frank H. Newcomb, a silver medal of honor to each officer, and a bronze medal of honor to each enlisted member of the crew.[74] The medal legislation would be passed by Congress on May 2, 1900 (31 Stat. 716), awarding each man the Cardenas Medal.[75]

The Revenue Cutter *Hudson* was built at Camden, New Jersey, under contract by J H. Dialogue on February 18, 1892. During the Spanish-American War, the cutter was under the command of Lieutenant Frank H. Newcomb with four additional officers and crew. At the time of the start of the war (operating under orders of the Navy), the cutter was stationed at Norfolk, Virginia, and outfitted with two six-pounder guns. After the end of hostilities, the cutter sailed back to Norfolk, Virginia, and then received orders to report to New York and arrived on October 6, 1898.[76]

---

[72] Edward W. Callahan, *List of Officers of the Navy of the United States and the Marine Corps from 1775-1900.* (New York: L.R. Hamersly & Company, 1901), 34, 54.

[73] *The United States Revenue Cutter Service in the War with Spain, 1898.* (Washington, DC; Government Printing Office, 1899), 21-22.

[74] Ibid., 10.

[75] Stephen W. Stathis. Congressional Gold Medals, 1776-2002. (New York: Nova Science Publishers, 2003), 40.

[76] *Record of Movements: Vessels of the United States Coast Guard 1790-December 31, 1933.* (Washington, DC: U.S. Coast Guard Headquarters, 1989), 34; and Dennis L. Nobile, *Historical Register U.S. Revenue Cutter Service Officers, 1790-1914.* (Washington, DC: U.S. Coast Guard Headquarters, 1990), 51.

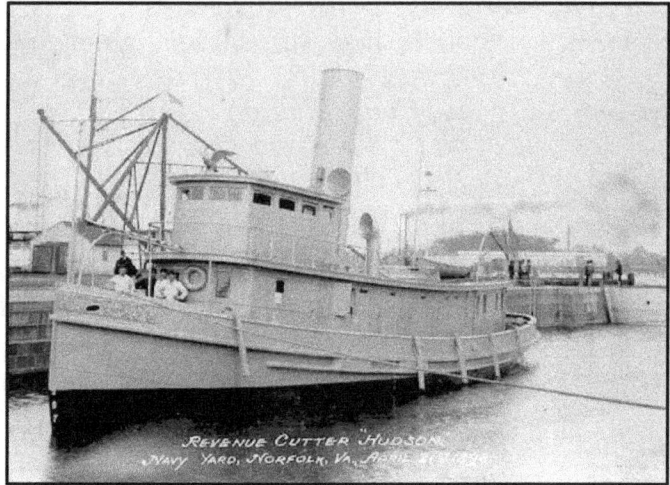

Figure 57: Courtesy of U.S. Coast Guard Historian   Figure 58: Courtesy of U.S. Coast Guard Historian

The above photographs show a uniformed Lt. Frank H. Newcomb (circa 1900) and the Revenue Cutter *Hudson* stationed at the Navy yard in Norfolk, Virginia, on April 21, 1898.

United States Revenue Cutter McCulloch

At the beginning of the Spanish-American War, the USRC McCulloch was stationed with Commodore George Dewey and the Asiatic Squadron. After the formal declaration of war between the United States and Spain, Dewey's fleet entered the approach of Manilla Bay in the Philippines under the cover of darkness on the night of April 30, 1898. As the fleet began to pass El Fraile Rock, guarding the bay entrance, the cutter's smokestack caught fire, which gave away the position of the attacking vessels. Now a lighted target, the fleet was fired upon by the batteries of the Spanish gun onshore, and the URRC *McCulloch*, along with the USS *Boston*, began to return fire, silencing the Spanish battery. The Chief Engineer, Frank B. Randall, tried to extinguish the fire and died from heat exhaustion.[77]

Engineer Randall became the only casualty of the battle at Manilla Bay. With the American fleet in the harbor, the Spanish fleet was defeated and surrendered. The *McCulloch* was one of the last vessels to offer resistance and fire at the enemy. After the engagement, Dewey dispatched the *McCulloch* to Hong Kong to cable the news of the victory to the United States Navy. The cutter was one of the squadron's more maneuverable and speedy steaming vessels. This made it practical to use the cutter to bring back news of Dewey's promotion to the rank of Admiral.[78]

---

[77] *The United States Revenue Cutter Service in the War with Spain, 1898.* (Washington, DC; Government Printing Office, 1899), 12-21.
[78] Captain Randolph Ridgely Jr. "The Coast Guard Cutter McCulloch at Manilla." *United States Naval Institute Proceedings.* 55 (May 1929): 417-426.

The Revenue Cutter *McCulloch* was built in Philadelphia, Pennsylvania, under contract by Wm. Cramp and Sons on February 28, 1896. During the Spanish-American War, the cutter was under the command of Captain Daniel B. Hodgsdon. The cutter consisted of six armament guns and had a crew of ten officers and ninety-five enlisted men. At the beginning of the war, the cutter was ordered to join the Asiatic Squadron under the command of Commodore George Dewey in Hong Kong, China. The Navy took command of the cutter two days later, on April 4, 1898. After the end of hostilities, the cutter was returned to the Revenue Cutter Service and the Department of the Treasury, setting sail for Honolulu, Hawaiian Territory, where it arrived on December 28, 1898. Later, the cutter was ordered to Mare Island (near San Francisco, California), where it arrived on January 19, 1899, for repairs.[79]

Figure 59: Courtesy of Harpers Weekly

Figure 60: Courtesy of Naval History and Command Center.

The above photographs show Captain Daniel B. Hodgsdon at the time of the battle of Manilla Bay in the Philippines and the Revenue Cutter *McCulloch* (circa 1900) in San Francisco, CA.

During the war, other service cutters to the United States Navy distinguished themselves, including the USRC *Manning* and the USRC *Woodbury*. They participated in numerous actions against the Spanish shore batteries while attached to the North Atlantic Squadron for blockade duty.

In the closing week of hostilities, the United States Navy returned the vessels' services to the Revenue Cutter Service on August 17, 1898.[80] One editorial in the *Army and Navy Journal* (dated November 26, 1864) not only recognized the value of the service but unknowingly

---

[79] *Record of Movements: Vessels of the United States Coast Guard 1790-December 31, 1933.* (Washington, DC: U.S. Coast Guard Headquarters, 1989), 370; and *Harpers Weekly*, September 30, 1899. The USRC *McCulloch's* armament was four 3-inch rifles, one 15-inch bow gun, and one torpedo tube.

[80] *CIS Index to Presidential Executive Orders & Proclamations* (Washington, DC: Congressional Information Services, Inc., 1987), 1121.

predicted both the motto of *"Semper Paratus"* and the future name of the Coast Guard. The editor wrote: *"Keeping always under steam and ever ready, in the event of extraordinary need, to render valuable service, the cutters can be made to form a coast guard whose value it is impossible at the present time to estimate."*[81]

The United States Coast Guard combined the former United States Live-Saving Service and the Revenue Cutter Service by an act of Congress on January 28, 1915 (38 Stat. 800), signed into law by President Woodrow Wilson. Later, on July 1, 1939 (53 Stat. 1216), the United States Lighthouse Service was incorporated and fell in line with the Department of Treasury, then Transportation, and later with Homeland Security.[82]

As a regular branch of the United States military, the Revenue Cutter Service closely followed the rank structure of the United States Navy. Original documents are located onsite at the National Archives and are included in Record Group 26, covering personnel stationed with the service. Most records are not digitized and are in the Washington, DC facility.

• Officers of the Revenue Cutter Service, 1791-1919.
• Muster Rolls/Revenue Cutter Service, 1833-1932
• Pay Rolls/Revenue Cutter Service, 1833-1932
• Shipping Articles, 1863-1915
• Logs of Revenue Cutters and Coast Guard Vessels, 1819-1941

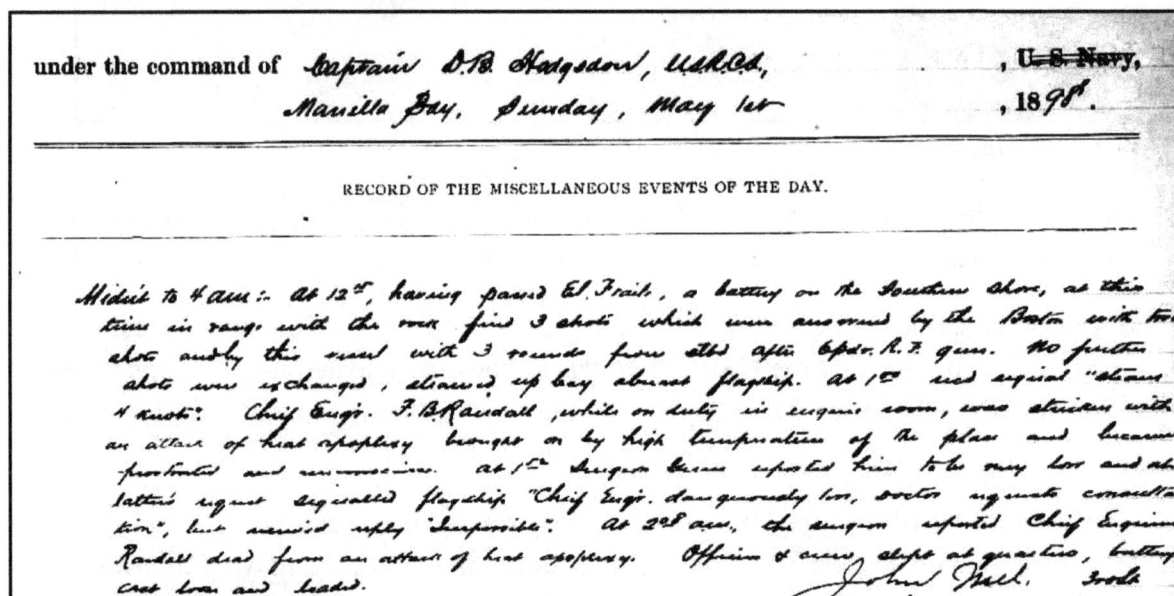

Figure 61: Courtesy of National Archives. RG26

---

[81] *The United States Army and Navy Journal.* (New York: Army and Navy Journal, Inc., 1864), 218. Assessed 13 September 2020. https://babel.hathitrust.org/cgi/pt?id=coo.31924069759862&view=1up&seq=2;

[82] Thomas P. Ostrom. *The United States Coast Guard and National Defense.* (Jefferson: McFarland and Company, 2012), 1-4, 11-12, 181.

The previous page contains logbook entries (dated May 1, 1898) for the USRC *McCulloch* under the command of Captain Daniel B. Hodgedon. The date of the log entry is the battle for Manilla Bay. During the 12-4 AM watch, the officer of the deck, 3rd Lieutenant John Mel, recorded the illness and death of Chief Engineer Frank B. Randall, who died of overexertion and heat exhaustion. Later that day, the ship chaplain performed services and had the body committed to the deep. The image is from Harpers Weekly magazine, reporting the victory at Manilla Bay.[83]

Figure 62: Courtesy of Harpers Weekly

Some records previously stated include after the dates of the merger in 1915. Located in RG26, some of the records are at the Archives II facility in College Park, Maryland. One extra set of records not included are the Official Registers of the United States (1816-1959). This source covers listings for persons employed by the United States Government and listed by department. Not only does this register list employees of the United States Revenue Cutter Service, it also includes the United States Life-Saving Service and the United States Lighthouse Service online at *Hathi Trust*: https://catalog.hathitrust.org/Record/002137439.

The United States Revenue Cutter Service is included in yearly volumes of published lists titled Annual List of Merchant Vessels, including the name of the cutters, call letters, tonnage, guns, homeport or station, and crew at *Hathi Trust* https://catalog.hathitrust.org/Record/008420432.

GENEALOGY CLUE When researching records of the United States Revenue Cutter Service during the Spanish-American War period consider looking at the records of the United States Life-Saving Service and the United States Lighthouse Service for personnel who may have served in all three organizations.

---

[83] National Archives and Records Administration (NARA). RG26. *Records of the United States Coast Guard*, 1785-2006. Logs of Revenue Cutters and Coast Guard Vessels, 1819-1941. *USCG McCulloch*, 12 December 1897-18 June 1898. Log dated 1 May 1898. Assessed 14 September 2020. https://catalog.archives.gov/id/70607509; and *Harpers Weekly*, September 30, 1899.

Cemeteries and Headstone Applications

The burial and recording of military dead precede many years from the start of the Revolutionary War, stretching back to biblical times. Over the centuries, many cultures have kept records of soldiers killed in battle, including the Egyptians, Greeks, and Romans.

Veteran Cemeteries

In the early days of the United States, no actual provisions were made to bury war dead at the national level. It was not until the Civil War that the idea of organizing a national cemetery system was suggested. Over time, veterans would be buried in non-federal or private cemeteries, post-cemeteries, and national cemeteries.

In the second year of the Civil War, Congress passed an Act on July 17, 1862 (12 Stat. 596), in Section 18 authorized President Lincoln *"Shall have the power, whenever in his opinion...to purchase cemetery grounds and cause them to be securely enclosed...used as a National Cemetery for soldiers who shall die in the service of the country."* This legislation would move towards a national cemetery system for deceased veterans after the end of the Civil War.[84]

Another act was passed to amend and protect National Cemeteries by Congress on June 8, 1872 (17 Stat. 345). It stipulated that each grave be marked with the name of the deceased. The act also called for privately sealed proposals from independent firms in business to provide the headstones.[85] This act called for the names of companies that the federal government would contract to design and make the headstones, including:

- S.G. Bridges, Keokuk, IA, owned by Samuel G. Bridges.
- Gross Brothers (William H. Gross and Frank S. Gross) of Lee, MA.
- Lee Marble Works, Lee, MA, owned by William H. Gross.
- William Manson, Albany, NY.
- Sheldon & Sons (William K Sheldon and Charles Sheldon), W. Rutland, VT.
- Stockbridge Marble Co. MA, owned by Henry V. Rathbun.
- Vermont Marble Co., Proctor, VT, owned by Redfield Proctor.
- D.W. Whitney, Troy, NY, owned by Daniel W. Whitney.
- D.L. Kent Company of East Dorset, VT, owned by Duane L. Kent, who took over the contract of D.W. Whitney, who couldn't meet the standards.[86]

---

[84] 37th Congress, Session II, Statutes at Large. Accessed 14 June 2023. https://www.loc.gov/law/help/statutes-at-large/37th-congress/session-2/c37s2ch200.pdf

[85] 42nd Congress, Session II, Statutes at Large. Accessed 14 June 2023. https://www.loc.gov/law/help/statutes-at-large/42nd-congress/session-2/c42s2ch368.pdf

[86] Headstones Provided for Union Civil War Veterans, ca 1879-1903. National Archives. Accessed 14 June 2020. https://www.archives.gov/research/military/civil-war/union/veteran-headstones.html.

On March 4, 1923, Congress passed an act (42 Stat. 1509) establishing the American Battle Monuments Commission (ABMC) to erect monuments and chapels in cemeteries in areas of Europe where fighting occurred during World War I.

Headstone Applications

Following the end of the Civil War, the United States Congress passed an Act on March 3, 1873 (17 Stat. 605) that authorized all honorably discharged Union soldiers, sailors, and marines who had served during the Civil War to be buried in any National Cemetery of the United States at no cost to the families. This act appropriated from Congress 1 million dollars to replace the older wooden headboards with more permanent and durable stone markers.

Another Act, passed by Congress on February 3, 1879 (20 Stat. 281), extended government headstones to Union soldiers, sailors, and marines who served in the Civil War to be now provided headstones in private village, and city cemeteries. No longer were headstones limited to National Cemeteries. The Secretary of War was required to keep a preserved record of the names and burial of all soldiers who were provided with a headstone.

The acts of 1873 and 1879 set in motion more permanent procedures when war erupted with Spain in 1898. The Quartermaster Department would bring to pass a burial corps and employ civilian contractors and work on exhuming the remains of soldiers who died in Cuba. This went beyond simply providing stones to identify remains and then providing a proper burial and headstone. One of the key figures in identifying the remains of soldiers was Adjutant General Charles Pierce, who also believed soldiers should be issued identification tags.[87]

Tombstone Styles

In 1873, the United States Secretary of War, William W. Belknap, adopted the first actual design of military tombstones that were to be erected in cemeteries. The tombstone was designed for Civil War dead from the Union side only. The design was an upright marble stone in size 36x10x4. As a logical military symbol, it was widely used until 1925. On October 30, 1925, the Joint Board of Interstate Highways adopted *"the use of the shield as a marker is limited to the United States highways."* The shield design was no longer used after this date.[88]

This design was also included for any soldier, sailor, or marine from the Revolutionary War, War of 1812, Mexican War, Civil War, and the periods afterward, including veterans of the Spanish-American War.

---

[87] Leo P. Hirrel, "The Beginnings of the Quartermaster Graves Registration Service." *Army Sustainment* 46:4 (July-August 2014): 64-67.

[88] Claire Prechtel-Kluskens, "Records for U.S. Military Veterans, Part I: Headstone Design." *NGS Magazine* 39:1 (January-March 2013): 28-31.

Plain Upright Design:

This was first introduced in May 1925, in the decade following World War I. A board of reviewing officers met to discuss and adopt a new design. This new design did not apply to veterans of the Civil War and the Spanish-American War. This stone was a slab plain upright design, also referred to as a "General" type of headstone, that was slightly rounded at the top of the base, constructed of American white marble, and 42x13x4 inches in size.

The headstone on the front included the soldier's name, rank, regiment, division, date of death, and, in most cases, his state of residence at the time of enlistment. The headstones were also allowed for the first time a new carved design for a religious emblem. Choices were limited to 2 styles, including the cross for protestants and others of the Christian faith, including Catholics, and the Star of David for persons of the Jewish faith.

Flat Marble or Granite Design:

This design type was first introduced in February of 1937. The option of using granite or marble was added in 1940. The marble or granite marker was measured 24x12x4 inches in size with an incised (or cut) style of inscriptions. Information included the name, military unit or organization, death date (and sometimes to include birth date), and the veteran's state of residence. An optional religious symbol (the same 2 available) was also available on the top of the stone from 1937 to 1973. After 1973, the Department of Veteran Affairs situated this symbol at the bottom of the stone for any headstones.[89]

Records of Headstones Applications, 1879-1903

Located in the collection of National Archives in RG92 of the Quartermaster General Individual card indexes measuring about 3x4 inches. Dating ca 1879-1903, these applications include more than 166,000 separate card indexes for veterans and typically include:

- Name of Deceased
- Rank of Soldier
- Military Unit or Organization
- Name of Cemetery to be interred
- Name of the Grave Marker (for national cemeteries)
- Contractor who supplied the Tombstone
- Date stone was contracted (often stamped on the index card)

The largest number of entries is for the Civil War, but it also includes some limited veterans of the Revolutionary War, the War of 1812, the Mexican War, and the Spanish-American War.

---

[89] Ibid., 28-31.

Ragland, Lewis L.
Pvt. Co. G, Regt. 2nd
Ark. Inf.
Cemetery Nat.
City or Town Chattanooga.
County and State Tenn.
Grave 13218.
died Aug. 15th 1898.
Headstone supplied .... 18 ......
by ....
....
Contract dated ....

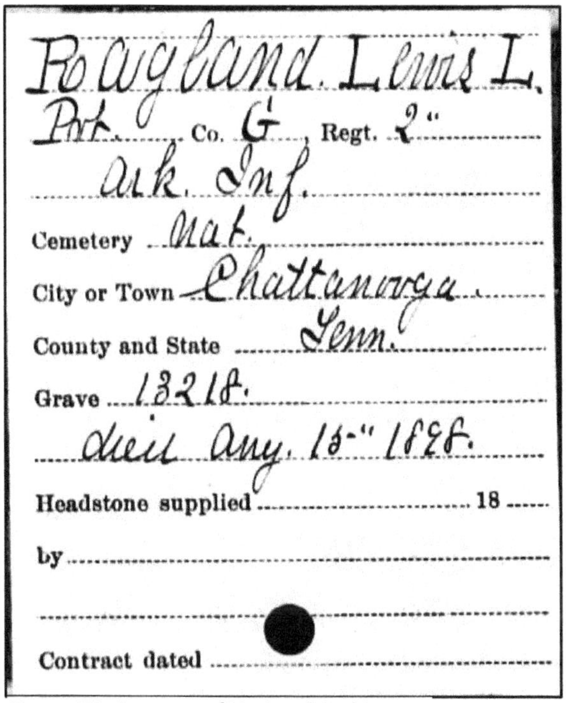

Figure 63: Courtesy of National Archives

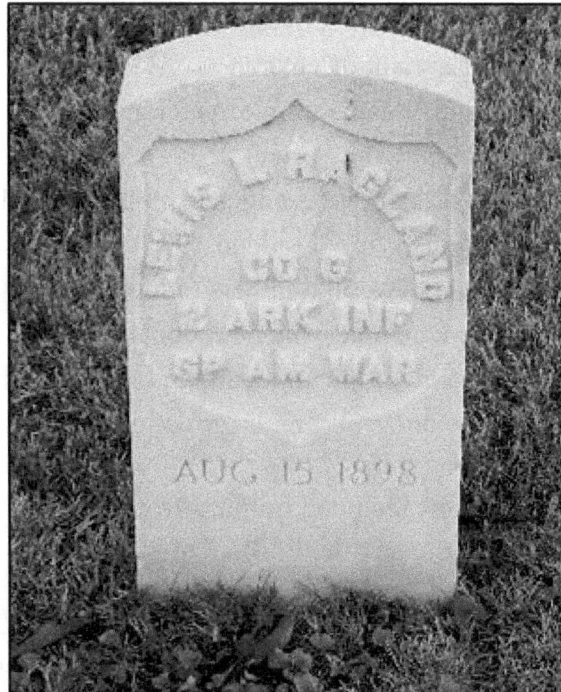

Figure 64: Courtesy of Find-A-Grave

The above headstone image and application for Lewis L. Ragland, who served as a private in Company G. 2nd Arkansas Infantry in the Spanish-American War. He died at Camp Thomas in Chickamauga Park, Georgia, of measles on August 15, 1898, and was buried at the Chattanooga National Cemetery in Tennessee.[90]

https://www.familysearch.org/search/collectio n/1913388 With *FamilySearch,* individual names can be searched, but it does not permit searching by war period. You must know the name.

https://www.ancestry.com/search/collections/1195 With *Ancestry,* individual names can be searched, allowing for keyword search by war period. The index covers 1861-1904.

U.S. Headstones for Veterans, 1925-1963

Applications card indexes for headstones of any military veterans issued from 1925-1963 are online, indexed, and located in RG92 of the office of the Quartermaster General. The cards are about 4x6 inches in size and are alphabetically digitized on the database and separated by ranges of dates. Not all the index cards in the series contain the exact same information, but most cards, including:

- Name of deceased veteran
- Birth date of veteran (after 1944)
- Death date of veteran

---

[90] *The Commercial Appeal,* August 18, 1898. Private Lewis L. Ragland was from Cabot, Arkansas.

- Dates of enlistment and discharge (added 1931)
- Military rank of veteran
- Military organization of veteran
- Death date of veteran
- Type of marker (changes in 1940, 1942, 1945, and 1947)
- Religious symbol (added 1925)
- Veteran pension numbers (added 1937)
- Veteran cemetery name & location
- The name of the applicant and the relationship are sometimes provided.
- Tombstone shipping information and location.

The applications included military from multiple wars, including the Spanish-American War, the Boxer Rebellion, and the Philippine Insurrection.

https://www.ancestry.com/search/collections/2375 With *Ancestry,* individual names can be searched, including cemetery filtering and keywords. It also allows for date-range searches.

https://www.fold3.com/title/926/headstoneapplications-1925-1963 With *Fold3,* individual names can be searched, and it allows for browsing by date ranges.

Orig — PLEASE MAKE OUT AND RETURN IN DUPLICATE — 27149

WAR DEPARTMENT

APPLICATION FOR HEADSTONE

Kent Harman Co. L 3 Tex. Inf. Sp.Am.War — Sp. War

NAME	RANK	COMPANY	U. S. Regiment, State Organization, or Vessel	DATE OF DEATH
KENT HARMAN	Pvt.	L Co	3rd Texas Inf.	10-13-1905

World War veteran— Division	State	Emblem	NAME OF CEMETERY	CITY	STATE
Spanish American War Veteran		Christian Hebrew None	Cleburne	Cleburne	Texas

TO BE SHIPPED TO American Legion Post (Name of consignee) at Cleburne Texas Johnson County (Give town, county, and State)

PERMANENT ADDRESS Cleburne Texas

DATE February 7th 1928

I hereby agree to accept the headstone at above destination, freight prepaid, and properly place same at decedent's grave.

Consignee.

DO NOT WRITE HERE

APR 24 1928

Verified

Ordered

From

Shipped AUG 9 1928

Address Cleburne Texas Date Feb. 7th 1928

This application is for the UNMARKED* grave of a† Soldier S.O. It is understood the stone will be furnished and delivered at the railroad station or steamboat landing above indicated, at Government expense, freight prepaid, and agreed it will be promptly removed and set up at private expense.

†State whether soldier, sailor, marine, Army nurse, etc.

T. E. Darcy S.O. Applicant.

*Should not be requested for any grave at which a private stone, monument, or other permanent marker is already erected or is to be erected.

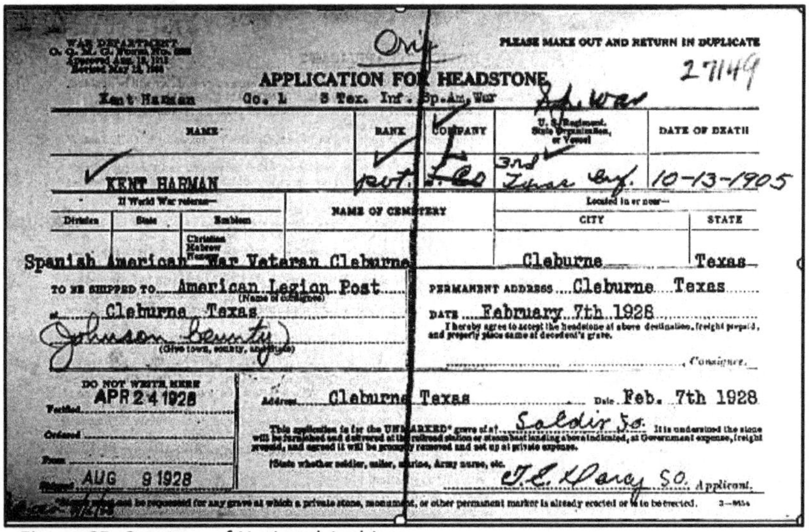

Figure 65: Courtesy of National Archives

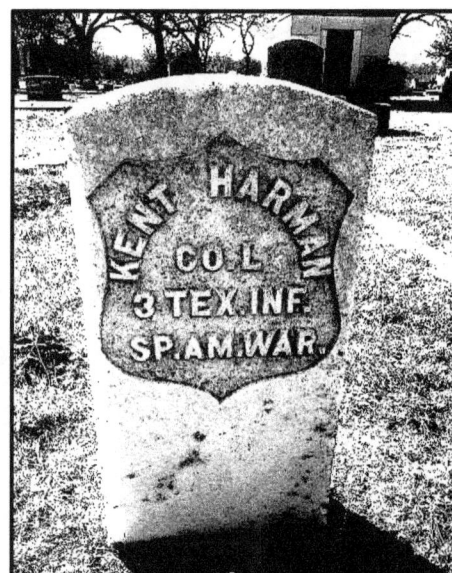

Figure 66: Courtesy of Find-A-Grave

The above veteran, Kent Harman, served in Company L of the 3rd Texas Infantry during the Spanish-American War and died on October 13, 1905 (not applied for until 1928).

Seldom did occasions arise when the military draped flags on the caskets as early as the Civil War. President Abraham Lincoln, at his death, received this high honor in 1865. The honored practice of draping a casket or coffin with an American flag has been more accepted and in place since the 1920s. This is another way to document an ancestor soldier, sailor, or marine during the Spanish-American War or later periods of conflict.

Figure 67: Courtesy of Library of Congress

The above photograph shows the graves of Spanish-American War dead draped with flags, ready to be interred at Arlington National Cemetery in Virginia in 1898. The casket on the right near the front is Charles Scott of Company C. 6th U.S. Cavalry (African American regiment), who was killed at the battle of San Juan Heights on July 2, 1898.[91] The Washington Monument can be seen in the distance.

On March 4, 1923, Congress passed an act that amended the War Risk Insurance Act of 1914 (43 Stat. 1521). It first authorized the use of burial flags for deceased veterans. Later, on June 7,

---

[91] Louis G. Prego, *The Battles of San Juan and El Caney or the Siege of Santiago* (Santiago: Heredia Alta, 1911), 30.

1924, the United States Congress passed an act (43 Stat. 616) that authorized the providing of burial flags to veterans "*for a flag to drape the casket, and after burial to be given to the next of kin of the deceased, a sum not exceeding $5; also, for burial expenses, a sum not exceeding $100, to such person or persons as may be fixed by regulations*". The amount of money provided for the flags changed when Congress passed another act on March 4, 1925 (43 Stat. 1305). It made provisions "*for a flag to drape the casket and after burial to be given to the next of kin...sum not exceeding $7*" with the same burial allowance as before.

Later acts in 1928 and 1930 made additional changes to the flags and the allotment for the burial of deceased soldiers. The new law took effect the following summer in 1931 when more flags became available for use on the caskets of veterans. The form required was Veterans Affair No. 2008 (application for United States flag for burial purposes), to be filled out to receive a burial flag. The flag burial forms are included in some deceased veterans' claims and pension files of men who served as early as the Civil War years and for several of the later war periods. The forms generally contain the relevant genealogical-related military information:

- Name of veteran
- Military unit and rank
- Date and place of death
- Claim file or pension application number

Searching these pensions and claim files is a means to find the application forms filled out by dependents. The current form online at the Veteran Administration can now be used for flags.

https://www.vba.va.gov/pubs/forms/VBA-272008-ARE.pdf This form is the same one that was issued earlier and revised numerous times.

 **GENEALOGY TOOL** When visiting veteran cemeteries and trying to decipher hard-to-read headstones due to soiling or damage, use the gentlest method possible to clean with soft natural brushes and use water to rinse without causing damage.

Veteran Organizations

Fraternal organizations and lineage societies date from as early as the colonial war era and can provide useful information not found in traditional records. The Spanish-American War and the Philippine Insurrection had several organizations. Research should be directed at state libraries and archives. Additional searches in local societies to locate manuscripts, photographs, and other useful material on veterans or their descendants can add to your family's history.

United Spanish War Veterans:

In 1899, after the end of the Spanish-American War, a group of veterans came together and organized a fraternal organization to keep in contact with former comrades. Membership was open to all veterans who served during the late wars:

- Spanish-American War, 1898-1899
- Boxer Rebellion, 1900
- Philippine Insurrection, 1899-1902

This group came together from three groups: Spanish-war veterans, Spanish-American War Veterans, and the Servicemen of the Spanish War. In 1906, another group called the Legion of Spanish War Veterans served as a female auxiliary. Later, in 1908, another independent group called the Veteran Army of the Philippines joined the United Spanish War Veterans organization. The group lasted until 1992, when the last member, a man named Nathan Cook, died. He had served in the United States Navy during the Philippine Insurrection.

DEPARTMENT DEATHS AND GRAVES REGISTRATION
DEPARTMENT OF OHIO
No. ______ UNITED SPANISH WAR VETERANS

NAME Porter, John E.
COMPANY ORGANIZATION OR SHIP Co. C, 2nd OVI
DATE OF BIRTH Nov. 4, 1868 DATE OF DEATH Feb. 3, 1955
CAUSE OF DEATH Info. via Dr. Hunter, Wapakoneta
NAME AND NO. OF CAMP CAPT. FRANK M. BELL NO. 38
CITY WHERE INTERRED Lima Sec. 7
CEMETERY WHERE INTERRED Woodlawn LOT NO. 69 GRAVE NO. ---
DATE RECORDED DATE FILED RECORDED G. O.
THIS CARD TO BE FILLED OUT BY CAMP ADJUTANT AND FORWARDED TO DEPARTMENT HEADQUARTERS AS SOON AS POSSIBLE AFTER BURIAL.

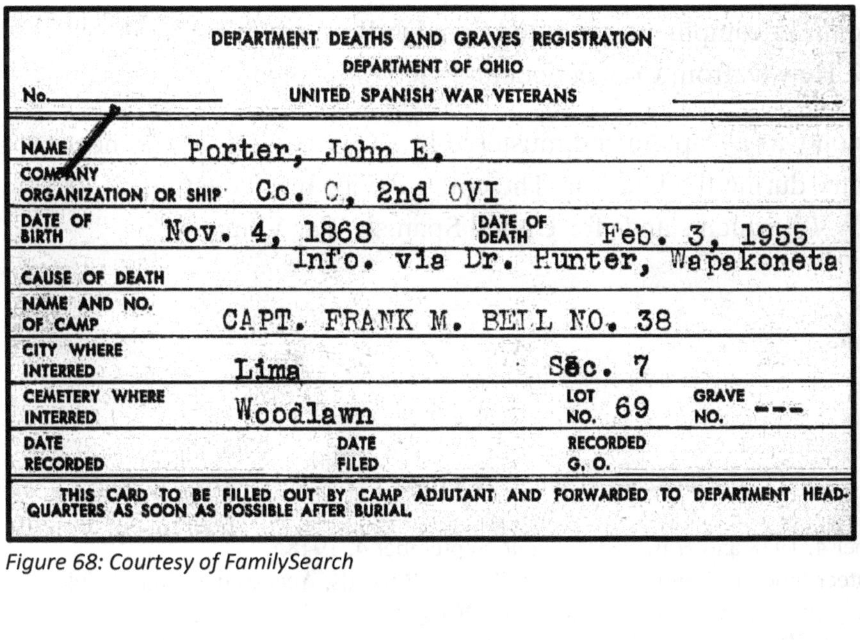

Figure 68: Courtesy of FamilySearch

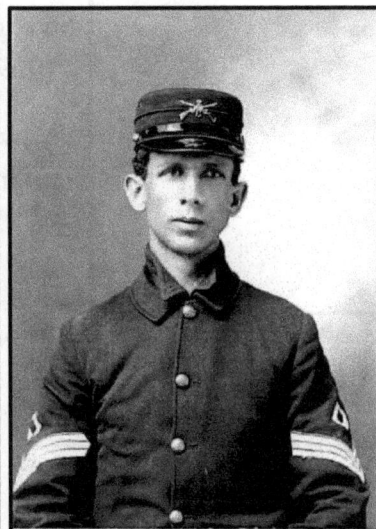

Figure 69: Courtesy of Michael L. Strauss

The previous page's images show the membership card for John E. Porter, who served during the Spanish-American War. A native of Lima, Ohio, and a former member of the Ohio National Guard, Porter was mustered in on May 10, 1898, in Lima as the 1st Sergeant in Company C. 2nd Ohio Volunteer Infantry. Porter was promoted regimental Sergeant-Major in January 1899 and mustered out at Bellefontaine, Ohio on January 25, 1899.[92]

After his discharge, Porter returned back to civilian life and joined the Captain Frank M. Bell Post No. 38 (formally numbered 128) in Lima, Ohio. He worked as a merchant in town in business with his father for many years and died on February 3, 1955, in Lima, OH.[93]

Members of the United Spanish-American Wars wore medals issued to active organization participants on their uniforms or other suits. The medal measures about 4 x 1 ½ inches with a ribbon of 13 stars and stripes. The bottom of the ribbon is a saber, rifle, and anchor, all crossing the other, representing different branches of service.

On the medal below are the words *"Porto Rico, Cuba, and the Philippines," where the fight occurred, with the* USA printed on the bottom.

Yearly encampments were held to spur comradeship. Former veterans were placed in command of the yearly camp and invited all current members. The listing of former commanders from 1904-1992, with images of many officers, is located online, browsable by years of service at https://web.archive.org/web/20090318131310/http:/freepages.military.rootsweb.ancestry.com/~sunnyann/commanders-photos.html.

Charles W. Newton served as the Commander-In-Chief of the National Encampment of United Spanish War veterans from 1908-1909. He was from Connecticut and died on September 4, 1948.[94]

Newton was a Captain and mustered into Company F. 1st Connecticut Infantry during the late war. The collar device has the letters "USWV," which stands for United Spanish War Veterans.[95]

Figure 70: Courtesy of Spanish War Veterans

---

[92] *The Official Roster of Ohio Soldiers in the War with Spain*, (Columbus: Edward T. Miller, 1916), 71, 88.
[93] *Lima News*, February 3, 1955.
[94] *The Bridgeport Telegram*, September 4, 1948 and *Hartford Courant*, September 4, 1948.
[95] U.S. Spanish-American War Volunteer Index to Compiled Military Service Records, Accessed 14 May 2024. https://www.ancestry.com/imageviewer/collections/2400/images/32803_261690-02519?treeid=&personid=&hintid=&queryId=948f83ad3547bc0737382037ebaaa877&usePUB=true&_phsrc=Pjx4&_phstart=successSource&usePUBJs=true&_ga=2.39755878.494245050.1596501988-1259336514.1596501988&pId=62954.

Sons of Spanish American War Veterans:

Founded in 1927 as a fraternal organization in Philadelphia, PA, the group is open to all male descendants over the age of 14. Their purpose is to perpetuate the memory of those who served in any of the three wars:

- Spanish-American War, 1898-1899.
- Boxer Rebellion, 1900
- Philippine Insurrection, 1899-1902

The organization today is very active and participates in yearly events. Six camps of the order that recruit for membership with the camp numbers and locations:

- Fighting Joe Wheeler Camp No. 14, located in Chattanooga, TN
- Colonel Andrew S. Rowan Camp No. 117 in California
- Egbert-Wetherill Reed Camp No. 167 in Kentucky
- Joseph Melvin Leonard Camp No. 168 in New York
- Alexander M. Quinn Camp No. 173 in Lebanon, PA
- USS Olympia Camp No. 174 in Philadelphia, PA

The society has an active online presence with information on the several chapters and the history of the veteran organization. The statement of purpose can be found on their website at https://ssawvhq.org. More information about membership for descendants can be directed to the National Secretary.

The organization has a female auxiliary called "*Daughters of 98*" that meets regularly and is active in events open to any female descendant of the war period. Following is a link from the main website for the SSAWV for more information on the daughters: https://ssawvhq.org/daughters-of-98 (contact the national captain).

Veterans of Foreign Wars:

Organized on September 29, 1899, during the Philippine Insurrection, it was founded by thirteen veterans of the Spanish-American War who wanted to promote the high ideals of an organization created to care for veterans of all wars. The VFW was organized partly to help secure benefits for returning veterans who arrived home sick or wounded. This is done by programs in place in local communities that both support veterans and their extended families.

VFW membership grew in large numbers following the end of World War I in 1918 and continues today as an active organization with the same ideals that advocate the benefits for veterans through our most recent conflicts. The organization has an active website where more information and membership details can be reviewed online: https://www.vfw.org.

Grand Army of the Republic

Organized in 1866 at the end of the Civil War, the GAR comprised the Union Army, Navy, Marines, and the Revenue Cutter Service veterans. The organization remained very active with members through the end of the twentieth century, with local post-level activities and larger national-level events. The GAR supported the veterans from other wars and often involved themselves in parades with Spanish-American War veterans.

Figure 71: Courtesy of Michael L. Strauss

The GAR had an active female auxiliary called Ladies of the GAR who supported the activities of their husbands. The last active member died in 1956 with the death of Albert Woolson.

GENEALOGY TIP An often-overlooked resource for finding useful information about military personnel can be found in newspapers. Many newspapers are being digitized and available online to help locate where someone served, their military unit, or if a veteran died while in service.

Soldier Home Records

The origin of soldiers' homes for disabled veterans started with the passage of government legislation by Congress on February 26, 1811 (2 Stat. 650), with the establishment of a Navy asylum for both disabled sailors and marines located in Philadelphia, PA. The construction of the building did not begin until 1827.[96]

The United States Army proposed the establishment of a veteran home as early as 1827. It was not until after the end of the Mexican War in the years following that Congress passed national legislation. This act, called *"An Act to Found a Military Asylum for the Relief and Support of Disabled Soldier of the Army of the United States"*, was passed by Congress on March 3, 1851 (9 Stat. 595), and provided care for men with service disabilities who had served at least twenty years and were honorably discharged. Funds were generally paid through the soldier's career over the course of service until being discharged.[97]

In the closing months of the Civil War, sweeping changes for the care of elderly, infirmed, or invalid veterans were brought up on the floors of Congress. The act entitled *"An Act to Incorporate a National Military and Naval Asylum for the Relief of the Totally Disabled Officers and Men of the Volunteer Forces of the United States"* was passed by unanimous vote by the members of Congress on March 3, 1865 (13 Stat. 509), accounting for volunteer soldiers, sailors, and marines.

Originally called the National Asylum of Disabled Volunteer Soldiers in 1873, the name was changed to the National Home for Disabled Volunteer Soldiers. The change was done to remove the negative imagery of the word asylum.

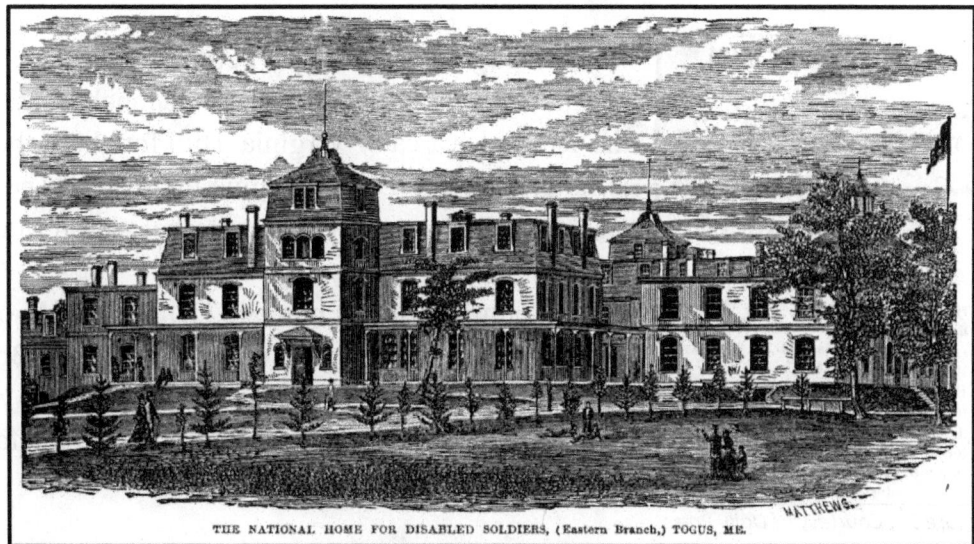

THE NATIONAL HOME FOR DISABLED SOLDIERS, (Eastern Branch,) TOGUS, ME.

Figure 72: Courtesy of Gazetteer of the State of Maine, 1881.

---

[96] United States Statutes at Large. Accessed 25 November 2022 at: https://www.loc.gov/law/help/statutes-at-large/11th-congress/session-3/c11s3ch26.pdf.

[97] United States Statutes at large. Accessed 25 November 2022 at: https://www.loc.gov/law/help/statutes-at-large/31st-congress/session-2/c31s2ch25.pdf.

The previous image shows a hand-drawn rendition of the National Home for Disabled Soldiers from the Eastern Branch at Togus near Chelsea, Maine.[98]

Records for veterans who lived in the homes are searchable online at Ancestry by researching the database of the *United States National Home for Disabled Volunteer Soldiers, 1866-1938* at: https://www.ancestry.com/search/collections/1200. Records extend back to 1866.

The records cover multiple federal homes for disabled soldiers:

- Bath Branch located in Bath, NY from 1876-1934.
- Battle Mountain Sanitarium was in Hot Springs, SD, from 1907 to 1934.
- Central Branch was in Dayton, OH, from 1867 to 1935.
- Danville Branch was in Danville, IL, from 1898 to 1934.
- Eastern Branch located in Togus, ME, from 1866 to 1934
- Marion Branch was in Marion, IN, from 1890 to 1931.
- The Mountain Branch was in Johnson City, TN, from 1903 to1932.
- Northwestern Branch was in Milwaukee, WI, from 1867 to 1934.
- Pacific Branch located in Sawtelle, CA, from 1888 to 1933.
- Roseburg Branch was in Roseburg, OR, from 1894 to 1937.
- Southern Branch was in Hampton, VA, from 1871 to 1933.
- The Western Branch was in Leavenworth, KS, from 1885 to 1934.

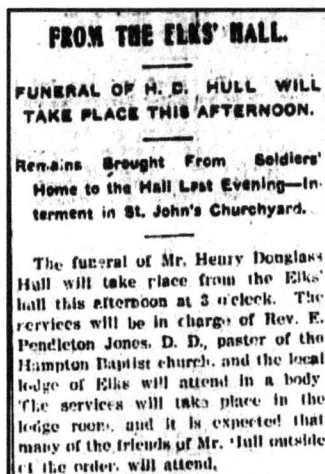

FROM THE ELKS' HALL.

FUNERAL OF H. D. HULL WILL TAKE PLACE THIS AFTERNOON.

Remains Brought From Soldiers' Home to the Hall Last Evening—Interment in St. John's Churchyard.

The funeral of Mr. Henry Douglass Hull will take place from the Elks' hall this afternoon at 3 o'clock. The services will be in charge of Rev. E. Pendleton Jones, D. D., pastor of the Hampton Baptist church, and the local lodge of Elks will attend in a body. The services will take place in the lodge room, and it is expected that many of the friends of Mr. Hull outside of the order, will attend.

Figure 73: Courtesy of Daily Press

Henry Douglas Hull died on February 21, 1905, in Hampton, Virginia, and lived at the Southern Branch Soldiers Home located in the Tidewater area of Virginia. Hull fought in the Spanish-American joining Company D. 4th Virginia Infantry and became ill while in Cuba with his regiment, being discharged on May 11, 1899.

He was admitted to the home in Hampton, VA, on April 18, 1901, and remained there until he died in 1905. His Brother, Amos Tyler Hull of Hampton, was his closest next of kin to whom his effects were sent, along with his body for burial in the family plot in St. John's Cemetery in Hampton, Virginia.[99]

The image on the following page shows the National Soldiers Home record for Henry D. Hull, who resided at the Southern Branch in Hampton, VA, from 1901-1905. Besides his military service, the records detail his domestic history, including his physical description and occupation before joining the military during the Spanish-American War.

---

[98] George J. Varney, *A Gazetteer of the State of Maine* (Boston: B.B. Russell, 1881), 170-172.
[99] *The Daily Press*, February 22, 1905.

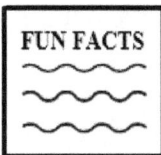

Figure 74: Courtesy of National Archives

Several states operated their own soldiers' homes for veterans of former wars. This was generally outside the control of the United States government. In 1886, the State of Ohio authorized the creation of a soldier's home in Sandusky, Ohio, which operated when the Central Branch for the National Soldiers Home was opened in Dayton, Ohio.

Outside of checking the registers of veterans in national or state homes, searching inside pension files often yields clues if the soldier, sailor, or marine lived in a soldier's home as part of obtaining their benefits from the pension. The chapter on pensions in this volume will provide the steps to locate this information.

In 1921, the United States Congress created the Veterans Bureau for soldiers to file for benefits. Later, in 1930, President Hoover combined the Veterans Bureau with the Bureau of Pensions and Home for Disabled Veterans to create a single office called the Veterans Administration. By 30 June 1932, the number of veterans in the home totaled 22,503, including 5,572 veterans from the Spanish-American War. The organization is now called Veterans Affairs.[100]

FUN FACTS

DID YOU KNOW the United States formally annexed Hawaii through a joint resolution on 7 July 1898, during the Spanish-American War? The sinking of the USS *Maine* helped to influence these events for heightened strategic considerations for a possible naval base in the Pacific.

---

[100] Trevor K. Plante "The National Home for Disabled Volunteer Soldiers" *Prologue: Quarterly of the National Archives* 36:1 (Spring 2004): 56-61.

African Americans in the Military

In the decades leading up to the Revolutionary War, very few blacks in the colonies were free, with most in the bonds of slavery. Some were indentured servants, while others were given their freedom through manumission. Persons of African American descent served in some of the colonial-era conflicts. A pattern began to emerge in the colonies where the English crown permitted blacks to enlist in times of war. However, they were excluded (due to the passage of session laws for each colony) from military service during times of peace.

Following the end of the Revolutionary War in 1783, the United States Congress passed the first Act calling upon militia on May 2, 1792 (1 Stat. 264). The act was amended six days later to exclude African Americans from militia service, with only free, white, able-bodied citizens who were at least 18 years of age and under 45 years eligible for service. This was further reinforced when, on February 18, 1820, the United States Army issued a general order barring both "Negroes" and "Mulattos" from military service.[101]

The following year, the United States Army regulations interpreted as meaning, "*All free white male persons above 18 and under 35 years, who are able-bodied, active, and free from disease, may be enlisted,*" with the ban lasting until the passage of the Militia Act of 1862.[102]

For the first time since 1792, African American males could now be recruited, and this was the basis for the formal establishment of the Bureau of Colored Troops on May 22, 1863, by issuing General Order No. 143. This organization was later called the United States Colored Troops.[103]

The end of the Civil War in 1865 brought about the reorganization of the United States Army, and the United States Congress passed an act on July 28, 1866 (14 Stat. 332). This decreased the size of the standing army and called for the raising of four infantry and two cavalry regiments of all black soldiers. In 1869, the number of regiments was lowered to two regiments of cavalry and two of infantry, giving birth to the famed "Buffalo Soldiers" and their service.[104]

The post-Civil War years witnessed the first commissioned black officers in the regular United States Army and graduates from West Point.

- Henry O. Flipper- graduated in 1877 and was assigned as 2nd Lieutenant to the 10th U.S. Cavalry.
- John H. Alexander-graduated in 1887 assigned as 2nd Lieutenant to 9th U.S. Cavalry.

---

[101] Hael D. Doubler and John W. Listman Jr. *The National Guard: An Illustrated History of America's Citizen Soldiers*, (Washington, DC: Brassey's Inc., 2003), 18.

[102] *General Regulations for the Army*. United States War Department, (Philadelphia, PA: M. Carey and Sons, 1821), 312. Accessed 27 April 2024 at: https://babel.hathitrust.org/cgi/pt?id=hvd.hxjg8p&view=1up&seq=13.

[103] Christine Compston and Rachel F. Seidman Editors, *Our Documents: 100 Milestone Documents from the National Archives*, (New York: Oxford University Press, 2003), 91-92.

[104] Jerold E. Brown, *Historical Dictionary of the U.S. Army*, (Westport: Greenwood Press, 2001), 39-40.

Both officers failed to have long military careers. Flipper was cashiered out of the Army in 1882, and Alexander died at the age of 30 in 1894. As the frontier wars with the Indians were less frequent, the United States, with the Buffalo Soldiers on military duty, would face a new threat from Spain and be called to action.[105]

The 9th and 10th U.S. Cavalry and the 24th and 25th U.S. Infantry were composed of black troops and led by white officers. In addition to regular army units, there were five regiments of the volunteer army, the "USV," consisting of the 7th, 8th, 9th, 10th, and 11th United States Volunteer Infantry.

The United States government believed these men were better suited to the climatic changes for fighting in Cuba and the Philippines. The regiments gained the nickname "Immune Regiments," with only one, the 9th United States Volunteer Infantry, having served overseas.[106]

During the war, seven regiments of volunteers were called up as state-designated regiments, most of which were led by black officers. The regiments were the 3rd Alabama Infantry, the 8th Illinois Infantry, Companies A and B of the 1st Indiana Infantry, the 23rd Kansas Infantry, the 3rd North Carolina Infantry, the 9th Ohio Infantry, and the 6th Virginia Infantry.[107]

Lt. Charles Young (pictured to the left) was a graduate of West Point in the class of 1889, the third black officer to graduate at the time. Young was assigned to the 10th and later 9th United States Cavalry until the war in 1898. He was appointed Major on May 14, 1898, in the volunteers and given command of the 9th Ohio Infantry. After the war, he was transferred back to the 9th United States Cavalry in 1899.[108]

Figure 75: Courtesy of Army Heritage Center

---

[105] Francis B. Heitman, *Historical Register and Dictionary of the United States Army from its Organization, September 29, 1789 to March 2, 1903*, (Washington, DC: Government Printing Office, 1903), 156, 425.

[106] Roger D. Cunningham, "An Experiment which may or may not turn out Well," *Journal of American History*, 10:4 (2005): 9-17.

[107] Edward A. Johnson, *History of Negro Soldiers in the Spanish-American War and other Items of Interest*, (Raleigh: Capital Printing Company, 1899), 92-112.

[108] Heitman, *Historical Register and Dictionary of the United States Army,* 1066 and Brian G. Shellum, *Black Officer in a Buffalo Soldier Regiment: The Military Career of Charles Young*, (Lincoln: University of Nebraska, 2010), 70-93. Charles Young was the first black officer to be promoted to Colonel in the United States Army when he retired at the end of World War I in 1918. Young, while on a reconnaissance mission, became ill and died on January 8, 1922, in a British hospital in Lagos, Nigeria. After his death, he received many honors and was buried at Arlington National Cemetery in Virginia.

Some of the heaviest fighting in Cuba involved the 9th and 10th United States Cavalry in the thick of the action during the battle of San Juan Hill on July 1-3, 1898. On the neighboring hill, the 25th United States Infantry took part in the El Caney, Cuba battle on July 1, 1898.[109]

At the end of the Spanish-American War, the United States was fighting during the Philippines Insurrection; the 24th United States Infantry was deployed to fight in the islands until the end of the Philippine War on July 2, 1902. Two other USV regiments of all-black troops were formed. These included the 48th and 49th United States Volunteer Infantry, which were organized and sent to the Philippines.

One of the more interesting stories during the Philippine Insurrection concerns the account of David Fagen, who, as a member of the 24th United States Infantry and with other regiment men, deserted on November 17, 1899, while in the Philippines.

Figure 76: Courtesy of Salt Lake Herald

David Fagen was born circa 1875 in Tampa, Florida, to parents who were former slaves. He enlisted on February 9, 1899, in Ft. McPherson, Georgia. Shortly after his enlistment, his father died, and he was transferred with his regiment to Fort Douglas near Salt Lake City, Utah.

After Fagen deserted his regiment, he defected to join the local insurgent Filipino Army fighting against United States forces. Over time, he became an efficacious guerrilla leader, gaining promotion to the rank of Captain in the belligerent's military. Often referred to as General Fagen, the United States Army put a price on his head for his capture. By the end of the war in 1902, Fagen's death was reported, but with no positive proof that he had died.[110]

Locating African-American soldiers during either the Spanish-American War or the Philippine Insurrection can be done by following the steps using the Compiled Military Service Records (previously discussed) or with the United States Regular Army records already mentioned.

Additional resources for Buffalo Soldiers can be found by digging further into the records of the returns of the specific regiments. One of the records to be searched is entitled *U.S. Buffalo*

---

[109] Jerome Tuccille, *The Roughest Riders: The Untold Story of the Black Soldiers in the Spanish-American War*, (Chicago: Chicago Review Press Incorporated, 2015), 47-85.
[110] Michael C. Robinson and Frank N. Schubert, "David Fagen: An Afro-American Rebel in the Philippines, 1899-1901" *Pacific Historical Review* 44:1 (February 1975): 68-83.

Soldiers, Returns from Regular Army Cavalry Regiments, 1866-1916, where the records are searchable on *Ancestry* at https://www.ancestry.com/search/collections/1934

Another entitled *U.S. Returns from Regular Army Infantry Regiments, 1821-1916* is available on Ancestry at https://www.ancestry.com/search/collections/2229 and is indexed by the number of the regiment. Once located, browse the military unit by the sub-grouped dates.

GENEALOGY CLUE When researching in cemeteries for military ancestors who served in the Spanish-American War, Boxer Rebellion, or the Philippine Insurrection, consider looking at reference books and other sources of information that cover the subject of tombstone symbolism and the meaning behind carved words or marks.

Women in Military Service

Life for American women historically has often been burdened with setbacks. Limited by society without voting rights, restricted educational opportunities, and virtually no legal identity, women sought to be equals in society. One area where woman sought equality was serving their country.

From the time of the Revolutionary War, women who wanted to serve in the military would likely have to disguise themselves as men. Many became camp followers, serving by cleaning and cooking. In the years preceding the turn of the twentieth century, women became more accepted in the military ranks. The establishment of the Army Nursing Corps in 1901 saw the first large-scale enlistment of women, followed in 1908 by the Navy Nursing Corps. The other military branches took longer to accept women. The Marine Corps followed the Navy's lead in 1918 and the Coast Guard in 1917.[111]

In the weeks immediately preceding the formal declaration of war against Spain in 1898, President William McKinley received a letter from national celebrity Annie Oakley. In her letter (April 5, 1898), Oakley (pictured below) offered her expert marksmanship services to the United States by raising an all-female regiment composed of fifty sharpshooters. The women supplied their own arms and ammunition if the United States went to war.

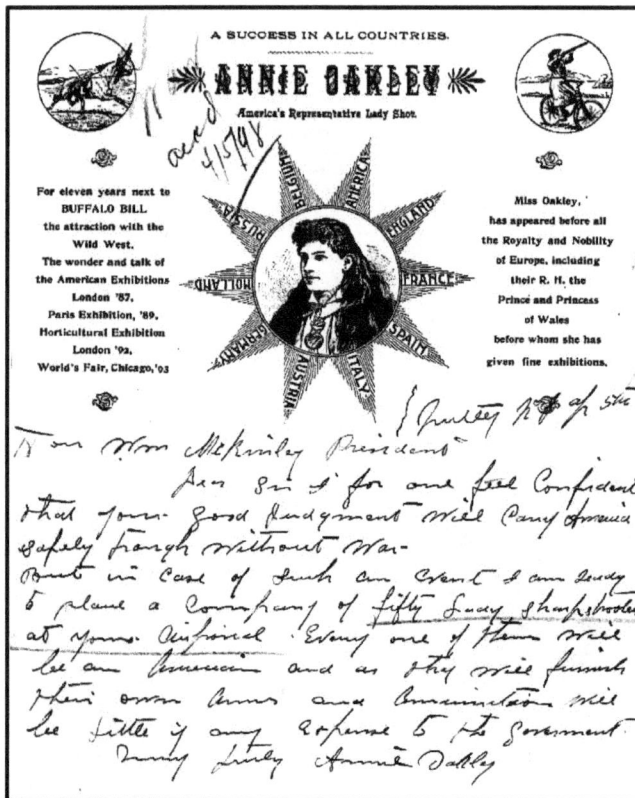

Figure 77: Courtesy of National Archives

Figure 78: Courtesy of Library of Congress

---

[111] Barton C. Hacker and Margaret Vining, *A Companion to Women's Military History,* (Boston: Brill, 2002), 137-232.

Oakley's request was passed from the President to the War Department, where it was declined, which did not dissuade Oakley from trying again when the United States entered World War I in 1917 with a similar offer to President Woodrow Wilson. Again, her offer was turned down.[112]

From the end of the Civil War in 1865, men served in the Army as hospital stewards and assistants tending to the wounded. Their numbers were inadequate for the start of the Spanish-American War. This was especially apparent in military camps where outbreaks of illnesses such as typhoid were depleting their already small numbers of medical staff. To solve the problem, the United States War Department authorized the recruitment of Army nurses, mostly under contract, to serve during the war. In turn, this volunteer force officially helped to organize the Army Nursing Corps in 1901.[113]

RG112 in the National Archives in Washington, DC, has records for military and civilian contracted personnel who served during the Spanish-American War, Boxer Rebellion, and the Philippine Insurrection.[114]

Entry 103: *Historical Files of the Army Nurse Corps, 1900-1947.* Collection of records loosely organized and unarranged.

Entry 104: *Case Files of Candidates Seeking Appointments as Army Nurses, 1898-1917.* Nice collection of files for Army nurses classified into two subgroups: candidates who were accepted into the Corps as well as those disqualified.

Entry 105: *Register of Military Service of Members of the Army Nurses Corps, 1901-1902.* It contains a listing of military nurses, arranged by the surname of the nurse, with a single volume containing a name index.

Entry 106: *Monthly Strength Return of Nurses, 1899-1917.* Small collection containing information on the monthly strengths of nursing stations.

Entry 107: *Station Books of Nurses, 1899-1903, 1911-1916.* Contained in two volumes. The record books are arranged by date of the nurses' arrival onsite.

Entry 108: *Annual Efficiency Reports on Nurses, 1898-1917.* Arranged chronologically by date and then indexed by station.

---

[112] *Annie Oakley the Feminist.* The Annie Oakley Center Foundation, Inc. Accessed 28 October 2024 at: https://www.annieoakleycenterfoundation.com/faq6.html.

[113] Mercedes Graf "Women Physicians in the Spanish-American War" *Army History.* 56:1 (Fall, 2002), 5-14.

[114] Patricia Taylor and Garry Ryan, *Preliminary Inventory of the Textual Records of the Office of the Surgeon General Army. RG112. Reprint* (Westminster: Heritage Books, 2001), 13.

During the Spanish-American War, the United States Army hired female civilian nurses and surgeons under contract. Contact records are included in the Records of the Surgeon General for the Army found in RG112 at the National Archives. Many case files with personal data for contract nurses are arranged alphabetically.[115]

Entry 147: *Correspondence Relating to Spanish-American War Contract Nurses, 1898-1910.* The files are loosely organized and unarranged.

Entry 148: *Register of Service of Spanish-American War Contract Nurses, 1898-1900.* The eight volumes are arranged by the date of the nurse's contract. Each volume has an index to names.

Entry 149: *Personal Data Cards of Spanish-American War Contract Nurses, 1898-1939.* The cards are arranged alphabetically by the surname of the nurses.

Entry 150: *Correspondence Relating to the service of Spanish-American War contract nurses, 1898-1939.* The files cover decades of records and are arranged alphabetically by the name of the nurses. The National Archives card catalog has a name index to 761 of the nursing files at: https://catalog.archives.gov/search?q=*:*&f.parentNaId=2561136&f.level=fileUnit&sort=naIdSort%20asc.

After the start of the war in 1898, outbreaks of typhoid and yellow fever ran unchecked among the troops in Cuba, Puerto Rico, and the Philippines. The small organization that would become the Army Nurse Corps grew to more than 1,500 nurses, mostly under contract, and paid the wages of $30 monthly. The nurses held no official military status while serving at military hospitals, ships, and stations from 1898 to 1901.

Figure 79: Courtesy of U.S. National Library of Medicine

Dita Hopkins Kinney was one of the more well-known figures who led the nursing field during the war. Born in New York City in 1855, she trained as a young adult as a nurse in Massachusetts. Later, Kinney worked in Minnesota and California before joining the Army as a contract nurse in 1898 during the Spanish-American War.

She was to become the first superintendent of the Army Nurse Corps from 1901 to 1909. After resigning her post, she became active during World War I in the American Red Cross and died on April

[115] *Ibid.*, 18.

16, 1921, in Bangor, Maine, being buried next to her husband in New York.[116]

Another leader in the field of nursing was Esther Voorhees Hasson. Born in Baltimore, MD, on September 20, 1870, she was the daughter of Major Alexander B. Hasson, a surgeon during the Civil War. In 1898, she enrolled in the Army Nurse Corps as a contract nurse and was discharged in 1901. Esther later helped organize the Navy Nurse Corps in 1908 and served as the first superintendent until her resignation in 1911.

When the United States entered World War I in 1917, Hasson again rejoined the Army Nurse Corps until being discharged in 1919. The image below shows the first 20 Navy nurses in 1908. They were called "The Sacred Twenty", Hasson being identified with an "X" below her image. Esther Voorhees Hasson died in Washington, DC, on March 9, 1942, and is buried in Arlington National Cemetery in Virginia.[117]

Figure 80: Courtesy of Naval Historical Center

[116] Benjamin F. Shearer, *Home Front Heroes: A Biographical Dictionary of Americans During Wartime. Vol 2,* (Westport: Greenwood Press, 2007), 484-486; *The Bangor Times*, April 18, 1921.
[117] Captain Doris M. Sterner, *In and Out of Harm's Way: A History of the Navy Nurse Corps*, (Seattle: Navy Nurse Corps Association, 1997), 19-35; and *Cumberland Evening Times*, March 9, 1942.

Ellen May Tower of Bryon, Michigan, was the first Army nurse to die on foreign soil during the Spanish-American War. After her enlistment, she was sent to Point Montauk at Camp Wikoff in New York, then to Puerto Rico, where she became sick and contracted Typhoid and died on December 9, 1898. Afterward, her body was repatriated back to the United States, where she was buried in Michigan with a full military funeral.[118]

One of the most noted female doctors to serve during the war was Anita Newcomb McGee (pictured on the inset), who was born on November 4, 1864, in Washington, DC. She was educated at Columbian College, receiving her medical degree in 1892, and went on to post-graduate work at John Hopkins University in Baltimore, MD.

McGee went into private practice between 1892 and 1896 in Washington, DC, before the beginning of the war in 1898. Appointed to Acting Assistant Surgeon on August 29, 1898, she was placed in charge of the Army nurses then under the control of the Army Surgeon General Department.

Figure 81: Courtesy of U.S. National Library of Medicine

Dr. Anita Newcomb McGee is perhaps best known for organizing the Spanish-American War Nurse Corps, which became the structure for the permanent Army Nurse Corps in 1901. McGee died on October 5, 1940, in Washington, DC, and was buried with full military honors in Arlington National Cemetery in Virginia.[119]

Another excellent website to locate Army Nurse Corps records is found in the United States Army Medical Department Center of History and Heritage located at Ft. Sam Houston in Texas with an online finding aid at: https://api.army.mil/e2/c/downloads/342056.pdf. Some of the records in their inventory include:

Series 31 Folder 2-Deaths during the Spanish-American War with the Army Nursing Corps.
Series 39: Folder 7-Spanish-American War pensions for members of the Army Nursing Corps.
Series 40: Folder 10-African-Americans within the Army Nursing Corps.
Series 41: Folder 1-Male nurses in the Army Nursing Corps during the Spanish-American War.
Series 44: Folders 78-80-Newsletters and correspondence during the Spanish-American War.
Series 60: Folder 1-Army Nursing Corps records during the Boxer Rebellion-1900-1901.
Series 72: Folder 7-Transportation of Army Nurses during the Spanish-American War.

---

[118] *Detroit Free Press*, December 15, 1898; and *Owosso Times*, January 20, 1899.
[119] Mercedes Graf "Women Physicians in the Spanish-American War" *Army History* 56:1 (Fall 2002): 5-14.

The Army Nursing Corps had a booklet titled: *"Manual for the Medical Department: Compiled under the Direction of the Surgeon General"* with details on duties, responsibilities, and military status on *Hathi Trust* at https://babel.hathitrust.org/cgi/pt?id=uc1.$b171542&view=1up&seq=7

The *American Red Cross* was founded in 1881 by Clara Barton. Clara Barton recruited nurses to serve with the troops despite the Army surgeon general's reluctance to allow women to care for the wounded. Barton soon overcame those obstacles.

Figure 82: Courtesy of Library of Congress

Secretary of War R.A. Alger sent her a letter on June 6, 1898, telling her that the "tender of services of the American National Red Cross . . . for medical and hospital work as auxiliary to the hospital service of the Army of the United States is accepted" and adding that her workers would be "subject to orders according to the rules and discipline of war, as provided by the 63 Articles of War." By 1899, Barton had recruited some 700 nurses.

Barton was disheartened to see that camp conditions had not changed significantly since the Civil War, including treatment of the wounded. The soldiers wore winter weather uniforms in the tropical summer heat, and countless numbers fell ill to yellow fever, typhoid fever, and dysentery. Medical officers credited the Red Cross with helping them sustain their operations under difficult circumstances.

https://www.plantmuseum.com/exhibits/online-exhibits/red-cross-nursing-and-the-war-of-1898

https://redcrosschat.org/2013/02/15/from-the-archives-4

GENEALOGY TOOL Watching television documentaries on A&E, C-Span, Corporation for Public Broadcasting, the History Channel, or the Biography Channel can help to learn about the military conflicts, adding depth to research on the Spanish-American War, Boxer Rebellion, or the Philippine Insurrection.

Identification Tags, Military Awards and Medals

Inside the majestic gates of the Arlington National Cemetery in Virginia lies the Tomb of the Unknown Soldier, where active-duty personnel stand as sentinels, remembering our fallen soldiers since the monument was solemnized in 1921. Many cemeteries have the remains of soldiers from wars past marked with a single word identifier "Unknown". Identification tags were created to remember those who sacrificed everything to serve their country.[120]

The Civil War brought changes in the way battlefield deaths were recorded. The task of identifying those killed who were unknown was considerably difficult. On April 3, 1862, the Adjutant General Office (AGO) issued General Order No. 33, which, in effect, stated: "*To secure as far as possible the decent internment of those who have fallen or may fall in battle...lay off lots of ground in suitable spot near every battlefield and... register of each burial ground will be preserved*". It was the large numbers of casualties that prompted some soldiers and civilians to consider other ways of identifying fallen soldiers.[121]

In the second year of the war, a resident of New York City named John Kennedy wrote on 3 May 1862 to the Secretary of War Edwin M. Stanton and proposed a plan for a badge of medal to be distributed to all officers and enlisted men to be worn under the clothing. The War Department rejected Kennedy's request.[122]

Spanish-American War

War with Spain erupted on April 25, 1898. Government thoughts again turned to the numbers of fallen soldiers and the identification of men. With soldiers fighting in Cuba and the Philippines, the San Francisco Red Cross Society took on the challenge of providing identification tags for soldiers (when individual states failed to furnish tags to their volunteers) that were roughly the size of a half-dollar made of aluminum.[123]

The discs were inscribed with the soldier's company, regiments, and the number of each soldier's listed numerical identifier (corresponding to the CMSR). On the other side of the disc was the visual design of the Red Cross with the letters "RED" inscribed.[124] The tags furnished by the Red Cross were only for troops embarking for Manilla and were not provided to soldiers or regiments that fought in Cuba.

---

[120] H.P. Caemmerer, *Washington the National Capital* (Washington, DC: Government Printing Office, 1932), 587.
[121] Michael Sledge, *Soldier Dead: How we Recover, Identify, Bury, and Honor our Military Fallen* (New York: Columbia University Press, 2005), 33.
[122] Larry B. Maier and Joseph W. Stahl, *Identification Discs of Union Soldiers in the Civil War: A Complete Classification Guide and Illustrated History* (Jefferson: McFarland and Company, 2008), 14.
[123] Stephen D. Coats, gathering *at the Golden Gate: Mobilizing for the War in the Philippines, 1898* (Ft. Leavenworth: Combat Studies Institute Press, 2006), 155, 160.
[124] *The San Francisco Call*, May 15, 1898.

The following year, in 1899, United States Army Chaplain Charles C. Pierce, who ran and established the Quartermaster Graves Registration Service, wrote to the AGO office: "*It is better that all men should wear these marks as a military duty than one should fail to be identified.*" Pierce was referring to government-issued ID tags for all men in the military. Six more years would pass before official tags were adopted.[125]

Figure 83: From the Authors Private Collection (Front and Back)

The above-pictured identification tag issued by the San Francisco Red Cross belonged to Charles Henry LaFever (1877-1951), who served in Company C. 13th Minnesota Infantry. He mustered in at St. Paul, MN, on June 13, 1898, and mustered out on October 3, 1899, in San Francisco, CA.[126] The unit was attached to the 1st Brigade of the 2nd Division in the 8th Army Corps under the command of General Arthur MacArthur (the father of General Douglas MacArthur of World War II fame) and stationed in the Philippines. The men of the 13th Minnesota Infantry participated in some of the heaviest fighting on the islands during the Philippines' Insurrection.[127]

Official Military Tags Introduced

The United States Army formally adopted Identification Tags by issuing General Order No. 204 on December 20, 1906. This order stated: "*An aluminum Identification tag the size of a silver half dollar...stamped with name, rank, company, regiment, or corps of the wearer will be worn by each officer and enlisted man...whenever the field kit is worn.*" The tag had a cord attached through a small hole. This began using dog tags by the different branches of the military.[128]

---

[125] Edward Steere, *The Graves Registration Service in World War II, No. 21* (Washington, DC: United States Government Printing Office, 1951), 41.

[126] Holbrook, *Minnesota in the Spanish-American War and the Philippine Insurrection*, 219-220.

[127] Ibid, 36-72.

[128] *General Orders and Circulars, War Department, 1909* (Washington, DC: United States Government Printing Office, 1910), 2.

Several medals based on prior military service in the Army, Navy, and Marine Corps during the late Spanish-American War were authorized either through acts of Congress or the issuing of General Orders of the War Department.[129]

United States Army Spanish Campaign Medal

This was a military award that recognized those members of the U.S. military who served in the Spanish-American War. Although a single decoration, there was more than one version of the Spanish Campaign Medal. It was established on January 11, 1905, and awarded for service performed between May 11, 1898, and August 16, 1898, in Cuba; July 24, 1898, and August 13, 1898, in Puerto Rico; and June 30, 1898, and August 16, 1898, with service in the Philippine Islands.[130]

Another minting of the medal and badge was for service during the Spanish-American War with the United States Navy or Marine Corps. It was authorized on June 27, 1908, for personnel who served in the Philippine Islands between May 1, 1898, and August 16, 1898.[131]

United States Army Spanish War Medal

Established by an Act of Congress on July 9, 1918 (40 Stat. 873), this bronze medal with a suitable ribbon was for Army personnel who served during the Spanish-American War for at least 90 days and received an honorable discharge. The wording in the congressional record indicated that this medal was to be presented to state units federalized during the war. This decoration recognized members of the Army on active duty during the Spanish-American War but who did not receive the Spanish Campaign Medal.[132]

---

[129] *Annual Reports, War Department. Report of the Secretary of War to the President 1922*, (Washington, DC: Government Printing Office, 1922), 220-223. The War Department authorized 7,652 Spanish Campaign Medals, 12,967 Spanish War Medals, 3,897 Cuban Occupation Medals, and 281 Puerto Rico Occupation Medals.

[130] *Compilations of General Orders Circulars and Bulletins of the War Department Issued between February 15, 1881, and December 31, 1915* (Washington, DC: Government Printing Office, 1916), 164. On the reverse are the words United States Army: Foster, Frank. *United States Army Medals, Badges, and Insignia* (Fountain Inn: MOA Press, 2011), 96. The image can be found on the pages of the book.

[131] Ross F. Collins, *Decorations and Medals of the U.S. Bureau of Naval Personnel Information Bulletin*, No 318 (September 1943), 22-23. On the reverse, the United States Navy and the United States Marine Corps.

[132] 65th Congress, Session II, Statutes at Large. Accessed 9 October 2020. https://www.loc.gov/law/help/statutes-at-large/65th-congress/session-2/c65s2ch143.pdf. All images of medals Accessed 9 October 2022 and from Wikipedia at http://www.en.wikipedia.org/wiki/main_page.

United States Army of Occupation Cuban Medal

Established by the War Department of the United States Army under General Order No. 40 issued on June 28, 1915, this medal included a service badge and ribbon issued to both officers and enlisted personnel who served on active duty with the Cuban occupational forces between July 18, 1898, and May 20, 1902. An amended badge was authorized for soldiers who served between 1906 and 1909.[133]

United States Army of Occupation Puerto Rico Medal

This medal was established by the War Department of the United States Army under the Compilation of Orders No. 15, issued on February 4, 1919. It included a service badge and ribbon issued to officers and enlisted personnel who served on active duty with the Puerto Rico occupational forces between August 14, 1898, and December 10, 1898.[134]

The Manila Bay Medal

Established by an Act of Congress on June 3, 1898 (30 Stat. 742) by joint resolution No. 42, this bronze medal with a suitable ribbon was for men who served under the command of Commodore George Dewey, commemorating the battle at Manila Bay in the Philippines. It is often called the "Dewey Medal" and is named after the commander. By the same resolution, Dewey was presented with a sword of honor. The award was to have the likeness of Dewey on one side, with the reverses depicting a sailor at rest on a ship gun.

---

[133] *Compilations of General Orders Circulars and Bulletins of the War Department Issued between February 15, 1881 and December 31, 1915*, (Washington, DC: Government Printing Office, 1916), 167; *Medals of the Spanish and Philippine War Era* Accessed 9 October 2020 at: https://tpcgs.org/Medals_Spanish%20War%20Era_V4.pdf.
[134] *Annual Reports, War Department. Report of the Secretary of War to the President 1922*, (Washington, DC: Government Printing Office, 1920), 300; *Army Regulation 600-8-22 Personnel-General Military Awards* (Washington, DC: Headquarters Department of the Army, 2006), 70.

Those authorized to wear the medal included both the Navy and Marine Corps, who participated with Dewey at the battle of Manila Bay.[135]

Most vessels attached to Dewey's Asiatic fleet were authorized to receive the medal. This included the USS Baltimore, USS *Boston*, USS *Concord*, USS *Olympia*, USS *Petrie*, USS *Raleigh*, and the Revenue Cutter *McCulloch*. Not included were the two colliers.[136]

The United Spanish War Veterans Medal

Members of the United Spanish-American Wars had medals issued to active organization participants worn on their uniforms or other suits. The medal measures about 4 inches x 1 ½ inches with a ribbon of 13 stars and stripes. The bottom of the ribbon is a saber, rifle, and anchor, all crossing the other, representing different branches of service.

On the medal below are the words Porto Rico, Cuba, and the Philippines, where the fighting took place, with the USA on the bottom.[137]

Philippine Insurrection War Medals

Several medals based on prior military service in the Army, Navy, and Marine Corps during the late Philippine Insurrection were authorized either through acts passed by Congress or the issuing of General Orders and Special Orders of the War or Navy Department.[138]

United States Navy Philippine Campaign Medal

This medal was established by the War Department of the United States Army under General Order No. 129, issued on August 13, 1908. It included a badge issued to officers and enlisted men who served on active duty in the Philippine Islands between February 4, 1899, and July 4, 1902, or during the Philippine Insurrection during specific expeditions or engagements in the islands.[139]

---

[135] *The Statutes at Large of the United States of America, 1897-1899*, 55th Congress, Session II, Resolutions (Washington, DC: Government Printing Office, 1899), 746; W. Augustus Steward, War Medals and Their History (London: Stanley, Paul & Company, 1915), 368. The image of the medal is shown in the pages.
[136] *The Statutes at Large of the United States of America, 1897-1899*, 55th Congress, Session II, Resolutions (Washington, DC: Government Printing Office, 1899), 746.
[137] Ibid.
[138] *Annual Reports, War Department. Report of the Secretary of War to the President 1922*, 220-223. The War Department authorized 32,694 Philippine Campaign Medals and 5,601 Philippine Congressional Medals.
[139] Ibid., 220-223.

The medal was authorized for veterans of the United States Army, with the Navy authorizing issuing their own version of the medal by Special Order No. 81 on June 27, 1908.[140]

Philippine Congressional Medal

Established by an Act of Congress on June 29, 1906 (34 Stat. 621), this bronze medal was a suitable device for officers and enlisted men who volunteered and enlisted under the direction of the President of the United States to fight in the war with Spain. To be eligible for the medal, the recipient had to serve beyond their regular enlistment (during the Spanish-American War) and serve during the Philippine Insurrection. Recipients had to have been honorably discharged from the Army. The United States Treasury authorized five thousand dollars to appropriate the medals.[141]

West Indies Campaign Medal

The United States Navy Department authorized this medal by issuing Special Order No. 81 on June 27, 1908. The decoration and ribbon were authorized to be worn by men of the United States Navy and Marine Corps (based on an Act of Congress on March 3, 1901) for service in the West Indies aboard Navy ships during the Spanish-American War. The first recipient of this award was Rear Admiral John E. Pillsbury of the USN. It was rarely bestowed since most sailors were awarded the Sampson Medal. The two awards were not authorized for the same service as the West Indies medal and were discontinued in 1913.[142]

---

[140] *Origin of Navy Service Medals*. Special Order No. 81. Naval History and Heritage Command. Accessed 9 October 2020 at: https://www.history.navy.mil/browse-by-topic/heritage/awards/special-order-81.html.

[141] 59th Congress, Session I, Statutes at Large. Accessed 9 October 2020. https://www.loc.gov/law/help/statutes-at-large/59th-congress/session-1/c59s1ch3613.pdf.

[142] Origin of Navy Service Medals. Naval History and Heritage Command. Navy Department Special Order No. 81 Issued 27 June 1908. Accessed 10 October 2024 at: https://www.history.navy.mil/browse-by-topic/heritage/awards/special-order-81.html. The list of vessels authorized by the Navy are listed by name and dates https://web.archive.org/web/20131208082930/http://www.history.navy.mil/medals/phil.htm.

Sampson Medal

Not to be confused with the previously listed West Indies Campaign Medal, this medal was authorized by an act of Congress by joint resolution No. 18 (dated March 3, 1901) as a bronze medal for fighting in the Philippines and the waters of Cuba. Sometimes referred to as the West Indies Naval Campaign Medal, it was considered a higher-level award than persons awarded the Dewey Medal.[143]

Boxer Rebellion

China Campaign Medal

This medal was established by the War Department of the United States Army under the issuing of General Orders No. 5 on January 1, 1905. It was made of bronze and included a service ribbon issued to officers and enlisted personnel that recognized service during the China Relief Expedition under the command of the United States Army during the Boxer Rebellion.

The medal was awarded for Army service between June 20, 1900, and May 27, 1901. It included an Imperial Chinese dragon with the words *"China Relief Expedition"* and the years 1900-1901. On the reverse of the medal was an eagle perched on a cannon with the words *"For Service"* with the border at the top stating *"United States Army"* as the command.[144]

China Relief Medal

The United States Navy Department authorized this medal by issuing Special Order No. 81 on June 27, 1908. This same order authorized the West Indies Medal. This order was issued to the members of the United States Navy. The Marine Corps issued Special Order No. 82 on the same date that authorized their personnel stationed during the Boxer Rebellion to be issued the medal. The eligible active-duty military service dates were

---

[143] *The Statutes at Large of the United States of America, 1899-1901*, 56th Congress, Session II, Resolutions (Washington, DC: Government Printing Office, 1899), 1465.

[144] *Annual Reports, War Department. Report of the Secretary of War to the President 1922*, (Washington, DC: Government Printing Office, 1922), 222. The China Campaign Medal was authorized for 1,673 medals.

May 24, 1900, to May 17, 1901. The medal has a suitable ribbon issued with the words *"China Relief Expedition"* in 1900 on the face.[145]

Special, Military Unit, State, and Campaign Medals

Cardenas Medal

Established by an Act of Congress on May 3, 1900 (31 Stat. 716), this medal was for the crew of the Revenue Cutter Hudson for gallantry in action on May 11, 1898, at the battle of Cardenas. The commander, Lt. Frank Newcomb, received a gold medal, his fellow officers each a silver medal, and the enlisted men all received bronze medals. The medal appears in uniform regulations as late as 1930.[146]

Brooklyn Medal

This special medal was presented to United States sailors and marines who served onboard the USS *Brooklyn* and participated in the battle of Santiago on July 3, 1898. The medal was heavy and completed by Robert Stoll, a jeweler at 19 John Street in Manhattan.[147]

Rough Riders Medal

This privately minted medal for the 1st United States Volunteer Cavalry was originally believed to be a reunion badge of the veterans. In his book The Rough Riders, Roosevelt wrote that this medal was the one he gave to his men. Las Guasimas, San Juan, and Santiago battles are listed on the medal with the unit designation and year.[148]

California Veterans Medal

The state issued a bronze medal to veterans of the Spanish-American War. It was engraved by the firm of Hammersmith & Field Jewelers, located at 36 Kearny Street in San Francisco. One side depicts a soldier and sailor standing before the figure from the California coat of arms.

Figure 84: Courtesy of The Jeweler Circular and Horological Review

---

[145] John Langellier, *U.S. Armed Forces in China, 1856-1941*, (New York: Osprey Publishing, 2012), 47.

[146] *The Statutes at Large of the United States of America, 1899-1901*, 56th Congress, Session II, Resolutions (Washington, DC: Government Printing Office, 1899), 716.

[147] *The Brooklyn Daily Eagle*, September 15, 1898.

[148] Alejandro De Quesada, *Roosevelt's Rough Riders*, (New York: Osprey Publishing, 2009), 61.

On the reverse are both the United States and the state flag of California with the words "*The People of California...For Service in the Spanish-American War 1898-1899*" struck on the same side that signified the conflict the state fought.[149]

Rhode Island Veterans Medal

This state medal was authorized by a joint resolution on November 23, 1898, by the Rhode Island legislature (Stat. § 13. 1898) for soldiers, sailors, and marines who served during the Spanish-American War of 1898. Produced by the Gorham Manufacturing Company, the bronze medal has the Rhode Island state seal with the reverse inscription "*The State of Rhode Island to her sons who on land and sea defended the nation's honor in the War with Spain, 1898*". Afterward, the state set out to distribute the medals to veterans.[150]

New Jersey Veterans Medal

This medal was authorized by a joint act passed by the New Jersey State legislature (Stat. § 217. 1898) on March 22, 1899, to prepare medals for all honorably discharged officers and enlisted men who served in the Spanish-American War. The medal bears the coat of arms for New Jersey along with a crossed saber, rifle, and anchor representing the different military services.[151]

Michigan State Commemorative Medal

This state-issued medal was authorized by the Michigan Session Laws (Stat. § 223. 1901) by joint resolution on September 5, 1901. The medal was to be presented to every state citizen who had enlisted in the regular or state army or navy and who served in the Spanish-American War of 1898 or the Philippine Insurrection until January 1, 1901. The medal was also authorized for any family member of a soldier or sailor who died while in service.[152]

New York Volunteers Medal

This state-issued medal was for New York Army, Navy, and Marine Corps servicemen. The front scene depicts a soldier with a setting sun in the background. The words "*To one who served the national with honor, 1898, 1899, 1900*" are on the reverse. The medal was presented to men

---

[149] *The Jewelers Circular and Horological Review*, 39:2, (9 August 1899), 1; and *Los Angeles Evening Express*, November 30, 1899.
[150] *Acts of a Local and Private Nature Including Act of Incorporation. Passed in November Session of the State of Rhode Island 1898*, (Providence: State Printer, 1898), 13; *The Jewelers Review*, 32:26, (28 Jun 1899), 825.
[151] *Acts of the One Hundred and Twenty-Third Legislature of the State of New Jersey 1899*, (Trenton: New Jersey State Printers, 1899), 217; and *The Numismatist: An Illustrated Monthly for Those Interested in Coins, Medals, and Paper Money*. 35:1 (January 1922), 222-223; and *Monmouth Democrat*, October 26, 1899.
[152] *The Compiled Laws of the State of Michigan, 1915* (Lansing: State Printers, 1916), 617.

who served during the Spanish-American War, the Boxer Rebellion, and the Philippine Insurrection.[153]

Connecticut Volunteers Medal

Two special acts passed by the State of Connecticut General Assembly in 1915 and 1917 authorized a badge and device for persons who served in the Army, Navy, and Marine Corps during the Spanish-American War between April 21, 1898, and December 10, 1898.[154]

Twentieth Kansas Volunteer Infantry Medal

This rarely seen medal was presented to soldiers of the 20th Kansas Volunteer Infantry who served in some of the fighting during the Philippine Insurrection. The Kansas Grand Army of the Republic (GAR) raised the necessary funds. The medals were struck by melting down a captured piece of artillery.[155]

Sixth Missouri Volunteer Infantry Medal

This was another rare medal presented to soldiers who served in the 6th Missouri Volunteer Infantry during the Spanish-American War. The unit served as part of the occupation force in Cuba. The reverse of the medal stated the regiment mustered in at St. Louis in July 1898 and mustered out after service at Camp Onward near Savannah, Georgia, on May 10, 1899.

First Montana Volunteer Infantry Medal

The 1st Montana Volunteer Infantry was mustered in at Helena, MT, between May 5-10, 1898, for service in the Philippine Islands during the Spanish-American War. The regiment stayed during the Philippine Insurrection, being mustered out on October 17, 1899, in San Francisco, CA. All regiment members were presented the medals of honor on October 23, 1899.[156]

Third United States Volunteer Cavalry Medal

Known as Grigsby's Rough Riders, commanded by Colonel Melvin Grigsby, the regiment comprised mostly Montana troopers who served with the First Corps during the Spanish-American War in 1898. Like the medal issued to the 1st Montana Volunteer Infantry, this was a unique medal authorized by a state for a United States Volunteer regiment.[157]

Pennsylvania Marksman Medal

---

[153] *The Numismatist: An Illustrated Monthly for Those Interested in Coins, Medals, and Paper Money.* 35:1 (January 1922): 222-223.
[154] *Public Documents of the State of Connecticut, 1918.* Volume 3. Part I, (Hartford: State Printer, 1919), 28-29.
[155] *Abilene Week Chronicle and the Dickinson County News*, October 20, 1899.
[156] *Butte Daily Post*, October 24, 1899.
[157] Ibid., October 24, 1899.

This award was given to officers and men of the Pennsylvania National Guard who qualified as either sharpshooters or marksmen in 1897 and later entered United States service in the war against Spain in 1898. The medal was suspended with a bar listing the class soldier qualified.[158]

Other Medals

Medal of Honor

This is the highest military decoration awarded by the United States government. It is bestowed on members of the military who distinguish themselves: "*Conspicuously by gallantry and intrepidity at the risk of his life above and beyond the call of duty while engaged in an action against an enemy of the United States*". First established during the Civil War on July 12, 1862, for non-commissioned Officers and enlisted men, the award lists the recipients by name, military branch, rank, date of honor, and the conditions of the award.[159]

Example of Medal of Honor Winner:

The image to the right exemplifies a Spanish-American War Medal of Honor recipient. Edward L. Baker Jr. was born in Laramie, Wyoming in 1865. He enlisted as a private in the United States Army on July 27, 1882, in Cincinnati, Ohio, and served with the 9th United States Cavalry. Being of African American descent, he was relegated to enlisted status but was promoted to the rank of Sergeant Major.

Figure 85: Courtesy of National MOH Museum

At the battle of Santiago, Cuba, on July 1, 1898, Baker received a citation for extraordinary heroism for saving the life of one wounded trooper of his regiment from drowning while under fire.[160]

The Medal of Honor was awarded for his heroism on July 3, 1902. He was promoted for his bravery, being commissioned a 1st Lieutenant of Company A. 10th United States Volunteer Infantry. Baker was promoted to captain during the United States' involvement in the Philippine Insurrection and then transferred to the 49th United States Volunteer Infantry. This regiment was an African American regiment serving on the Philippine Islands. He stayed in the Army after the

---

[158] *Annual Report of the Adjutant General of Pennsylvania for the Year 1898*, (Harrisburg: William Stanley Ray, State Printer, 1900), 592.
[159] *Medal of Honor, 1863-1968*, (Washington, DC: U.S. Government Printing Office, 1968), X, 1-17; The image of the award is depicted in the pages of the reference source.
[160] Ibid., 355.

war ended, being recommissioned with the Philippine Scouts. He resigned from the United States Army on October 31, 1909. Baker moved to California after his retirement, where he died a few years later on August 26, 1913, in San Francisco, California.[161]

Locating Military Medals

Medals awarded for military service are like any other item of ephemera. Families may have original items in their own collections, or they can be found online through dealers of military collectibles. Other sources for locating medals include online searches on eBay, Etsy, and other auction houses for antiques. If a rim number or medal is located, every attempt to know to whom the medal was awarded is the next methodological step in the research process.

United States Army

The National Archives in Washington, DC, has compiled an incomplete list of medal recipients based on engraved rim numbers. Information on some of the medal recipients is in RG92 of the Quartermaster General Office and available on microfilm series M2159. The National Archives has an online, downloadable finding aid breaking down the two rolls of microfilm.[162]

The microfilmed lists of records are arranged by the award and then listed numerically by the rim numbers. Many of the card numbers were filmed out of sequence (as noted in each film's description). Four application cards are listed for each page filmed.

The cards are about 8.75 x 4.25 inches in size. Each contains the name of the recipient, medal serial number, rank, and military designation. In a few cases, card applications were canceled and reissued to another recipient. Prior to 1919, some terminology referred to the medals as badges. Afterward, the Quartermaster Department lists them as medals.[163]

United States Army Spanish War Medal

The serial numbers on the rim are listed and run from 1-16,670 as the complete set of numbers assigned. Rim numbers 1-2,310 are identified as former state national guard federalized. Some cards were intentionally blank (16,651-16,670 and 1,901-1,910). The filming was not complete and was out of order. For national guard recipients, their home address was often recorded in place of their former military units.

---

[161] *The Bystander*, October 13, 1899. James B. Martin, Editor. *African American War Heroes*, Denver, CO: ABC-CLIO Publishing, 2014), 10-12.

[162] Claire Prechtel-Kluskens, *Serial Lists of Spanish War Service Medals, Philippine Congressional Medals, Philippine Campaign Medals, Army of Cuban Pacification Medals, Mexican Service Medals, and Mexican Border Service Medals Issued from 1907-1925*. M2159. RG92. National Archives and Records Administration. Accessed 11 October 2020 at: https://twelvekey.files.wordpress.com/2014/10/m2159-final-revised.pdf.

[163] Ibid., 1-8 and Mark C. Mollan, "The Army Medal of Honor: The First Fifty-Five Years" Prologue *Magazine: Quarterly of the National Archives* 33:2 (Summer 2001): 128-139.

Philippine Campaign Medal

The serial numbers on the rim are listed and run from 1 to 25,000 as the complete set of numbers assigned. The series is broken into filmed segments: 1-1,320 and 1,321-9,100. Rim numbers 9,101-9,010 were initially not filmed but were later included after the introduction notes to the series. The series continues 9,011-12,160 (with rim card numbers 12,151-12,160 misfiled). Near the end of the series, it continues 12,171-23,250 (numbers 23,251-23,500 are blank with no additional information provided) and ending with 23,501-25,000. There is a notation that the card number continues beyond 25,001, but there is no indication of where these are located.

Philippine Congressional Medal

Limited rim number identification is available for serial numbers 5,801-6,179.

United States Marine Corps

The United States Marine Corps in RG127 at the National Archives in Washington, DC, has records of marines receiving badges and medals based on military service.[164]

Entry 106: *Register of Badges, Medals, and Bars Issued, 1908-1911*. The collection is arranged alphabetically by surname and dated by the year awarded beginning with 1908. The badges and medals are based on service during the Spanish-American War, the Boxer Rebellion, and the Philippine Insurrection. Entries in the register include the name of the marine, rank, serial or rim number of the badge, type of badge, and the aforementioned campaign or war fought.

---

[164] Maizie Johnson, *Records of the United States Marine Corps*. National Archives Inventory, RG127 (Washington, DC: National Archives and Records Administration), 23.

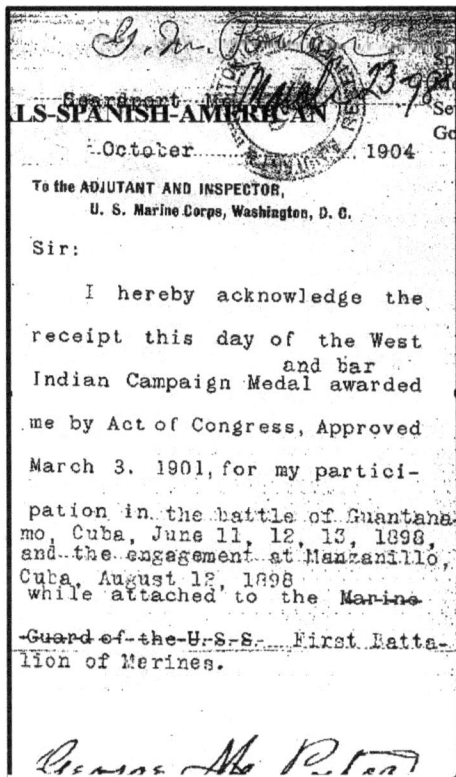
Figure 86: Courtesy of National Archives

The image at left acknowledges that in October 1904, United States Marine Corps private George Melvin Porter received the West Indies Campaign Medal for his military service during the Spanish-American War fighting with the 1st Battalion of Marines.

According to the award citation, Porter received his medal for participation in the battles of Guantanamo, Cuba (from June 11-13, 1898) and Manzanillo, Cuba (on 12 August 1898). Porter was born in Searsport, Maine, and joined the United States Marine Corps on March 23, 1898. He was discharged as a private on February 3, 1899. He returned home to Searsport following the war. That is where his medal was mailed.

Porter lived in Searsport, Maine, and was self-employed with a confectionary business in town for the remainder of his life. He died on 5 June 5, 1941. His obituary listed incorrectly that he served in the army during the war.[165]

United States Navy

The United States Navy in RG24 at the National Archives in Washington, DC, has records of naval personnel receiving badges and medals based on military service.[166]

Entry 69: *Letters Sent Forwarding Certificates, Appointment, and Badges, 1896-1903.* This collection is arranged chronologically and addressed to officers in command of ships and stations, and it relates to medals and badges presented to sailors.

Entry 70: *Letters sent Relating to Navy Medals and Badges, 1908-1911.* Copies of letters relating to awards and medals for participation in the Spanish-American War, Boxer Rebellion, the West Indian Campaigns (including the Philippine Insurrection), and the earlier Civil War.

Entry 210: *Record Cards for Recipients of Medals, Badges, Bars, and Pins Issued by the Navy Department, 1899-1910.* The records are arranged alphabetically by the recipient's name, giving the date, rim or certificate number, date, service awarded, and ship or station served.

Some medals allow rim numbers to identify the recipient, while others display numbers that cannot be tracked. One example of a medal with a number not trackable is the United Spanish

---

[165] *The Bangor Times*, June 6, 1941.
[166] Virgil E. Baugh. *Preliminary Inventories of the National Archives of the United States.* Records of the Bureau of Naval Personnel. RG24, (Washington, DC: National Archives and Records Administration, 1960): 29, 64.

War Veterans Medal, which had an inscribed number on the reverse. Other medals have the names, ranks, ships, or military units engraved directly into the medals.

Besides records in the National Archives, several reference books on the Spanish-American War, Boxer Rebellion, and Philippine Insurrection covering awards, badges, and medals offer research-finding aids to identify different medals and their recipients. The books available include detailed links to find the books either for sale or obtainable through interlibrary loan.[167]

Gleim, Albert F. *Cuban Occupation Medal Issue Records*. Ft. Myer, VA: Planchet Press, 1987.

_____. *Unclaimed Sampson Medals*. Arlington, VA: Planchet Press, 1985.

_____. *Porto Rico Occupation Medal Issue Records*. Ft. Myer, VA: Planchet, 1987.

_____. *CRE Reference Data*. Arlington, VA: Planchet Press, 1985.

Thomas D. Thiessen, Douglass D. Scott, and Albert F. Gleim. *Philippine Congressional Medal Issue Records*. Ft. Myer, VA: Planchet Press, 1994.

_____. *Army Spanish Campaign Medal Issue Records*. Ft. Myer, VA: Planchet Press, 1991.

Melvin D. Mueller and Albert F. Gleim. *Spanish War Service Medal Issue Records*. Ft. Myer, VA: Planchet Press, 1995.

Smith, Scott D. *Marine Corps 1898 Spanish & West Indies Campaign Medal: History and Campaign Medal Listing*. Private Printing.

_____. *Marine Corps 1899 Philippine Campaign: History and Campaign Medal Listing*.

_____. *Marine Corps 1900 China Relief Campaign "The Boxer Rebellion": Campaign Medal Listing*. Private Printing.

GENEALOGY TIP: To locate different laws or legislation relating to military service outside of the United States federal records, consider searching for state session laws to find needed material that covers military service with the Adjutant General Office, National Guard or other state record.

---

[167] World Cat library catalog at https://www.worldcat.org should be searched to find the listed reference books for a library or archive with the book. Searches should also be conducted on Ebay at https://www.ebay.com and on the Library of Congress card catalog https://catalog.loc.gov/vwebv/searchBrowse. All locations to find books.

Army Transport Service

The history of the Army Transport Service during the Spanish-American War begins as a division of the Office of the Quartermaster General. On November 16, 1898, the Secretary of War approved regulations that established and made the Army Transport Service responsible for transporting men and supplies to the war zone. Two ports were established, one in New York, New York, and the other in San Francisco, California, to ferry troops for the war.[168]

The start of the war in 1898 found the United States woefully unprepared to transport troops overseas. Vessels were speedily fitted or purchased to transport large numbers of soldiers to Cuba, Puerto Rico, Manilla, and China during the hostilities of the Boxer Rebellion. Under General Order No. 102 on August 4, 1917, the ATS was abolished, and the Embarkation Services (ES), part of the Quartermaster Corps.

United States Army Transport Ships between the United States, Cuba, and Puerto Rico. This list is complete through May 14, 1900. The U.S. Government owns transports are listed in *Italics*, while all others were under charter.[169]

Adria	Iroquois	*Relief* (hospital ship)
Alamo	Kanawha	Rio Grande
Allegheny	*Kearney*	Saratoga
Aransas	*Kilpatrick*	San Marcos
Arkadia	Knickerbocker	Santiago
Berkshire	La Grande Duchess	*Sedgwick*
Breakwater	Lampasas	Seguranca
Buford	Leona	Seneca
Burnside	*Logan*	*Sheridan*
Catania	Louisiana	*Sherman*
Cherokee	City of Macon	Specialist
Clinton	Manteo	Stillwater
Comal	Matteawan	*Sumner*
Comanche	*McClellan*	Tarpon
Concho	*McPherson*	*Terry*
Crook	*Meade*	*Thomas* (formally Minnewaska)
Cumberland	Miami	Unionist
Florida	D.H. Miller	Vigilancia
Gate City	*Missouri* (hospital ship)	Wanderer

---

[168] Erna Risch, *Quartermaster Support of the Army: A History of the Corps, 1775-1939*, (Washington DC: Quartermaster Historian Office, 1962), 566-567.

[169] Newton A. Strait, Alphabetical List of Battles, 1754-1900: *War of the Rebellion, Spanish-American War, Philippine Insurrection and all Old Wars with Dates* (Washington, DC: Newton A. Strait, 1914), 210.

Grant	Morgan	City of Washington
Gussie	Nueces	Whitney
Hooker (cable ship)	Olivette	*Wright*
Hudson	Orizaba	Yucatan[170]
Ingalls	*Rawlins*	

United States Army transports, including the Crook, Grant, Logan, Meade, Missouri, Relief, Sheridan, Sherman, Sumner, and Thomas, were all transferred to the Pacific following the end of the Spanish-American War. They were used to transport troops and supplies during the Philippine Insurrection. The USAT Hooker, a cable ship, was wrecked on August 11, 1899, when the vessel ran aground off the Island of Corregidor near Manilla in the Philippines.[171]

USAT ships between the United States and the Philippine Islands. This list is complete through May 14, 1900. Transports in *Italics* are owned by the U.S. Government, and all others are under charter.[172]

Arthenian	Indiana	City of Rio de Janeiro
Australia	*Lawton*	Roanoke
Aztec	Leelanaw	*Rosecrans*
Belgian King	Lennox	Senator
Benmohr	Mananense	*Seward*
Centennial	Morgan City	Siam
China	Charles Nelson	Sikh
Cleveland	Newport	St. Paul
Colon	Ohio	City of Sydney
Columbia	Olympia	Tacoma
Conemaugh	City of Para	Tacoma (sailing ship)
Dalny Vostock	Pathan	Tartar
Duke of Fife	City of Peking	Tealandia
George W. Elder	Pennsylvania	Valencia
Egbert	Peru	Victoria -1st
Flintshire	Port Albert	Victoria -2nd
Garonne	Portland	Westminster
Glenogle	Port Stephens	*Warren*
Hancock	City of Pueblo	Wyefield

---

[170] *Report of the Commission Appointed by the President to Investigate the Conduct of the War Department in the War with Spain*, (Washington, DC: Government Printing Office, 1900), 3212-3216. The *USAT Yucatan* transported eight companies of officers and men of the 1st United States Volunteer Cavalry under Colonel Theodore Roosevelt.
[171] *The Boston Globe*, August 15, 1899.
[172] Strait, Alphabetical List of Battles, 1754-1900, 210.

Over the course of all three war periods, the United States Army Transport Service periods ferried tens of thousands of men and supplies between key port cities to the combat zones. Lists of troopships are available, as well as the numbers of men carried, and the regiments transported. Often, these records provide the dates of either arrival or departure.[173]

Figure 87: Courtesy of Michael L. Strauss

The above image shows the United States Army Transport Ship *USAT Minnewaska* on December 19, 1898, in Savannah, Georgia, loading men from the 49th Iowa Infantry sailing for Havana, Cuba, where it arrived on December 23, 1898.[174]

The National Archives in Washington, DC, in RG92, has records for the Army Transport Service (ATS), including the names of the vessels and regiments transported during the Spanish-

---

[173] *Report of the Commission Appointed by the President to Investigate the Conduct of the War Department in the War with Spain*, 3212-3216; Strait, *Alphabetical List of Battles, 1754-1900*, 202-210; and *Report of the Commission Appointed by the President to Investigate the Conduct of the War Department in the War with Spain*, (Washington, DC: Government Printing Office, 1899), 29-43. All three reports provide details on the transports and regiments deployed.

[174] *The Austin Daily Herald*, December 23, 1898.

American War, Boxer Rebellion, and the Philippine Insurrection. Records of the ATS are onsite only and have not been digitized by the National Archives.[175]

Entry 1313: *Description of Army Transports, 1899-1901*. This series of records contains the descriptions of the Army transports used from 1899-1901. Included are telegrams received and a list of arrival and departures of transports in Havana, Cuba from 1899-1901.

Entry 1794: *Army Transport Service Circulars, 1899-1901*. Listing of ATS circulars that are arranged chronologically by publication.

Entry 1801: *Lists of Contents of Inward Army Transports, 1899-1901*. Lists are arranged by date chronologically from arriving transports. Volumes include a name index for consignees.

Entry 1818: *Logs of United States Army Transports, 1899-1901*. Very similar to Navy logs that record daily activities. The logs are alphabetical by the name of the army transport. In the NARA finding aids room, staff can provide a list of transport vessels.

Entry 1833: *Passenger Lists of Army Transports Arriving in New York, 1899-1900*. Lists arranged alphabetically by name of the army transport, then chronologically by date.

Entry 1839: *Abstracts of Logs of U.S. Army Transports, 1899-1916*. Arranged alphabetically by name of the army transport and then chronologically.

Entry 1848: *Cargo Lists of Army Transports, 1898-1900*. Arranged alphabetically by name of the army transport. Often provides the full lists of cargo onboard.

Entry 1867: *List of Arrivals and Departures of U.S. Army Transports, 1898-1917*. Arranged by sailing route for the army transports, then chronologically. Includes is a name index to vessels.

Entry 1870: *Registers of Movements of U.S. Army Transports, 1898-1916*. These registers cover a longer period than the Spanish-American War. The first set of registers from 1898-1901 are separated by the Atlantic and Pacific oceans. Later registers from 1901-1916 were arranged by the name of the army transport and provided indexes to vessels, persons, and locations.

Entry 2117: *Records Relating to U.S. Army Transports, 1899-1902*. These records cover ship manifest and sailor orders as well as shipboard specifications. Most lists relate to the 8th Army Corps (stationed in the Philippines) and their transportation with the ATS.

Entry 344: *United States Army Transport Vessels, 1898-1912*. Series of still photographs that cover the Army Transport Service depicting the vessels used from the Spanish-American War to the eve of World War I. The entire collection contains nearly two hundred images. Several vessels used during the Spanish-American War remained in active service through the end of

---

[175] Maizie H. Johnson, *Preliminary Inventory NM-81, Preliminary Inventory of the Records of the Office of the Quartermaster General* (Washington, DC: National Archives and Records Administration, 1967), 1-234.

World War I, being used again as troopship transports. An online collection at Ancestry: https://www.ancestry.com/search/collections/61464, is browsable by the names of the vessels.

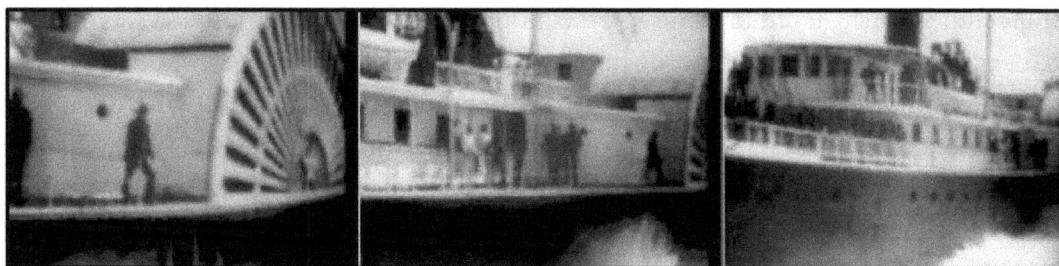

Figure 88: Courtesy of Library of Congress

The short video image above (30 seconds at 24 frames per second) shows the United States transport ship USS *Whitney* leaving for Cuba with men onboard from the 5th U.S. Infantry, available online at the Library of Congress at https://www.loc.gov/item/98500975. See the next chapter, which contains a full collection of short motion pictures from the war.

The Army Transport Service (ATS) is listed in the published yearly volumes containing the list of merchant vessels and warships entitled *Annual List of Merchant Vessels of the United States*. At the end of each volume (dated yearly) in Part V, under the heading of "List of vessels of the Quartermaster's Department, United States Army," are the name, tonnage, class, dimensions, when and where vessels were built, and by whom employed available online for free at *Hathi Trust*: https://catalog.hathitrust.org/Record/008420432

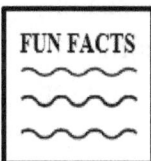

FUN FACTS

DID YOU KNOW Lt. Colonel Aaron S. Daggett who commanded the 25th U.S. Infantry at the battle of San Juan Hill, Cuba on July 1-3, 1898, had previously fought thirty-five years earlier to date in the battle of Gettysburg from July 1-3, 1863, as a Major in the 5th Maine Infantry? Daggett survived both wars despite being wounded.

Photographs and Motion Pictures

In the mid-nineteenth century, a remarkable intersection of time and technology came together. While personal accounts and military records preserve a wartime fighting record, the human experience lived on primarily through oral histories, aging memories, and yellowing documents. The veterans' experiences can be characterized by their unique stories during the war, which can be visualized when looking at their photographs even decades later, leaving the imagination to wonder what their eyes witnessed during this period of national crisis. Several key research facilities have collections that are searchable online, as outlined below.

National Archives

The United States Congress passed the act to create the National Archives on June 19, 1934 (48 Stat. 1122), while the building was under construction. Earlier on February 20, 1933, President Herbert Hoover celebrated the laying of the Archives cornerstone to commemorate the opening of the building that would occur later. Once completed, the first years were used to hire personnel, organize agencies, and appoint the first director, Dr. R.D.W. Conner of NC.[176]

One of the largest collections of government images and motion pictures is located inside the walls of the National Archives. Patrons should direct their searches to Archives II in College Park, Maryland, to the Still Picture Reference room on the 5th floor. The Archives holds over fourteen million images, roughly three million in digital format. On the 4th floor is the Motion Picture, Sound, and Video Research room, which is available to search historical films. The NARA card catalog at https://catalog.archives.gov/advancedsearch (using the advanced search) can only filter requested records. The National Archives has a feature for exploring record groups online for digital materials: https://www.archives.gov/findingaid/record-group-explorer.

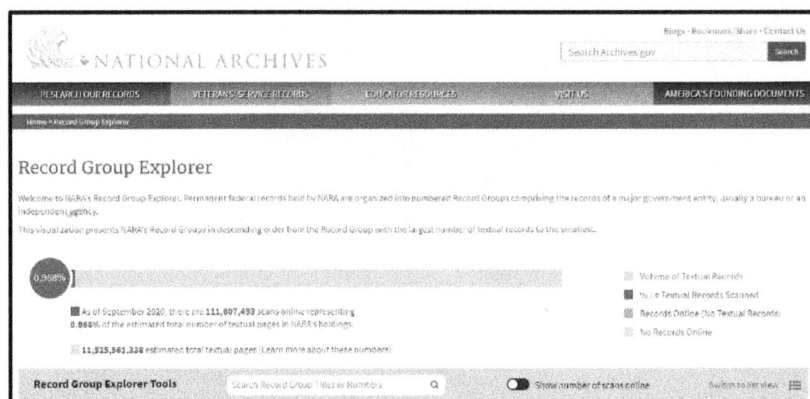

Figure 89: Courtesy of National Archives

---

[176] Our First Archivist, Robert D.W. Connor. Posted 1 June 2016 by Jessie Kratz. National Archives. Accessed 22 September 2020 at: https://prologue.blogs.archives.gov/2016/06/01/our-first-archivist-robert-d-w-connor.

Library of Congress

The Library of Congress is the official research library that served the United States Congress. It is also the national library of the United States. In 1800, the library was opened as President John Adams authorized the appropriation of funds to be used for books needed by Congress. By 1802, the library had acquired 3,000 volumes until the War of 1812. Everything was lost when the British Army burned down the Library of Congress in 1814. Located in Washington, DC, the Library of Congress has one of the world's largest collections of United States government records, documents, photographs, and motion pictures.[177]

The Library of Congress has a small collection of original silent motion pictures covering the Spanish-American War at https://www.loc.gov/collections/spanish-american-war-in-motion-pictures containing eighty-two short video clips, including the Philippine Insurrection.

Figure 90: Courtesy of Library of Congress

The above short video clip (51 seconds at 16 frames per second) shows the 25th United States Infantry returning from a march near Mt. Arayet, Philippines. The regiment was an all-African American regiment led by white officers.

The Library of Congress's overall collection of still pictures and images can be searched online through the Prints & Photograph Online Catalog at https://www.loc.gov/pictures

Smithsonian Institute

In 1826, English scientist James Smithson donated (from his written will) more than half a million dollars to open a library intended to increase the knowledge of mankind through collecting books, images, and materials of sociological, historical, and political interest. On August 10, 1846, the U.S. Congress passed an Act (9 Stat. 102) that opened the institute to research patrons.[178]

The photographic and image collection of the Smithsonian Institute can be searched online at https://siarchives.si.edu/what-we-do/photograph-and-image-collections.

---

[177] *The Library of Congress*, (Washington, DC: Government Printing Office, 1922), 5-7.
[178] Smithsonian Institute, Accessed 12 September 2021 https://siarchives.si.edu/history/general-history.

Located in Carlisle, Pennsylvania, this research facility has one of the largest collections of military images with particular emphasis on the Civil War. Other war periods are also available, including digitized images, which can be searched at https://arena.usahec.org/web/arena.

GENEALOGY CLUE Following the end of the Spanish-American War and the other two conflicts, there was a movement to erect monuments in remembrance of veterans who served, trained for war, or fought. Monuments can provide details on specific engagements or unit participation during one of the late wars.

Corps Badges and Pennants

During the Spanish-American War in 1898, the United States Army authorized changes in the corps badge designs and pennants used at the division and brigade level. The Army used Previous corps badges, with changes intended to distinguish them from the prior Civil War design. General Order No. 99 (dated July 15, 1898) from the office of the Adjutant General of the War Department lists each corps numerically and the different designs with an image. The corps badges were to be worn by officers on the uniform's left breast, and enlisted personnel were authorized to wear the design on the front of the cap or the center of the forage cap.[179]

Corps Badge Designs

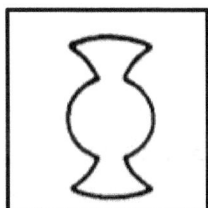

1st Corps badge design to be a circle over the letter "I" of special design.

2nd Corps badge design to be a four-leaf clover.

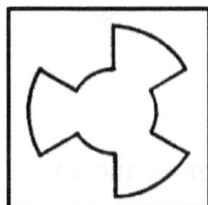

3rd Corps badge design to be a three-tooth clutch.

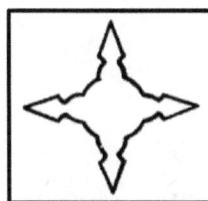

4th Corps badge design to be a four-pointed caltrop.

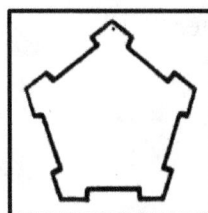

5th Corps badge design to be a five-pointed bastion fort.

---

[179] General Orders, 1898- General Order No. 99 Adjutant General for the War Department dated 15 July 1898, 239-245. All drawing of he badge designs courtesy of the Adjutant General Office of the United States War Department.

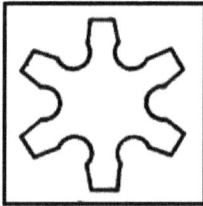

6th Corps badge design to be a six spoke hub.

6th Corps badge design to be a six spoke hub.

7th Corps badge design to be a seven-pointed star.

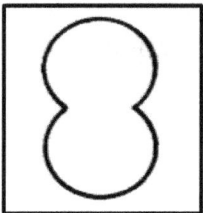

8th Corps badge design to be two circles overlapping the other 1/3 radius to resemble the figure "8".

9th Corps badge design to be a buzz saw with ninth teeth.

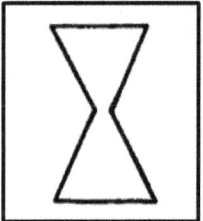

10th Corps badge design to be two triangles point to point to resemble the letter "X".

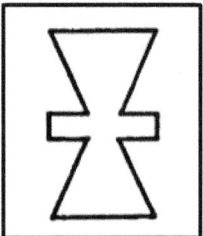

11th Corps badge design to be a near identical to the 10th Corps with a horizontal bar running through the center and to resemble the letter "XI".

12th Corps badge design to be a square with a clover leaf design on each of the four corners, which in turn displays twelve small circles.

13th Corps badge design to be a palm leaf with thirteen spikes.

14th Corps badge design to be a square with circles on each of the sides.

15th Corps badge design to be a bugle.

16th Corps badge design to be a spearhead.

17th Corps badge design to be a battle axe.

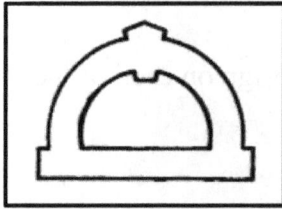

18th Corps badge design to be an arch.

2nd Lieutenant Orrin R. Grow served in Battery B. Utah Light Artillery and was commissioned on May 4, 1898, on the orders of the Governor of Utah, Heber M. Wells. The unit was mustered in on May 9, 1898, at Ft. Douglas and commanded by Captain Frank A. Grant. They were attached to the 2nd Brigade, 2nd Division, of the 8th Army Corps commanded by Major General Wesley Merritt.[180]

Grow remained with his battery until serious health issues forced his return to the United States, where he arrived on February 21, 1899. Afterward, he was discharged. Grow wears the 8th Army Corps badge on his left breast.[181]

Figure 91: Courtesy of Utah Volunteers in Spanish American War

Other Badge Designs

Artillery Corps design is crossed conical shaped projectiles, with a round shot above the center.

Cavalry Corps design is a winged horse foot.

The designs of the Army Corps used during both the Spanish-American War and the Philippine Insurrection were initiated to include the 8th Army Corps. The others were never activated.

---

[180] *Salt Lake Herald*, May 5, 1898; and *Correspondence relating to the War with Spain: Including the Insurrection in the Philippine Island and the China Relief Expedition* Volume 1. (Washington, DC: United States Government Printing Office, 1902), 556, 620.

[181] Charles R. Mabey, *The Utah Batteries: A History* (Salt Lake City: Daily Reporter Company, 1900), 110-111.

In General Order No. 99, the Army designated the use of flags and pennants for the armies. The designs varied by corps, division, and brigade using different colors to represent each command.

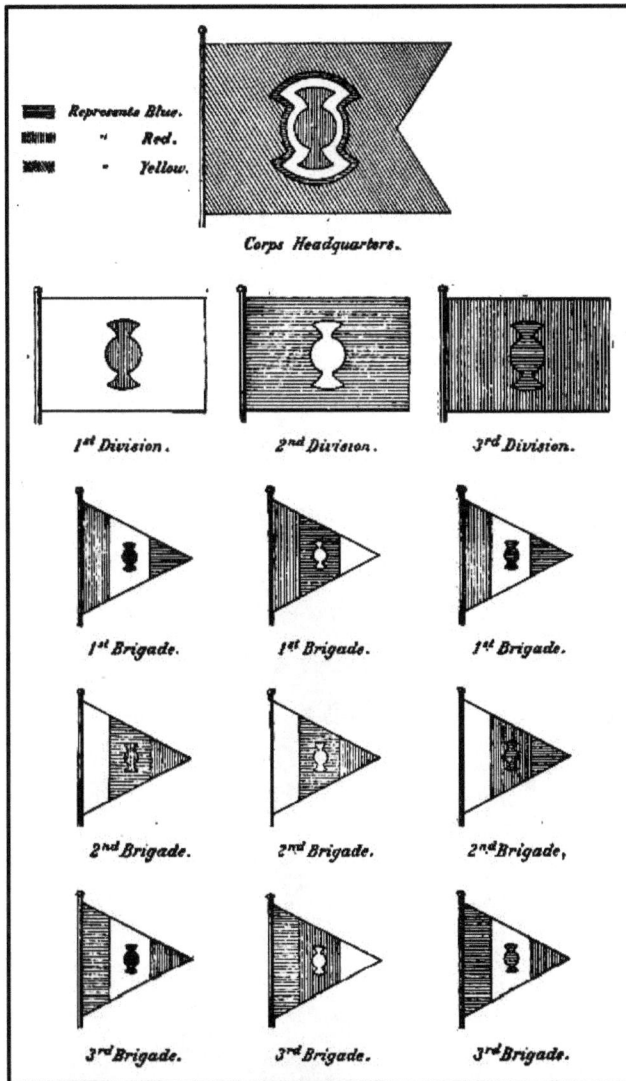

The pennant designs to the left represent the 1st Army Corps raised during the Spanish-American War issued in General Order No. 36 on May 7, 1898, comprising both volunteers and regulars.[182]

The flags in the 1st Corps (read down):
1st Division-white flag-corps symbol red
2nd Division-white flag-corps symbol white
3rd Division-white flag-corps symbol blue

The pennants of the 1st Division:
1st Brigade-red, white, blue-symbol red
2nd Brigade-white, blue, red-symbol red
3rd Brigade-blue, white, red-symbol red

The pennants of the 2nd Division:
1st Brigade-red, blue, white-symbol white
2nd Brigade-white, blue, red-symbol white
3rd Brigade-blue, red, white-symbol white

The pennants of the 3rd Division:
1st Brigade-red, white, blue-symbol blue
2nd Brigade-white, red, blue-symbol blue
3rd Brigade-blue, white, red-symbol blue

Figure 92: Courtesy of U.S War Department-1898

Not all Corp designs were used during the Spanish-American War or the Philippine Insurrection. The I Corps was stationed in Puerto Rico; the V and VII Corps were in Cuba; and the VIII Corps was on duty in the Philippines. The II, III, IV, and VI Corps remained in the United States and were never deployed.[183]

---

[182] General Orders, 1898- General Order No. 99 Adjutant General for the War Department dated 15 July 1898, 239-245; and General Orders, 1898-General Order No. 36. Adjutant General Office dated 7 May 1898, 94.
[183] *Correspondence relating to the War with Spain and Conditions Growing out of the same.* Volume 1, (Washington, DC: United States Government Printing Office, 1902), 509-579.

GENEALOGY TOOL Attend genealogy conferences and institutes either in person or online through webinars to take opportunities to watch topics relating directly to military records from not only the Spanish-American War, Boxer Rebellion, or the Philippine Insurrection but other war periods.

Military Abbreviations

Whether reading original documents found at the national archives or records from a local state resource found either online or onsite, the use of military abbreviations can often be listed to help distinguish a particular military unit, organization, or the work performed in service.

Commonly used Spanish-American War era abbreviations are found in different primary source documents, as listed below. At the time of the war in 1898, these listings would also apply to both the Boxer Rebellion and the Philippine Insurrection.[184]

A.A.A.G.	Acting Assistant Adjutant General
A. A. G.	Assistant Adjutant General.
A.C.	Army Corps.
Actg.	Acting.
A. D. C.	Aide-de-Camp.
Adj.	Adjutant.
A.G.	Adjutant General or A.G.O. Adjutant General Office
Amb.	Ambulance Corps.
Apptd.	Appointed
Artf.	Artificer
Art. or Arty.	Artillery
Asst.	Assistant.
Battn or BN.	Battalion
Baty.	Battery
Box.	Boxer Rebellion
Brig.	Brigade or Brigadier or BG for Brigadier General
C.A. and C.A.C.	Coast Artillery and Coast Artillery Corps
Capt.	Captain
Cas. Det.	Casual Detachment (men on detached service or duty)
Cav or Cavy.	Cavalry
Cert.	Certificate
Co.	Company
Col.	Colonel
CMSR or CSR	Compiled Military Service Record or Compiled Service Record
Comdg.	Commanding
Comsd.	Commissioned
Comy. or Comsy.	Commissary
Corp or Cpl.	Corporal

---

[184] Holbrook, *Minnesota in the Spanish-American War and the Philippine Insurrection,* 135-136; Stewart, *Records of Pennsylvania Volunteers in the Spanish-American War, 1898,* 7; and Patrick McSherry, *Military Abbreviations-A Primer* assessed 19 June 2020, http://www.spanamwar.com/genealogy5abbrev.htm.

Dept.	Department
Det.	Detached
Dischd. or Disch.	Discharged
Dist.	District.
Div.	Division
Enrd.	Enrolled
F.O.C.	Field Officer Court
F.C.M.	Field Court Martial
Far.	Farrier
Furl.	Furlough
G.C.M.	General Court Martial
Gen.	General
G.O.	General Orders
H.A.	Heavy Artillery
Hdq.	Headquarters or HQ for the same
Hosp.	Hospital
Hosp Corp.	Hospital Corps
Hosp. Stew.	Hospital Steward
I.D.P.I.E.F.	Independent Division Philippine Islands Expeditionary Forces
Ind.	Independent.
Infy.	Infantry
I.R.P.	Inspector of Rifle Practice
J.A. or J.A.G.	Judge Advocate and Judge Advocate General
Jnd.	Joined
L.A. or Lt. Art.	Light Artillery
LDS or lds.	Landsman (Navy Rank)
LG	Lieutenant General
Lieut. or Lt.	Lieutenant
Lt. Col.	Lieutenant Colonel
M.A.A.	Master at Arms (Navy Rank)
Maj.	Major
MG	Major General
M.I.	Mustered In
Mil.	Militia
Mily.	Military
M.O.	Mustered Out
M.O.H.	Medal of Honor
Mus.	Musician.
N.G.	National Guard or *example* of N.G.N.Y. National Guard New York
Non-Com or N.C.O.	Non-Commissioned Officer

Ord.	Ordnance.
O.V.I.	Ohio Volunteer Infantry or insert any other state volunteer regiment
Par.	Paragraph.
Phil.	Philippine Insurrection
P.I.	Philippine Islands or Philippine Insurrection
P.M.G. or P.M.G.O.	Provost Marshal General or Provost Marshal General Office
P.R.	Porto Rico or Puerto Rico.
Prin. Mus.	Principal Musician.
Priv or Pvt.	Private
Prom.	Promoted
Q.M.	Quartermaster
Q.M. Sgt.	Quartermaster Sergeant
Regt. or Reg.	Regiment
Red.	Reduced
RED	Red Cross (war era organization)
Res.	Residence
R.O.	Regimental Orders
SAW or Span. Am.	Spanish-American War
SP.	Spanish-American War
Sgt.	Sergeant
Sgt. Maj.	Sergeant Major
Sect. War.	Secretary of War
Sig. Corps.	Signal Corps
S.N.M.	State Naval Militia
S.O.	Special Orders
S.S.A.W.V.	Sons of Spanish American War Veterans (fraternal organization)
Stew.	Steward.
Sub.	Subsistence
Sum. Ct.	Summary Court
Surg.	Surgeon
Temp.	Temporary or Temporarily
Tr.	Troop (cavalry designation)
Tranfd.	Transferred
Trump.	Trumpeter
Unassnd.	Unassigned
U.S.	United States
U.S.A.T.	United States Army Transport
U.S.L.H.S.	United States Lighthouse Service (formed in 1789)
U.S.L.S.S.	United States Live-Saving Service (formed in 1878)
U.S.M.C.	United States Marine Corps

U.S.N.	United States Navy
U.S.N.M.C.	United States Navy Medical Corps
U.S.R.S.	United States Receiving Ship (training vessel for U.S.N. recruits)
U.S.V. or U.S. Vol.	United States Volunteer
U.S.S.	United States Ship
U.S.R.C.	United States Revenue Cutter
U.S.R.C.S.	United States Revenue Cutter Service (forerunner of U.S. Coast Guard)
U.S.T.B.D.	United States Torpedo Boat Destroyer
U.S.W.V.	United Spanish War Veterans (fraternal organization)
Vet.	Veteran
Vol.	Volunteer
Wag.	Wagoner
W. Dept.	War Department
W.C.	Widows Certificate (military pension)
W.O.	Widows Original (military pension)
XC or C	Pension Claim Prefixes the "X" indicates veteran was deceased
Yeo.	Yeoman

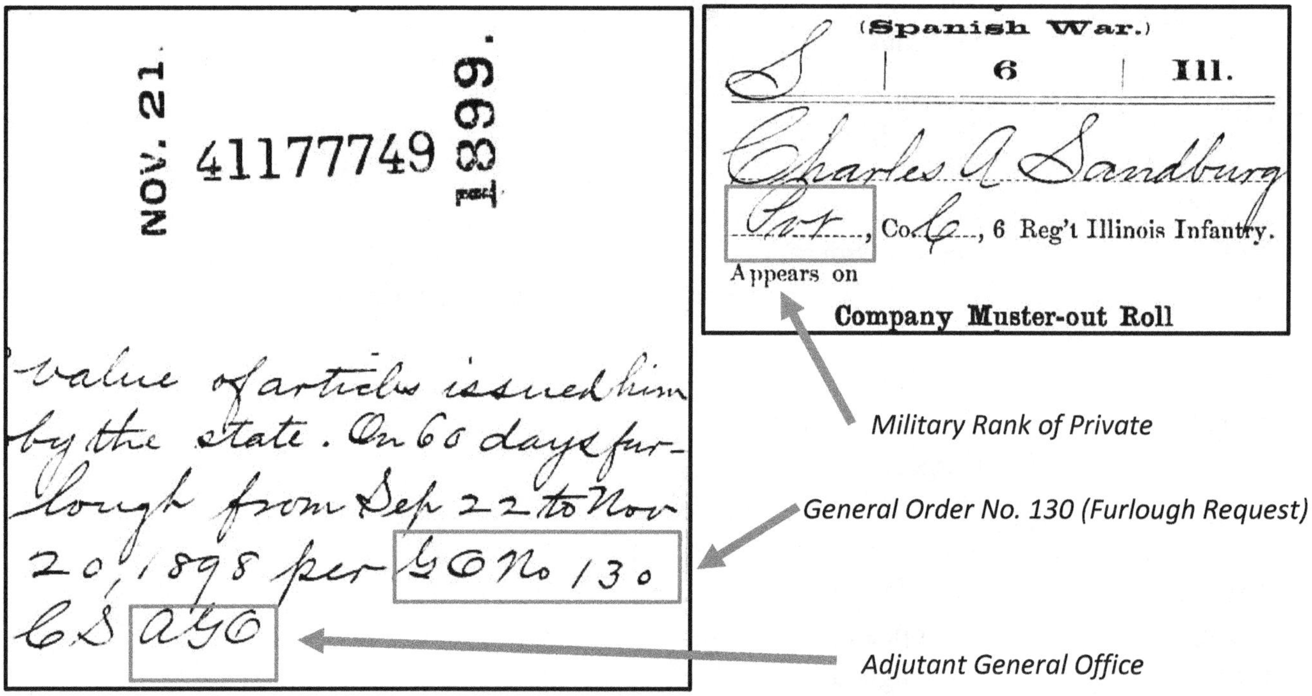

Figure 93: Courtesy of National Archives

The previous page example shows Private Charles A. Sandburg of Company C. of the 6th Illinois Infantry, who served during the Spanish-American War. The documents are found inside the compiled military service records. After returning to civilian life, Sandburg was a Pulitzer Prize winner for his complete biography told of the life of President Abraham Lincoln with two volumes published in 1926 and another four volumes published later in 1939.[185]

GENEALOGY TIP Consider searching in the online catalog called the Record Group Explorer on the National Archives website to locate published finding aids, online photographs, and documents related to specific record groups of interest.

---

[185] James Hurt "Sandburg's Lincoln within History" *Journal of the Abraham Lincoln Association* 20:1 (Winter 1999): 55-65.

State Genealogical Resources

Numerous genealogy records exist for state sources outside the large collection of records found at the National Archives and the National Personnel Record Center. The sources of state-related material come from online databases, digitized books, state archives, libraries, museums, and historical societies. Every effort was made to provide accurate links to each state record.

ALABAMA

FamilySearch

Muster Rolls of Alabama Volunteers in the Spanish-American War of 1898 online at: https://www.familysearch.org/search/catalog/666676?availability=Family%20History%20Library.

Spanish-American War service, 1898-1899 Alabama Department of Archives and History at: https://www.familysearch.org/search/catalog/632754?availability=Family%20History%20Library.

Fighting Joe Wheeler: Hero of Two Wars book by Allen P. Tankersley, published in 1954 online at: https://www.familysearch.org/library/books/records/item/399998-redirection

Hathi Trust

A History of Alabama's White Regiments during the Spanish-American War: Touching incidentally on the Experiences of the entire First Division of the Seventh Army Corps at: https://catalog.hathitrust.org/Record/009562157.

ARIZONA

FamilySearch

1st Regiment, U.S. Volunteer Cavalry, 1898: a brief study and indexed roster of the "Rough Riders" written by Howard M. Gabbert in 1992-Arizona State Genealogical Society: https://www.familysearch.org/search/catalog/2713763?availability=Mesa%20Arizona%20FamilySearch%20Library

Arizona State Library & Archives

Rough Riders and the Spanish-American War at: https://azlibrary.gov/dazl/learners/research-topics/rough-riders-and-spanish-american-war.

Hathi Trust

The Story of Arizona by Will H. Robinson https://catalog.hathitrust.org/Record/007702408 written in 1919 is one of the definitive works for the history of the state.

ARKANSAS

Hathi Trust

Report of the Adjutant General of the Arkansas State Guard, 1897-1900 Including the Period of the Spanish-American War at: https://catalog.hathitrust.org/Record/006584839.

World Cat

Arkansas Spanish-American War Soldiers at: https://www.worldcat.org/title/arkansas-spanish-american-war-soldiers/oclc/47630971&referer=brief_results.

Encyclopedia of Arkansas

Spanish American War at https://encyclopediaofarkansas.net/entries/spanish-american-war-4856

CALIFORNIA

FamilySearch

Illustrated roster of California volunteer soldiers in the war with Spain: enlisted under the President's proclamations of April 23rd and May 25th, 1898 authored by Horace W. Bachelder https://www.familysearch.org/search/catalog/666713?availability=Family%20History%20Library

Hathi Trust

California Volunteers in the Spanish-American War of 1898 published in Sacramento, CA in 1899 at: https://catalog.hathitrust.org/Record/006540174.

California Military Museum

California and the Spanish-American War and Philippine Insurrection on the museum website at: http://militarymuseum.org/HistorySpanAm.html

COLORADO

FamilySearch

Colorado's volunteer infantry in the Philippine Wars, 1898-1899 in 2006 by Geoffrey R. Hunt at: https://www.familysearch.org/search/catalog/1317960?availability=Family%20History%20Library

Just outside of Manila: letters from members of the First Colorado Regiment in the Spanish-American and Philippine-American wars published by Frank Harper in Denver, CO in 1992 at: https://www.familysearch.org/search/catalog/544097?availability=Family%20History%20Library

Hathi Trust

The Colorado Volunteers published by Arthur G. Baker including rosters printed in 1899 at: https://catalog.hathitrust.org/Record/008650684

Colorado State Archives

Historical Records Index Search at: https://catalog.hathitrust.org/Record/008650684

CONNECTICUT

Hathi Trust

Adjutant General. Record of Service of Connecticut Men in the Army, Navy, and Marine Corps of the United States in the Spanish-American War, Philippine Insurrection, and China Relief Expedition, from April 21, 1898 to July 4, 1904 https://catalog.hathitrust.org/Record/009262281

Ancestry

Connecticut service Spanish American War https://www.ancestry.com/search/collections/3803

Connecticut State Library

Military Records with sub grouped Spanish-American War service Records finding aid in RG 013 at: https://libguides.ctstatelibrary.org/hg/militaryrecords/spanish

DELAWARE

FamilySearch

Delaware Spanish-American War card file index, 1898-1899 from the Delaware Public Archives at: https://www.familysearch.org/search/catalog/2659873?availability=Family%20History%20Library

FLORIDA

FamilySearch

Soldiers of Florida in the Seminole Indian, Civil and Spanish-American Wars by Charles M. Wills at: https://www.familysearch.org/library/books/records/item/471291-redirection.

Ancestry

Florida, Spanish American War Compiled Service Records, 1898 from National Archives in RG94 at: https://www.ancestry.com/search/collections/2135

State Library and Archives of Florida

Florida Memory-Florida and Spanish-American War of 1899- https://www.floridamemory.com

University of Florida

George A. Smathers Libraries-1898 The Spanish American War & Florida online collection at: https://guides.uflib.ufl.edu/tampasoldiers

GEORGIA

FamilySearch

A Roster of Spanish American War soldiers from Georgia published b in 1984 at: https://www.familysearch.org/search/catalog/387?availability=Family%20History%20Library.

Soldier's & Widows Pensions, 1899-1921 Civil War, Spanish-American War and Mexican War at: https://www.familysearch.org/search/catalog/837091?availability=Family%20History%20Library

Hathi Trust

Georgia Archives

Virtual Vault of George Archives Spanish-American War Service Summary Cards online at: https://vault.georgiaarchives.org/digital/collection/swc

HAWAII

University of Hawaii at Manoa

The U.S. Philippines, and Hawaii Leap into Imperialism from the Center for Philippine Studies at: http://www.hawaii.edu/cps/US-Imperialism.html

IDAHO

Idaho Military Museum

The Spanish-American War: A brief history of the 1st Idaho Volunteer Infantry on their website at: https://museum.mil.idaho.gov

United States GenWeb Project Archives

Idaho in the Spanish-American War at: http://files.usgwarchives.net/id/statewide/spanamer.txt

ILLINOIS

FamilySearch

Spanish-American War soldiers with Decatur listed as their residence in the Central Illinois Genealogy Quarterly at: https://www.familysearch.org/search/catalog/1841725

History of the Fourth Illinois Volunteers in their relation to the Spanish-American War for the liberation of Cuba and other island possessions of Spain published by John R. Skinner in 1898 at: https://www.familysearch.org/search/catalog/3220843

Hathi Trust

Adjutant general's report containing the complete muster-out rolls of the Illinois volunteers who served in the Spanish-American War, 1898 and 1899 published by General James B. Smith at: https://catalog.hathitrust.org/Record/100641189?type%5B%5D=all&lookfor%5B%5D=illinois%20spanish%20american%20war&ft=

The Eighth Illinois published by Corporal W.T. Good in Chicago, Illinois in 1899 online at: https://catalog.hathitrust.org/Record/008719472?type%5B%5D=all&lookfor%5B%5D=illinois%20spanish%20american%20war&ft=

History of the Second regiment Illinois volunteer infantry from organization to muster-out published by Chaplain H.W. Bolton former veteran of the regiment in Chicago, Illinois in 1899: https://catalog.hathitrust.org/Record/006578918?type%5B%5D=all&lookfor%5B%5D=illinois%20spanish%20american%20war&ft=

The Cuban campaign of the First infantry Illinois volunteers April 25-September 9, 1898 / Illustrated with a series of views taken by the late Claron S. Wagar, member of drum corps published in 1899 in Chicago, IL at: https://catalog.hathitrust.org/Record/100171181.

Illinois Secretary of State

Illinois Spanish-American War Veterans database from the collection of the Illinois State Archives at: https://www.ilsos.gov/isaveterans/spanamericansrch.jsp.

Illinois Spanish-American War Veterans-duplicate database with commonly used abbreviations at: https://www.cyberdriveillinois.com/departments/archives/databases/spanam.html.

INDIANA

FamilySearch

Record of Indiana volunteers in the Spanish-American war 1898-1899: Issued by Authority of the Sixty-First General Assembly of Indiana published in Indianapolis, IN in 1900 by James K. Gore: https://www.familysearch.org/search/catalog/154561?availability=Family%20History%20Library.

Spanish American & World War veterans & nurses of Monroe County Indiana published in 1982 at: https://www.familysearch.org/search/catalog/221471?availability=Family%20History%20Library

Ancestry

Indiana Spanish American War Records published from *Record of Indiana Volunteers in the Spanish-American War* at: https://www.ancestry.com/search/collections/4305

Hathi Trust

Record of Indiana Volunteers in the Spanish-American War, 1898-99 available online at: https://catalog.hathitrust.org/Record/009834145

Memorial order of United Spanish War Veterans, Department of Indiana: Soldiers and Sailors Monument, Indianapolis, Indiana, June 8, 1947 published in 1947 by United Spanish War Veterans at: https://babel.hathitrust.org/cgi/pt?id=inu.30000110539909&view=1up&seq=1.

Record of Indiana volunteers in the Spanish-American war 1898-1899: Issued by Authority of the Sixty-First General Assembly of Indiana published in Indianapolis, Indiana in 1900 by James K. Gore at: https://catalog.hathitrust.org/Record/000776605

Indiana Historical Society

Spanish-American War and Philippine Insurrection War Collection ca 1898-1901 finding aid at: https://indianahistory.org/wp-content/uploads/spanish-american-war-and-philippine-american-war-collection.pdf

IOWA

FamilySearch

Black Hawk County, Iowa Military: Black Hawk Co. IA veterans, War of 1812, Mexican War, Indian Wars, Civil War, Spanish American War. Written by Northwest IA Genealogical Society https://www.familysearch.org/search/catalog/1196586?availability=Family%20History%20Library

Hathi Trust

From Iowa to the Philippines: A History of Company M, Fifty-first Iowa infantry Volunteers. https://babel.hathitrust.org/cgi/pt?id=cool.ark:/13960/t1zc8gb96&view=1up&seq=9.

The Story of the Forty-Ninth [Iowa, United States Volunteer Infantry], by James E. Whipple at: https://babel.hathitrust.org/cgi/pt?id=loc.ark:/13960/t3gx4d51g&view=1up&seq=7.

Iowa National Guard

The Spanish-American War and the Philippine Insurrection: History of the Iowa National Guard at: https://www.iowanationalguard.com/SitePages/Index.aspx.

KANSAS

FamilySearch

Manhattan area veterans of the Spanish-American War, Riley County, Kansas online at: https://www.familysearch.org/search/catalog/1162066?availability=Family%20History%20Library.

Hathi Trust

Kansas troops in the volunteer service of the United States in the Spanish and Philippine wars at: https://catalog.hathitrust.org/Record/009579067?type%5B%5D=all&lookfor%5B%5D=kansas%20spanish%20american%20war&ft=.

Kansas troops in the volunteer services of the United States in the Spanish and Philippine Wars, mustered in under the first and second calls of the President of the United States. May 9, 1898-- October 28, 1899. Published in Topeka, Kansas by W.Y. Morgan Iowa State Printers in 1900 at: https://catalog.hathitrust.org/Record/101851403?type%5B%5D=all&lookfor%5B%5D=kansas%20spanish%20american%20war&ft=.

Kansas State Historical Society

Spanish-American War (1898) and Philippine Insurrection (1899-1901) database searches at: https://www.kshs.org/p/spanish-american-war-1898-philippine-insurrection-1899-1901/11197.

Kansas Adjutant General's Reports, 1898-1899 direct link to records and database search at: https://www.kshs.org/p/kansas-adjutant-general-s-report-1898-1899/11174

KENTUCKY

FamilySearch

Report of the Adjutant General of the State of Kentucky: Kentucky volunteers, war with Spain, 1898-1899 printed in 1908 by authority of the Kentucky Adjutant General at: https://www.familysearch.org/search/catalog/125730?availability=Family%20History%20Library

Volunteer officers and soldiers of the Spanish American War, 1898-1899 online at: https://www.familysearch.org/search/catalog/255569?availability=Family%20History%20Library

Kentuckians in the war with Spain, 1898-1899 published by James G. Cornett at: https://www.familysearch.org/search/catalog/1181877?availability=Family%20History%20Library

Kentucky National Guard Museum

The Spanish-American War, 1898-1899 collection of records and finding aids at:
https://kynghistory.ky.gov/Pages/default.aspx

Lexington History Museum

The Spanish-American War at: http://lexhistory.org/wikilex/spanish-american-war

LOUISIANA

FamilySearch

Muster-in rolls, 1st & 2nd Infantry and Artillery, Spanish-American War, 1898 online at:
https://www.familysearch.org/search/catalog/581519?availability=Family%20History%20Library.

Index to compiled service records of volunteer soldiers who served during the war with Spain in organizations from the state of Louisiana with access online at the National Archives at:
https://www.familysearch.org/search/catalog/313086?availability=Family%20History%20Library

Hathi Trust

Index to compiled service records of volunteer soldiers who served during the war with Spain in organizations from the state of Louisiana published by the National Archives in Washington, DC
https://catalog.hathitrust.org/Record/102318801?type%5B%5D=all&lookfor%5B%5D=spanish%20american%20war%20louisiana&ft=.

The Spanish-American war of 1898: Liberty for Cuba and world power for the United States. "Remember the Maine." Louisiana's part in the accomplishment of the manifest destiny of the nation. Published by the Louisiana State Museum by James J.A. Fortier in 1939 at:
https://catalog.hathitrust.org/Record/000467294

Louisiana Digital Library

Spanish American War, 1898 located at: https://louisianadigitallibrary.org

MAINE

FamilySearch

Maine Veteran Cemetery Records, 1676-1918 database search at the Maine State Archives at:
https://www.familysearch.org/search/collection/1985567

Maine State Archives

Spanish-American War at: https://www.maine.gov/sos/cec/elec/voter-info/veteran/spanish.html.

MARYLAND

Hathi Trust

Roster of the soldiers and sailors who served in organizations from Maryland during the Spanish-American War authorized by the MD House of Delegates and published in 1901 at: https://catalog.hathitrust.org/Record/008731708

Maryland State Archives

Military Records at: http://guide.msa.maryland.gov/pages/viewer.aspx?page=military.

Maryland Spanish and Philippine American War Veteran Burials inventory from the archives at: https://msa.maryland.gov/megafile/msa/speccol/sc6200/sc6235/000000/000001/000000/000002/pdf/msa_sc6235_1_2.pdf.

MASSACHUSETTS

Hathi Trust

The First Regiment, Massachusetts Heavy Artillery, United States volunteers, in the Spanish-American War of 1898: with regimental roster and muster rolls by James A Frye https://www.familysearch.org/search/catalog/81552?availability=Family%20History%20Library

Twelve months with the Eighth Massachusetts infantry in the service of the United States. By Harry Endicott Webber printed in 1908 in Salem, Massachusetts online at: https://www.familysearch.org/search/catalog/102701?availability=Family%20History%20Library.

Greater Salem in the Spanish American War by Harry Endicott Webber printed in 1901 at: https://www.familysearch.org/search/catalog/228701?availability=Family%20History%20Library.

Springfield in the Spanish-American War published by Walter W. Ward in 1898 online at: https://www.familysearch.org/library/books/records/item/119286-redirection.

Northampton in the Spanish-American War by James R. Gilfillan published in 1898 at: https://www.familysearch.org/library/books/records/item/160833-redirection.

LuLu Publishing

Malden Soldiers Spanish-American War by Noreen Finneran published in 2015 available online at: https://www.lulu.com. Search catalog for book title.

Ancestry

Massachusetts Spanish American War Records from the 8th Massachusetts Volunteer Infantry at: https://www.ancestry.com/search/collections/5070.

MICHIGAN

FamilySearch

Michigan volunteers, Spanish American War muster out rolls, 1898-1899 from AGO at: https://www.familysearch.org/search/catalog/339768?availability=Family%20History%20 Library

Hathi Trust

Report of the Quartermaster General of Michigan: War with Spain from the State Printer in 1898: https://babel.hathitrust.org/cgi/pt?id=mdp.39015071163029&view=1up&seq=3

Ancestry

Michigan Men in the Spanish-American War database published in Detroit, Michigan in 1990 at: https://www.ancestry.com/search/collections/20048

Department of Military and Veteran Affairs

The Spanish-American War at: https://www.michigan.gov/dmva

MINNESOTA

FamilySearch

Minnesotans in the Spanish-American War and the Philippine Insurrection: April 21, 1898-July 4, 1902 by Antona Hawkins Richardson published in 1998 at: https://www.familysearch.org/search/catalog/821233?availability=Family%20History%20Library.

The Boys in Blue: Diaries of John Curtin, with information on other Sibley County, Minnesota soldiers in the Spanish-American War and Philippine insurrection, 1898-1902 at: https://www.familysearch.org/search/catalog/720649?availability=Family%20History%20Library.

Hathi Trust

Minnesota in the Spanish-American war and the Philippine Insurrection by Franklin F. Holbrook at: https://catalog.hathitrust.org/Record/000817628.

With the 13th Minnesota in the Philippines by John Bowe published in 1905 at: https://babel.hathitrust.org/cgi/pt?id=loc.ark:/13960/t76t1j60j&view=1up&seq=7

Ancestry

Minnesota in the Spanish-American War and the Philippine Insurrection published in 1923 at: https://www.ancestry.com/search/collections/23884.

Minnesota History Center

Military Service Records Research: Spanish American War Record located at the Gale Family Library at: https://libguides.mnhs.org/milservice/saw

MISSISSIPPI

FamilySearch

Mississippi, county rosters of military veterans, 1936-1939 from the Mississippi State Archives at: https://www.familysearch.org/search/collection/1919687

Hathi Trust

The Mississippi agricultural and mechanical college war record: the civil war; the Spanish-American war; the World War published by MS Agricultural and Mechanical College at: https://babel.hathitrust.org/cgi/pt?id=mdp.39015055281763&view=1up&seq=3

Mississippi Department of Archives and History

Remembering Veterans: Spanish-American War with online finding aids and microfilm reference at: https://www.mdah.ms.gov/senseofplace/tag/spanish-american-war

MISSOURI

FamilySearch

Missouri Infantry- Spanish-American War: [6th Missouri Infantry roster] online at: https://www.familysearch.org/search/catalog/2519370

Military records, Spanish-American War, 1897-1898 from the Missouri AGO at: https://www.familysearch.org/search/catalog/426861?availability=Family%20History%20Library

Missouri State Archives

Soldiers' Records: War of 1812-World War I database through Missouri Digital Heritage at: https://s1.sos.mo.gov/records/archives/archivesdb/soldiers/Default.aspx#soldierSearch.

MONTANA

FamilySearch

Montana Military Records, 1904-1918 https://www.familysearch.org/search/collection/3010075

Montana Memory Project

Military Enlistments, 1890-1918 https://mtmemory.org/digital/collection/p16013coll34/id/1775

Archives West

United Spanish War Veterans, Department of Montana Records, 1903-1950 finding aid online at: http://archiveswest.orbiscascade.org

NEBRASKA

FamilySearch

Spanish-American War veterans from Nebraska by K. H. Simons published in 2000 at: https://www.familysearch.org/search/catalog/998514?availability=Family%20History%20Library

Hathi Trust

Roster of soldiers, sailors and marines who served in the War of the Rebellion, Spanish-American War and World War at: https://catalog.hathitrust.org/Record/100786050.

History of the Operations of the First Nebraska Infantry, U.S.V. in the Campaign in the Philippine Islands at: https://catalog.hathitrust.org/Record/009577001.

The State of Nebraska

The Spanish-American War at: https://history.nebraska.gov/publications/spanish-american-war.

United Spanish War Veterans Records, 1907-1975. Includes finding aids of 22 cubic feet at: https://history.nebraska.gov/sites/history.nebraska.gov/files/doc/United%20Spanish%20War%20Veterans.%20Nebraska%20Department%20%5BRG0044%5D.pdf.

The Boys of our Regiment: Roster of the Second Nebraska Volunteer Infantry, 1898 published in Chattanooga, Tennessee with more details available online at the Nebraska State Historical Society at: https://nebraskahistory.pastperfectonline.com/webobject/4E50BEEB-1378-4435-94B8-263318703512

The image to the left shows Private Archie Raymond Miner in front of tents in Chickamauga Park at Camp Thomas in Chattanooga, Tennessee. He is pictured holding his standard-issued 1896 Krag-Jorgensen .30-40 caliber rifle that the regiment's men were all supplied.

Miner was born on June 18, 1872, in Graf, Nebraska, and was the son of Samuel and Mary (Holmes) Miner, where he spent his youth. A few months after the war began, he enlisted in Company I of the 2nd Nebraska Infantry on May 10, 1898.

His unit was never deployed to either Cuba or the Philippines. They were assigned to the 2nd Brigade, First Division, of the Third Army Corps. After leaving Lincoln, Nebraska, on May 19, 1898, they were sent to Camp Thomas, where they remained until the regiment was transferred to Fort Omaha, Nebraska, where the entire regiment, including Miner, was mustered out on October 24, 1898.

Figure 94: Courtesy of Michael L. Strauss

After the end of the war, Miner moved to Missouri, Colorado, and eventually to Amarillo, Texas, where he died on February 15, 1956, at the age of 83 years. He was an active member of the Veterans of the Spanish-American War. He lies interred in Springfield National Cemetery in Missouri, where his government-issued headstone records his prior military service.[186]

NEVADA

FamilySearch

Grave registration records: G.A.R. and Spanish-American War veterans buried in Nevada at:
https://www.familysearch.org/search/catalog/183528?availability=Family%20History%20Library

Revised and complete roster of Nevada veterans, Civil War, Spanish American War, Nevada National Guards to 1914, State Militia, Home Guards from the Nevada Historical Society at:
https://www.familysearch.org/search/catalog/708148?availability=Family%20History%20Library.

---

[186] *Springfield Leader and Press*, February 16, 1956.

Nevada Historical Society

Summer Soldiers: The First Battalion Nevada Volunteer Infantry in the Spanish-American War in the NV Historical Quarterly http://epubs.nsla.nv.gov/statepubs/epubs/210777-1990-3Fall.pdf.

Orders and Medals Society of America

Nevada's Spanish-American and Philippine War Medal with the history and background at: http://www.omsa.org/files/jomsa_arch/Splits/1979/27317_JOMSA_Vol30_12_04.pdf

NEW HAMPSHIRE

FamilySearch

New Hampshire, Spanish-American War records, 1898 from the NH Division of Archives at: https://www.familysearch.org/search/catalog/1880943?availability=Family%20History%20Library.

Naval History and Heritage Command

NH Spanish Prisoners of war, Seavey's Island New Hampshire. Spanish-American War, 1898 at: https://www.history.navy.mil/our-collections/photography/numerical-list-of-images/nhhc-series/nh-series/NH-121000/NH-121096.html

New Hampshire Division of Archives

Records of the Spanish-American War and the Philippine Insurrection through finding aids at: https://sos.nh.gov/archives-vital-records-records-management/archives/archival-holdings

NEW JERSEY

FamilySearch

Soldiers and sailors of New Jersey in the Spanish-American War: embracing a chronological account of the army and navy at: https://www.familysearch.org/search/catalog/666875.

Index to records of Spanish American war, books 1-122 from the NJ State Library at: https://www.familysearch.org/search/catalog/208563?availability=Family%20History%20Library.

A history of the Second Regiment, N. G. N. J, Second N. J. Volunteers, Spanish War, Fifth New Jersey Infantry: together with a short review covering early military life in the state of New Jersey at: https://www.familysearch.org/search/catalog/1381476

Hathi Trust

Roster and addresses of the Second New Jersey Volunteer Infantry in the Spanish-American War, 1898 https://babel.hathitrust.org/cgi/pt?id=loc.ark:/13960/t5p84cd2j&view=1up&seq=7

Internet Archives

Soldiers and Sailors of New Jersey in the Spanish American War in 1898 by Bernard McNally at: https://archive.org/details/soldierssailors00mcna.

New Jersey State Archives

Department of Defense-Spanish American War and Related Record with the finding aids at: https://www.state.nj.us/state/archives/catsedefen5.html.

Photographs of Officers of the New Jersey Volunteer Infantry, 1898-1904 with scanned images at: https://www.nj.gov/state/archives/sdea5005.html.

NEW MEXICO

The Spanish American War Website

A List of Spanish American War Veterans buried in New Mexico with names and links to more at: https://www.spanamwar.com/NewMexico.htm

The American History and Genealogy Project

Regiments-Spanish American War, New Mexico 1898 with list of regiment rosters and names at: https://nmahgp.genealogyvillage.com/Military/regiments_spanish_american_war_1898.html

NEW YORK

FamilySearch

New York in the Spanish American War, 1898: Part of the report of the Adjutant-General of the state for 1900 found in three volumes published in 1900 by the AGO of New York located at: https://www.familysearch.org/search/catalog/165424?availability=Family%20History%20Library

Index to the New York Spanish-American War Veterans, 1898 edited by Richard H. Saldana at: https://www.familysearch.org/search/catalog/607641?availability=Family%20History%20Library

New York and the War with Spain: History of the Empire State digital copy published by Argus Co. in 1903 at: https://www.familysearch.org/search/catalog/1932307.

Proceedings of the United Spanish War Veterans, Department of New York, for the year 1919 at: https://www.familysearch.org/search/catalog/1852095?availability=Los%20Angeles%20Californ ia%20FamilySearch%20Library

Hathi Trust

Our Heroes of the Spanish-American War published by Central Bureau of Engraving in New York at: https://babel.hathitrust.org/cgi/pt?id=loc.ark:/13960/t6930xg2p&view=1up&seq=5.

Index to the New York Spanish-American War Veterans, 1898 online and digitized at: https://catalog.hathitrust.org/Record/009597970.

New York Military Museum

New York Spanish-American War Units at: https://dmna.ny.gov/historic/reghist/spanAm.

New York State Archives

War Service Records and Searches with finding aids for military records from the Colonial era to World War II and later at: http://www.archives.nysed.gov/research/res_topics_mi_warsvc.shtml.

Ancestry

New York Spanish American War Military and Naval Service Records, 1898-1902 from the NY State Archives Series B-0809 at: https://www.ancestry.com/search/collections/5351.

All New York Military Service Cards, 1816-1979 from the New York National Guard at: https://www.ancestry.com/search/collections/2340. Example from this database below.

COAN, CLARENCE ARTHUR

RANKS	Sep. Co.	Bat'n	Reg't	Brig.	Div.	A.G. Rept. Year	Register Page No.
2nd Lt.			9	1		1892	41
1st Lt.			9	1		1894	48
Capt.			9	1		1895	59
1st Lt.			23	2		1900	144

Register of Officers whose services terminated prior to Jan. 1, 1916.

Figure 95: Courtesy of New York State Archives

Figure 96: Courtesy of Michael L. Strauss

The above military service card for the New York State militia relates to the National Guard service of Clarence Arthur Coan, who was born on 16 December 1867 in Ottawa, IL, and lived in New York since childhood. He joined the NYNG in 1892 with the rank of 2nd Lieutenant, being assigned to the 9th NY Infantry which served during the Spanish-American War as a Captain in Company L. His unit was never deployed to Cuba and he was discharged from federal service after the war. Coan was reduced in rank to 1st Lieutenant and transferred to the 23rd NY National Guard regiment where he retired. He died in South Nyack, NY, on 17 August 1934.[187]

---

[187] *Poughkeepsie Eagle-News*, August 18, 1934.

NORTH CAROLINA

FamilySearch

North Carolina's role in the Spanish-American War by Joseph F. Steelman online at:
https://www.familysearch.org/search/catalog/545767?availability=Family%20History%20Library

Roster of the North Carolina Volunteers in the Spanish-American War, 1898-1899 at:
https://www.familysearch.org/library/books/records/item/29302-redirection

Hathi Trust

Roster of the North Carolina Volunteers in the Spanish-American War, 1898-1899 available at:
https://catalog.hathitrust.org/Record/009578857.

Ancestry

North Carolina Volunteers, Spanish American War from the NC Adjutant General Office at:
https://www.ancestry.com/search/collections/4136.

North Carolina State Archives

Military Collection of Spanish-American War, 1898-1949 with finding aid online to search at:
https://files.nc.gov/dncr-archives/documents/files/milcoll_spanishamericanwar.pdf.

NORTH DAKOTA

Hathi Trust

Volunteer-service in the Philippines: Remarks of Hon. H.C. Hansbrough, of North Dakota, in the Senate of the United States, May 4, 1900 published in Washington, DC in 1900 online at:
https://babel.hathitrust.org/cgi/pt?id=loc.ark:/13960/t9j39mt97&view=1up&seq=3

The North Dakota State Historical Society

Military-Philippine Insurrection and Spanish American War manuscript guide by subject at:
https://www.history.nd.gov/archives/manuscripts/military/philippine_spanamer.html.

North Dakota National Guard in the Spanish American War in lessons and topics at:
https://www.ndstudies.gov/gr8/content/unit-iii-waves-development-1861-1920/lesson-4-alliances-and-conflicts/topic-9-spanish-american-war/section-2-north-dakota-national-guard-spanish-american-war.

World Cat

The Boys: 1st North Dakota Volunteers in the Philippines at: https://www.worldcat.org/title/boys-1st-north-dakota-volunteers-in-the-philippines/oclc/467254571.

OHIO

Hathi Trust

The official roster of Ohio soldiers in the war with Spain, 1898-99: Under Direction of Frank B. Willis Governor at: https://catalog.hathitrust.org/Record/000776607.

Ohio History Connection

Official Roster of Ohio Soldiers in the War with Spain, 1898-99 searchable online at: https://ohiohistory.on.worldcat.org/oclc/784129

Spanish American War Rolls at: https://aspace.ohiohistory.org/repositories/2/resources/9820

Grave Registration Cards, A-Z Spanish-American War from 1920-1970 at: https://aspace.ohiohistory.org/repositories/2/resources/25660

Correspondence to the Governor and Adjutant General of Ohio, 1861-1898 online at: https://aspace.ohiohistory.org/repositories/2/resources/9443

OKLAHOMA

FamilySearch

LeFlore County, OK, World War I Military Discharge records including the Spanish-American War: https://www.familysearch.org/search/catalog/779246?availability=Family%20History%20Library.

Military Discharge Records, 1917-1952. From Latimer Co. including the Philippine Insurrection at: https://www.familysearch.org/search/catalog/821630?availability=Family%20History%20Library.

Hathi Trust

Oklahoma Rough Rider: Billy McGinty's Own Story published in 2008 by University of OK at: https://catalog.hathitrust.org/Record/007150585?type%5B%5D=all&lookfor%5B%5D=spanish%20american%20war%20oklahoma&ft=.

The Oklahoma Historical Society

https://www.okhistory.org/publications/enc/entry.php?entry=RO034

OREGON

FamilySearch

The Official records of the Oregon volunteers in the Spanish War and Philippines insurrection https://www.familysearch.org/search/catalog/18187?availability=Family%20History%20Library amilySearch

Oregon in the Philippines: 2nd Division, 8th Army Corps, Second Regiment, Oregon Volunteer Infantry in Two Wars published in 1899 by William S. Gilbert and digitized online at: https://www.familysearch.org/search/catalog/2370270?availability=La%20Grande%20Oregon% 20Family%20History%20Center

Hathi Trust

The Official Record of the OR Volunteers in Spanish War & Philippine Insurrection online at: https://catalog.hathitrust.org/Record/000776563

Ancestry

Oregon Volunteers, Spanish American War and Philippine Insurrection at: https://www.ancestry.com/search/collections/4830

Oregon Historical Society

Oregon Soldiers in the Spanish-American and Philippine Wars, 1898-1899 on OR Encyclopedia https://www.oregonencyclopedia.org/articles/oregon_unit_in_the_phillipines/#.X35J22hKiUl

PENNSYLVANIA

FamilySearch

A Bibliography of Sources for Civil War, Mexican War, and Spanish American War research at: https://www.familysearch.org/search/catalog/45468?availability=Family%20History%20Library

Hathi Trust

Record of Pennsylvania Volunteers in the Spanish-American War, 1898 available for free online at https://catalog.hathitrust.org/Record/008588041 with online rosters from all the regiments.

Pennsylvania in the Spanish American War: a commemorative look back by Richard A. Sauers: https://catalog.hathitrust.org/Record/102777276?type%5B%5D=all&lookfor%5B%5D=spanish %20american%20war%20maine&ft=.

Pennsylvania State Archives

Spanish American War Veterans card File of United States Volunteers Indexes database at: http://www.digitalarchives.state.pa.us/archive.asp?view=ArchiveIndexes&ArchiveID=8

Pennsylvania National Guard Veterans Card Files, 1867-1921, Index database online at: http://www.digitalarchives.state.pa.us/archive.asp?view=ArchiveIndexes&ArchiveID=21

Ancestry

Pennsylvania Spanish War Compensation, 1898-1934 database covers Spanish-American War, Philippine Insurrection, and the Boxer Rebellion available and digitized online at: https://www.ancestry.com/search/collections/2392. Example from this database.

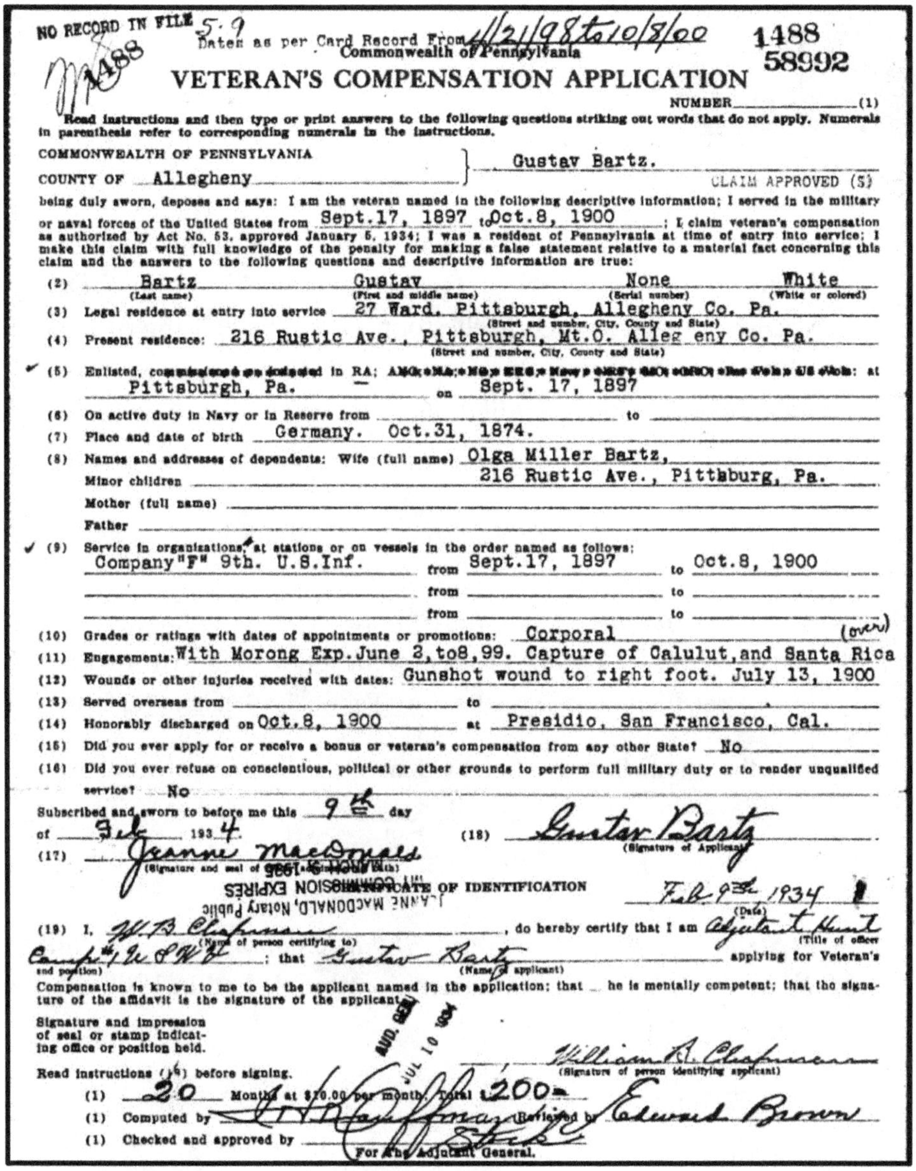
NO RECORD IN FILE 5-9

Dates as per Card Record From 11/21/98 to 10/8/00 1488

Commonwealth of Pennsylvania 58992

VETERAN'S COMPENSATION APPLICATION

NUMBER ________ (1)

Read instructions and then type or print answers to the following questions striking out words that do not apply. Numerals in parenthesis refer to corresponding numerals in the instructions.

COMMONWEALTH OF PENNSYLVANIA } Gustav Bartz.

COUNTY OF Allegheny

CLAIM APPROVED (S)

being duly sworn, deposes and says: I am the veteran named in the following descriptive information; I served in the military or naval forces of the United States from Sept.17, 1897 to Oct.8, 1900 ; I claim veteran's compensation as authorized by Act No. 53, approved January 5, 1934; I was a resident of Pennsylvania at time of entry into service; I make this claim with full knowledge of the penalty for making a false statement relative to a material fact concerning this claim and the answers to the following questions and descriptive information are true:

(2) Bartz (Last name) Gustav (First and middle name) None (Serial number) White (White or colored)

(3) Legal residence at entry into service 27 Ward, Pittsburgh, Allegheny Co. Pa. (Street and number, City, County and State)

(4) Present residence: 216 Rustic Ave., Pittsburgh, Mt.O. Alleg eny Co. Pa. (Street and number, City, County and State)

(5) Enlisted, commissioned or inducted in RA; at Pittsburgh, Pa. on Sept. 17, 1897

(6) On active duty in Navy or in Reserve from ________ to ________

(7) Place and date of birth Germany. Oct.31, 1874.

(8) Names and addresses of dependents: Wife (full name) Olga Miller Bartz,

Minor children 216 Rustic Ave., Pittsburg, Pa.

Mother (full name)

Father

(9) Service in organizations, at stations or on vessels in the order named as follows:

Company "F" 9th. U.S.Inf. from Sept.17, 1897 to Oct.8, 1900

from ________ to ________

from ________ to ________

(10) Grades or ratings with dates of appointments or promotions: Corporal (over)

(11) Engagements: With Morong Exp.June 3,to8,99. Capture of Calulut,and Santa Rica

(12) Wounds or other injuries received with dates: Gunshot wound to right foot. July 13, 1900

(13) Served overseas from ________ to ________

(14) Honorably discharged on Oct.8, 1900 at Presidio, San Francisco, Cal.

(15) Did you ever apply for or receive a bonus or veteran's compensation from any other State? No

(16) Did you ever refuse on conscientious, political or other grounds to perform full military duty or to render unqualified service? No

Subscribed and sworn to before me this 9th day of Feb 1934.

(17) Jeanne MacDonald (Signature and seal of ...)

(18) Gustav Bartz (Signature of Applicant)

JEANNE MACDONALD, Notary Public
COMMISSION EXPIRES

CERTIFICATE OF IDENTIFICATION Feb 9th 1934 (Date)

(19) I, W. B. Chapman (Name of person certifying to), do hereby certify that I am Adjutant Hunt Camp #1 U.S.W.V. (Title of office and position); that Gustav Bartz (Name of applicant) applying for Veteran's Compensation is known to me to be the applicant named in the application; that he is mentally competent; that the signature of the affidavit is the signature of the applicant.

Signature and impression of seal or stamp indicating office or position held.

AUD. GEN. JUL 10 1934

William B. Chapman (Signature of person identifying applicant)

Read instructions (4) before signing.

(1) 20 Months at $10.00 per month Total $200.-

(1) Computed by ________ Revised by Edward Brown

(1) Checked and approved by ________ For the Adjutant General.

Figure 97: Courtesy of Pennsylvania State Archives

The previous image shows the Spanish-American War-era veteran compensation application for Gustave Frederick Bartz. Pictured at left, Bartz was born in Germany on October 31, 1874, and emigrated to the United States in 1890. He joined the United States Regular Army in Pittsburgh, PA, on September 17, 1897, and was assigned to Company F of the 9th U.S. Infantry.

Bartz was engaged with his regiment in San Juan, Cuba, on June 1, 1898. Afterward, he was sent to fight in the Philippines, where he participated in an engagement in Angelis, P.I from August 9-12, 1899, and the capture of Bambon, P.I on November 11, 1899.

With the fighting being diverted to other units, his regiment was sent to China during the Boxer Rebellion and participated in the assault on the city of Tientsin on July 13, 1900.[188] During the engagement in Tientsin, he was shot and wounded in the foot. With the ceasing of hostilities with the Boxers, the 9th U.S. Infantry was sent to San Francisco, CA, where Bartz was discharged at the Presidio on October 8, 1900. He died on June 21, 1954, in Mt. Oliver, PA.[189]

RHODE ISLAND

FamilySearch

Rhode Island in the War with Spain: Compiled from the Official Records of the Executive Department of the State of Rhode Island by Frances E. Kinnicutt published in 1900 at: https://www.familysearch.org/search/catalog/666952?availability=Family%20History%20Library.

Military Records, 1847-1900 from the Rhode Island Adjutant General Office on microfilm at: https://www.familysearch.org/search/catalog/728946?availability=Family%20History%20Library.

Hathi Trust

Rhode Island in the War with Spain: Compiled from the Official Records of the Executive Department of the State of Rhode Island by Frances E. Kinnicutt published in 1900 digitized at:

---

[188] *Pittsburgh Post-Gazette*, August 4, 1900.
[189] Ibid., June 22, 1954.

https://catalog.hathitrust.org/Record/006252435?type%5B%5D=all&lookfor%5B%5D=rhode%20island%20spanish%20american%20war&ft=.

Rhode Island Department of State Archives

Spanish American War Rhode Island Militia Volunteers, 1898 with finding aid to records at: https://catalog.sos.ri.gov/repositories/2/archival_objects/763.

Spanish American War Military Record at: https://catalog.sos.ri.gov/repositories/2/resources/648

SOUTH CAROLINA

World Cat

Roster and Itinerary of South Carolina Volunteer Troops who served in the late war between the United States and Spain, 1898 printed in 1901 authored by General Joseph W. Floyd cataloged on: https://www.worldcat.org/search?q=au%3AFloyd%2C+J.+W.&qt=hot_author.

Amazon

Roster and Itinerary of South Carolina Volunteer Troops who served in the late war between the United States and Spain, 1898 printed in 1901 authored by General Joseph W. Floyd available for purchase https://www.amazon.com/South-Carolina-Spanish-American-War/dp/0893087815.

University of South Carolina

South Carolina and Spanish American War online https://digital.library.sc.edu/collections/south-carolina-and-spanish-american-war.

SOUTH DAKOTA

FamilySearch

Spanish American War members that served in the Philippines; First South Dakota Inf: material taken from the Sioux Falls Daily Argus Leader, Friday 13 Oct 1899 & History of SD online at: 1 https://www.familysearch.org/search/catalog/225113?availability=Family%20History%20Library.

South Dakota State Historical Society

Spanish American War Roster, 1898 at: https://history.sd.gov/Archives/spanishwar.aspx.

TENNESSEE

FamilySearch

Overton County Veterans: Spanish American War-Vietnam War from the VFW from Overton, TN https://www.familysearch.org/search/catalog/1015493?availability=Family%20History%20Library.

Hathi Trust

The First Tennessee Regiment, United States Volunteers published in 1899 in Nashville, TN and digitized online at: https://catalog.hathitrust.org/Record/009605069.

The Spanish American War Centennial Website

The Fourth Tennessee Souvenir and Roster, Spanish American War, 1898-1899 located at: https://www.spanamwar.com/4thTennesseeroster.html.

Tennessee State Library and Archives

The Volunteer State Goes to War: Spanish-American War and Philippine Insurrection finding aid at: https://sharetngov.tnsosfiles.com/tsla/exhibits/veterans/spanishamerican.htm.

Spanish-American War Index to Abstracts of Tennessee Volunteer Units searchable online by names at: https://tslaindexes.tn.gov/database-military-records/spanish-american-war.

TEXAS

Texas State Library and Archives Commission

Texas Adjutant General Service Records at: https://www.tsl.texas.gov/arc/service/introhelp.html with a searchable roster of men who served.

Inventory of Spanish-American War Military Rolls with an online finding aid for the materials at: https://legacy.lib.utexas.edu/taro/tslac/30076/tsl-30076.html.

Texas Military Forces Museum

Spanish American War history at: http://www.texasmilitaryforcesmuseum.org/index.html.

UTAH

FamilySearch

Spanish American War roster of Utah units, 1898 from the Utah State Archives and Records at: https://www.familysearch.org/search/catalog/596365?availability=Family%20History%20Library.

Utah's Roll of Honor (Spanish American War) from the Utah State Archives and Record Service at: https://www.familysearch.org/search/catalog/596377?availability=Family%20History%20Library.

Spanish-American War: Index to Utah Units from the Utah State Archives digitized online at: https://www.familysearch.org/search/catalog/172767?availability=Family%20History%20Library.

Index to Utah Spanish-American War Veterans, 1898 published in 1988 by Richard H. Saldana online at: https://www.familysearch.org/search/catalog/1935339?availability=Logan%20Utah%20FamilySearch%20Library\

Spanish War Veterans, Utah, Medals Undelivered from the Utah State Archives and Records at: https://www.familysearch.org/search/catalog/596401?availability=Family%20History%20Library.

Hathi Trust

The history of the Utah volunteers in the Spanish-American War and in the Philippine Islands. A complete history of all the military organizations in which Utah men served digitized at: https://babel.hathitrust.org/cgi/pt?id=uc1.$b52587&view=1up&seq=9.

The history of the Utah volunteers in the Spanish-American war and in the Philippine Islands at: https://babel.hathitrust.org/cgi/pt?id=loc.ark:/13960/t19k51j25&view=1up&seq=9.

The Utah Batteries: A history: a complete account of the muster-in, sea voyage, battles, skirmishes and barrack life of the Utah batteries, together with biographies of officers and muster-out rolls by Charles R. Mabey published in 1900 in Salt Lake City and digitized at: https://babel.hathitrust.org/cgi/pt?id=uc2.ark:/13960/t4th8dq4v&view=1up&seq=7.

Utah Division of Archives and Record Services

Department of Administrative Services. Division Archives and Records Service Spanish American War and Philippine Insurrection service cards with finding aid online for records at: http://www.archives.state.ut.us/research/inventories/24048.html.

VERMONT

FamilySearch

Vermont in the Spanish-American War published by Herbert T. Johnson of the AGO of Vermont at: https://www.familysearch.org/search/catalog/2290238?availability=Family%20History%20Library.

Record of the soldiers of the Civil War, Spanish American War and the World War from the town of Manchester, Vermont published by Alice E. Bennett in Rutland, Vermont digitized at: https://www.familysearch.org/search/catalog/186677?availability=Family%20History%20Library.

Hathi Trust

Vermont in the Spanish-American War. Prepared and published under the direction of Herbert T. Johnson, by authority of the General Assembly, 1929. Printed by authority of the AGO in Vermont at: https://babel.hathitrust.org/cgi/pt?id=miun.adh2510.0001.001&view=1up&seq=5.

Internet Archives

Vermont in the Spanish-American War published by Herbert T. Johnson Adjutant General of Vermont at: http://archive.org/stream/adh2510.0001.001.umich.edu#page/n3/mode/2up.

Vermont States Archives and Records Administration

Spanish-American War finding aids guides at: https://sos.vermont.gov/vsara/research/guide.

Vermont Historical Society

United Spanish War Veterans Records MSA 789 with historical notes, and finding aid online at: https://vermonthistory.org/documents/findaid/UnitedSpanishWarVets.pdf.

VIRGINIA

FamilySearch

The history of Appomattox, Virginia: Also, World War II-I and Spanish American War service record published by Nathaniel R. Featherston of the American Legion Post No. 104 online at: https://www.familysearch.org/search/catalog/2733035?availability=Family%20History%20Library.

State Library of Virginia

Virginia's Participation in the Spanish American War, 1898; The Philippine Insurrection, 1899-1901; and the China Relief Expedition, 1900-1901 with an online finding aid to the records at the State Library at: https://www.lva.virginia.gov/public/guides/vmd/SpanishAmWarBbliography.pdf.

University of Richmond

A History of Virginia in the Spanish-American War by Virginia Rowe Christian digitized online: https://scholarship.richmond.edu/cgi/viewcontent.cgi?referer=https://www.google.com/&httpsredir=1&article=1087&context=masters-theses.

JSTOR Database of Journals

Virginia's Negro Regiment in the Spanish-American War: The Sixth Volunteers by Willard B. Gatewood Jr. published in the Virginia Magazine of History and Biography Vol 80, No. 2 (April 1972) viewable online at: https://www.jstor.org/stable/4247720?seq=1

WASHINGTON

FamilySearch

United Spanish War Veteran Death Announcement from organization in Washington and Alaska at: https://www.familysearch.org/search/catalog/1614940.

Washington History Link

First Washington Volunteer Infantry Regiment Musters for the Spanish-American War on May 1, 1898 with online https://www.historylink.org.

Washington State University

Guide to the First Washington Infantry, U.S.V Records, 1899 with an online finding aid located at: http://ntserver1.wsulibs.wsu.edu/masc/finders/cg619.htm.

WEST VIRGINIA

FamilySearch

Lewis County in the Spanish-American War published by Roy Bird Cook in 1925 and digitized at: https://www.familysearch.org/search/catalog/2135337.

Records of veterans buried in Brooke County: Includes veterans from the Revolutionary War, Spanish American War, War of 1812, Civil War, and World War I published by Bobbie Elliott https://www.familysearch.org/search/catalog/1045856?availability=Family%20History%20Library.

Soldiers of Wayne County, West Virginia: Revolutionary War, War of 1812, Mexican War, Civil War, Spanish-American War published by Rennie Talbert and Mary Lou Workman at: https://www.familysearch.org/search/catalog/1023452?availability=Family%20History%20Library.

West Virginia State Archives

Collection of Spanish-American War records online at: http://www.wvculture.org/index.aspx.

West Virginia University

Spanish-American War, 1898 for records found in seventeen different collections online at: https://archives.lib.wvu.edu/subjects/835.

WISCONSIN

FamilySearch

Wisconsin Spanish American War soldiers in soldier's homes from the War Department, Office of the Inspector General, Washington D.C. December 9, 1916 by Bev Hetzel and available at: https://www.familysearch.org/search/catalog/1567414?availability=Family%20History%20Library.

Hathi Trust

Company G. Third Wisconsin edited by Rosemary Rick in 1996 with a limited search of the book at: https://babel.hathitrust.org/cgi/pt?id=wu.89058573775

Proceedings of the United Spanish War Veterans Annual Encampment of the Department of Wisconsin published between 1925-1948 with limited online searches for each yearly catalog at:

https://catalog.hathitrust.org/Record/009629260?type%5B%5D=all&lookfor%5B%5D=spanish%20american%20war%20wisconsin&ft=.

Wisconsin Historical Society

Spanish American War in Wisconsin includes a history of the state in this conflict and online at: https://www.wisconsinhistory.org/Records/Article/CS1793.

Wisconsin Veterans Museum

Search the Spanish-American War Roster Database online by name, rank, unit, city, or notes online at: http://museum.dva.state.wi.us/spanishamericanwarroster.

WYOMING

Wyoming State Historical Society

Spanish-American War references at https://www.wyohistory.org/tags/spanish-american-war.

Internet Archives

History of Wyoming by Ichabod S. Bartlett contains rosters of Spanish-American War soldiers (pages 287-303), at: https://archive.org/details/historyofwyoming01bart/page/n5/mode/2up.

DISTRICT OF COLUMBIA

District of Columbia National Guard

History of the District of Columbia's involvement in the National Guard throughout history at: https://dc.ng.mil/About-Us/Heritage/History/Past-and-post-war.

Fort Wiki

History of the 1st District of Columbia Volunteer Infantry at: http://www.fortwiki.com/Fort_Wiki.

The list of state-related websites isn't entirely exhaustive. Researchers of the Spanish-American War are recommended to look at other online resources.

GENERAL WEBSITES

The Church of Jesus-Christ of Latter-day Saints has the *FamilySearch Research Wiki* to aid in genealogy on a broad range of topics at: https://www.familysearch.org/wiki/en/Main_Page.

Figure 99 Courtesy of FamilySearch

In this volume are numerous references to websites containing in-depth genealogical and historical information at the federal, state, or local level on the Spanish-American War, Boxer Rebellion, and Philippine Insurrection. One excellent online source not covered previously that contains detailed historical research on the war and related materials is on the Spanish-American War Centennial Website located at https://www.spanamwar.com.

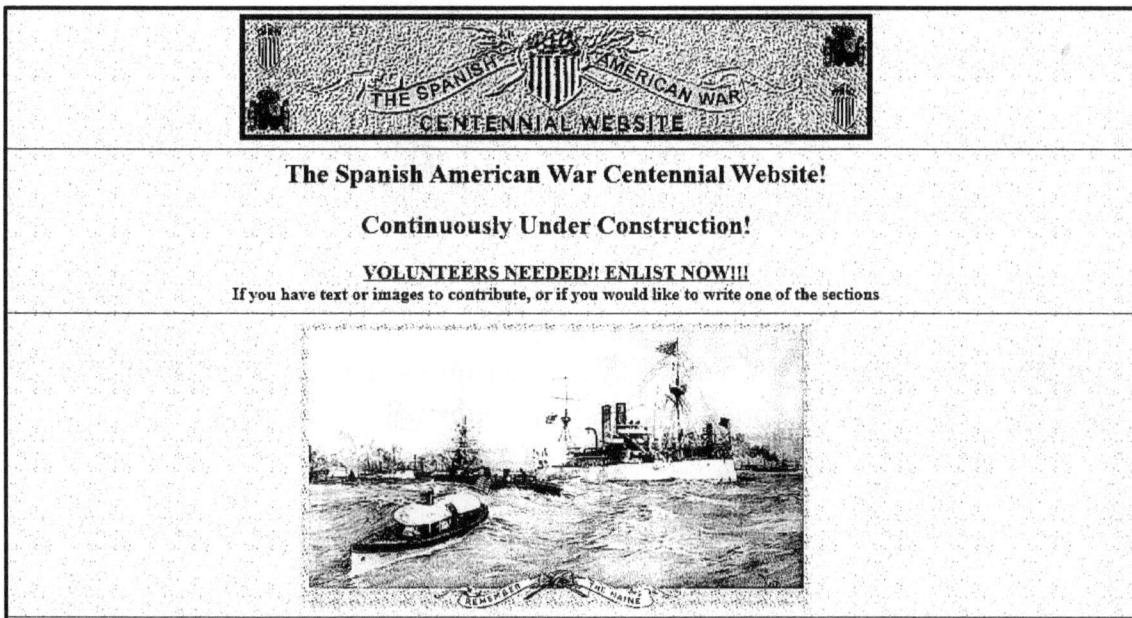

Figure 100: Courtesy of the Spanish-American War Centennial Website

Another excellent research website on the Philippine Insurrection covers, in detail, the fighting of the war from 1899-1902 and the continued insurgent fighting for another decade. The website is called Philippine-American War, 1899-1902 at https://philippineamericanwar.webs.com

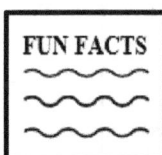

Figure 101: Courtesy of Philippine-American War, 1899-1902 Website

GENEALOGY WEBINARS

In addition to the many websites, genealogists can watch full-length instructional webinar tutorials on the war and genealogical records that can help find wartime ancestors. Below are three online webinars with links to access the videos.

FUN FACTS

DID YOU KNOW that John Hay, who served as the United States Secretary of State under President William McKinley, is often credited with the term *That Splendid Little War* when describing the Spanish-American War? Hay believed the conflict would be brief, bloodless, and ultimately successful.

Military Ephemera

Historical documents and research methodology provide solid clues about the lives of our military ancestors. However, another approach to research is the importance of ephemera items like photographs, letters, diaries, identification cards, posters, engravings, broadsides, medals, and periodicals. Each item has a unique story about a military ancestor who may have fought in the Spanish-American War, Boxer Rebellion, or the Philippine Insurrection.

Examples of Ephemera:

Albert Pike Smith

Items of historical ephemera can be found in many forms. When veterans applied for pension claim benefits based on their former military service, the Veterans Administration provided the recipient with an identification card containing their name, address, birth date, and military claim number assigned when the application was filled out. Albert P. Smith was born on April 12, 1875, in Jefferson, Pennsylvania, and served in the Spanish-American War, enlisting in Company K of the 10th Pennsylvania Volunteer Infantry on June 21, 1898, in Waynesburg, PA. Smith joined his regiment in Manilla in the Philippines on December 2, 1898, and fought at the battle of La Loma on 5 February 5, 1899, before coming back to the United States and being discharged on August 22, 1899, at the Presidio in San Francisco, California.[190] Smith returned home and worked as a bank examiner for the United States Department of Justice and died on March 5, 1955, in Pittsburgh, Pennsylvania.[191]

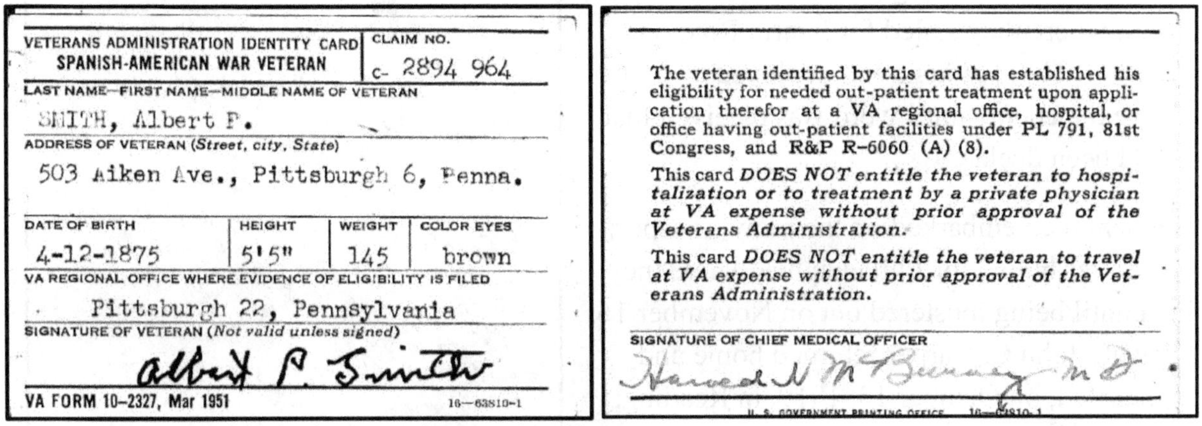
VETERANS ADMINISTRATION IDENTITY CARD
SPANISH-AMERICAN WAR VETERAN
CLAIM NO. C- 2894 964
LAST NAME—FIRST NAME—MIDDLE NAME OF VETERAN: SMITH, Albert P.
ADDRESS OF VETERAN (Street, city, State): 503 Aiken Ave., Pittsburgh 6, Penna.

DATE OF BIRTH	HEIGHT	WEIGHT	COLOR EYES
4-12-1875	5'5"	145	brown

VA REGIONAL OFFICE WHERE EVIDENCE OF ELIGIBILITY IS FILED: Pittsburgh 22, Pennsylvania
SIGNATURE OF VETERAN (Not valid unless signed): Albert P. Smith
VA FORM 10-2327, Mar 1951 16—63810-1

The veteran identified by this card has established his eligibility for needed out-patient treatment upon application therefor at a VA regional office, hospital, or office having out-patient facilities under PL 791, 81st Congress, and R&P R-6060 (A) (8).

This card *DOES NOT entitle the veteran to hospitalization or to treatment by a private physician at VA expense without prior approval of the Veterans Administration.*

This card *DOES NOT entitle the veteran to travel at VA expense without prior approval of the Veterans Administration.*

SIGNATURE OF CHIEF MEDICAL OFFICER: Harold N McBurney M.D.
U. S. GOVERNMENT PRINTING OFFICE 16—63810-1

Figure 102: Courtesy of Michael L. Strauss (Front and Back)

[190] Stewart, *Record of Pennsylvania Volunteers in the Spanish-American War, 1898*, 433-436, 480.
[191] *Pittsburgh Press*, March 6, 1955.

Letters, diaries, and journals can provide clues leading to information regarding the military service and unit where an ancestor served during any military conflict. Look at the letter below, dated July 4, 1898, from Camp Thomas near Chickamauga Park, Georgia. The author signs it, John C. Harper, who wrote to his father, Thomas G. Harper, living at 549 N. 9th Street in Reading, Pennsylvania. The return address on the envelope indicates that Harper served in Company A of the 4th Regiment of Pennsylvania Volunteer Infantry.

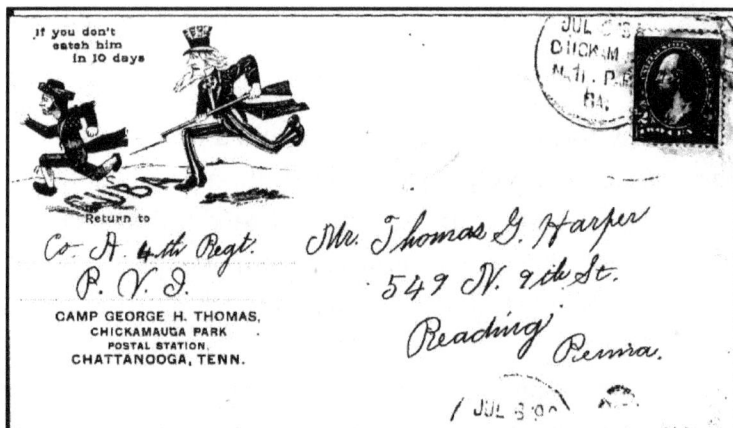

Figure 103: Courtesy of Michael L. Strauss

The 4th Pennsylvania Infantry was called up for duty pursuant to General Order No. 7 of the Adjutant General Office of Pennsylvania on April 28, 1898. Harper enlisted in the regiment two months later June 15, 1898, in Reading, PA. He joined the his new regiment at Chickamauga Park, GA regiment, and wrote his father, Thomas Harper, on July 4, 1898.

Three weeks later, his regiment broke camp, being sent first to Rossville, Georgia, and then to Newport News, VA, where they sailed for Puerto Rico on July 27, 1898. The regiment was deployed to find and engage the enemy until word was received that a truce had been declared.

The regiment then embarked on the army transport *City of Chester* bound for Philadelphia, where they remained until being mustered out on November 16, 1898. Private John C. Harper returned home and died, unmarried, on October 13, 1919, in Reading, Pennsylvania.[192]

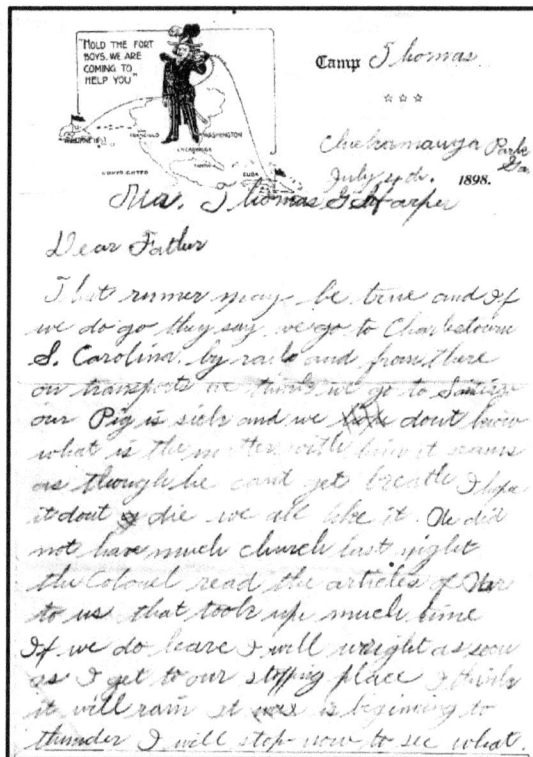

Figure 104: Courtesy of Michael L. Strauss

---

[192] Stewart, *Record of Pennsylvania Volunteers in the Spanish-American War, 1898*, 157-159, 177; *Reading Times*, October 15, 1919.

Benjamin M. Snow

Historical images and pictures of soldiers or civilians who lived through the Spanish-American War can provide personal information on family members where very little is known. Benjamin M. Snow was born in 1837 in Eastport, Maine, and moved to Massachusetts when he was young. He lived in Boston for many years, working in a theater as a stage manager and actor for the Bowdoin Square Theatre in downtown Boston. After the Spanish-American War, one of the more popular plays was called "Dewey" and named for the hero of the Battle of Manilla in the Philippines, Admiral George Dewey. Snow, who resembled Dewey, was cast as the main character in the play, which ran for several months. The *Boston Post* advertised the play at the theater with the below ad (dated February 16, 1902).[193] Snow died on November 9, 1912, in Boston, Massachusetts, and was buried in the Woodlawn Cemetery in Everett, MA.[194]

Figure 105: Courtesy of Michael L. Strauss

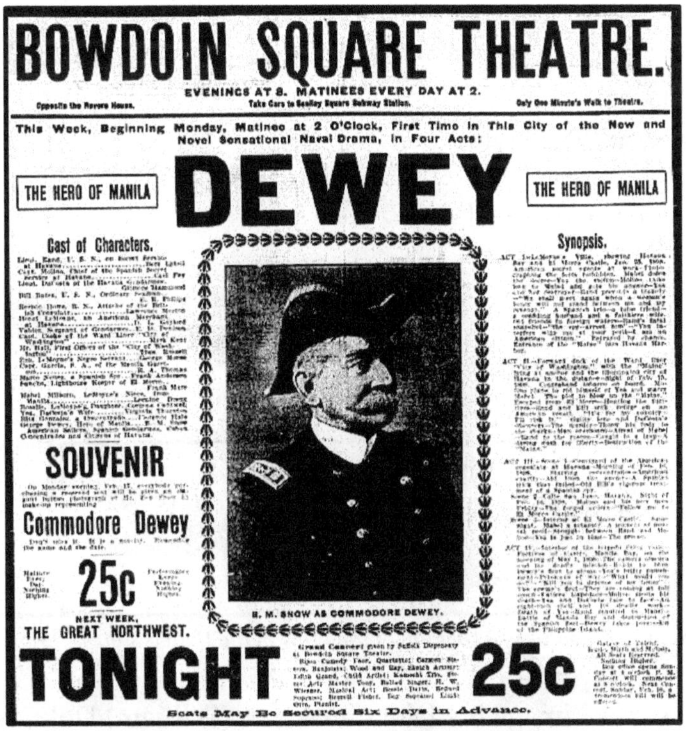

Figure 106: Courtesy of the Boston Post-1902.

GENEALOGY CLUE We may not realize the genealogical value of personal items in our own possession. However, items of military historical value can also be found online at eBay, Etsy, auction houses, or dealers who specialize in military antiques and surplus supplies where items purchased can be identified.

---

[193] *The Boston Post*, February 16, 1902.
[194] *The Boston Globe*, October 10, 1912.

Uniforms, Ranks and Insignia

Each of the military branches involved in the Spanish-American War (Army, Navy, Marine Corps, and Revenue Cutter Service) are examined. Their officer and enlisted rank structure and some major changes in the uniforms, rank structure, and insignia used are discussed. Both officers and enlisted personnel represent each of the branches.

United States Army

The United States Army uniform regulations for the period dating from 1882, 1889, and 1908 all contain details about the different ranks and insignia. Many changes occurred in the style of uniforms, hats, breeches, and colors indicating the branch of service in the Army.[195]

United States Army Officer Ranks

Lieutenant General
Major General
Brigadier General
Colonel
Lieutenant Colonel
Major
Captain
1st Lieutenant
2nd Lieutenant
Chaplain

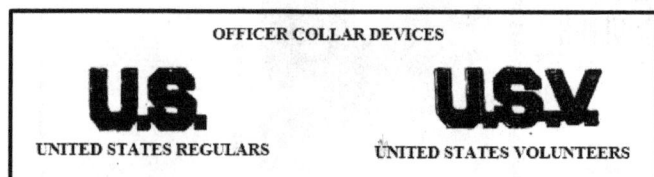

OFFICER COLLAR DEVICES

U.S.
UNITED STATES REGULARS

USV
UNITED STATES VOLUNTEERS

Figure 107: Courtesy of Uniform of the Army of the United States.   Figure 108: Courtesy of Michael L. Strauss

The above image is Major Guillermo (William) Dolz, who served as the Brigade Surgeon with the United States Army in Cuba. His collar device has the distinctive USV on both collars. This indicates he was a United States Volunteer officer. Dolz was appointed to New York on October 20, 1898, and discharged from the Army on April 5, 1899. He lived in Cuba after the end of the war and was later appointed the Governor of Pinar del Rio. He died on 7 November 1911 in Paris, France.[196]

---

[195] *Uniform of the Army of the United States, 1882*, (Philadelphia, PA: Thomas Hunter, 1882), 1-23; *The Uniform of the Army of the United States, 1908,* (Washington, DC: Government Printing Office, 1908), 1-129; Jerome A. Greene, *U.S. Army Uniforms and Equipment, 1889.* Reprint, (Lincoln, NE: University of Nebraska Press, 1986), 1-371 and William H. Emerson, *Encyclopedia of United States Army Insignia and Uniforms*, (Norman, OK: University of Oklahoma Press, 1996), 1-674.
[196] *The Evening Star*, April 3, 1899.

The image below shows officers' shoulder straps or boards during the Spanish-American War, the Boxer Rebellion, and the Philippine Insurrection. Each of the military ranks is displayed. The color of the strap was different for the type of service: general staff or staff wore dark blue, infantry wore white, artillery wore scarlet, and cavalry was yellow.[197]

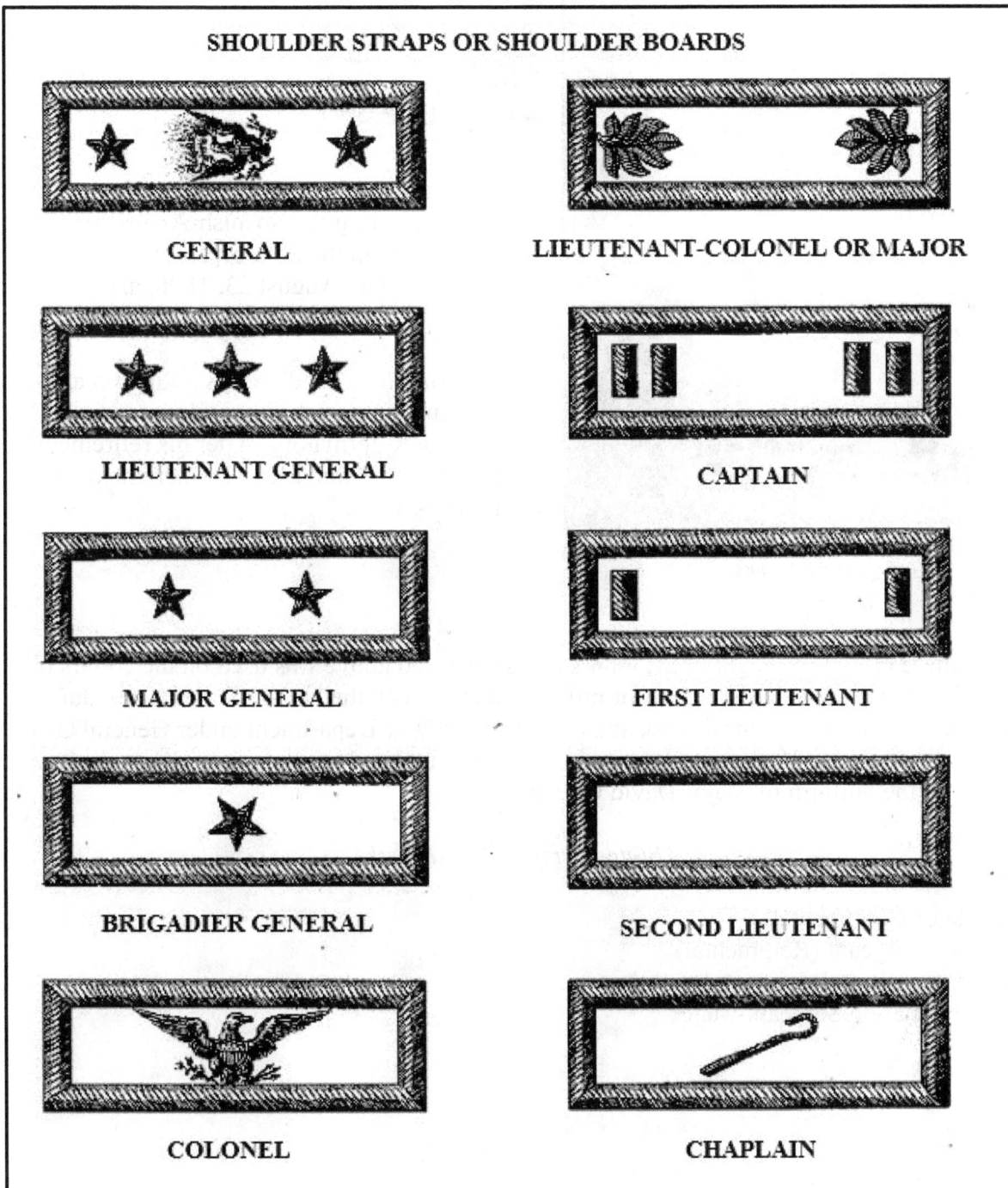

Figure 109: Courtesy of the Uniform of the Army of the United States, 1882.

---

[197] *Regulations and Decisions Pertaining to the Uniform of the Army of the United States*, (Washington, DC: Government Printing Office, 1897), 16-18.

The image at left is Major David C. Peyton, who served during the Spanish-American War with the Army in the 2nd Corps. He was commissioned on August 23, 1898, and discharged in 1899.

Peyton continued his duties as a surgeon after the war and later worked as superintendent of the Indiana Reformatory. After his retirement, he lived in Jeffersonville, IN, where he died on February 6, 1923.[198]

Figure 110: Courtesy of Michael L. Strauss

The tiny Maltese cross (or Knight of St. John's cross) pictured above was used on the collars of military officers who served as surgeons or military doctors with the United States Army during the Spanish-American War. This design, authorized by the War Department under General Order No. 39 issued August 18, 1896, was changed in 1904 with updated regulations and was the same design used on the uniform of Major David C. Peyton.[199]

United States Army Enlisted Ranks

Sergeant-Major (Regimental)
Quartermaster Sergeant (Regimental)
Commissary Sergeant (Regimental)
Squadron or battalion Sergeant-Major
Chief Musician
Chief Trumpeter
Principal Musician
Drum Major
Ordnance Sergeant

---

[198] *The Indianapolis News*, August 23, 1898; and February 6, 1923.
[199] *General Orders and Circulars: Adjutant General Office, 1896* (Washington, DC: Government Printing Office, 1897), 227-228 for General Order No. 39 issued 18 August 1896; and Emerson, *Encyclopedia of United States Army Insignia and Uniforms*, 180-181.

Quartermaster Sergeant (Post)
Commissary Sergeant (Post)
Hospital Steward
Acting Hospital Steward
Sergeant 1st Class of the Signal Corps
Sergeant of the Signal Corps
Corporal of the Signal Corps
First Class Private
Electrician Sergeant
First Sergeant
Troop, Battery, or Company Quartermaster Sergeant
Sergeant (Regimental or Battalion)
Lance Corporal
Cook
Farrier
Saddler
Mechanic and Artificer
First Class Gunner

Sergeant Major Frank W. Pullen-25th U.S. Infantry

Figure 111: Courtesy of Google Books

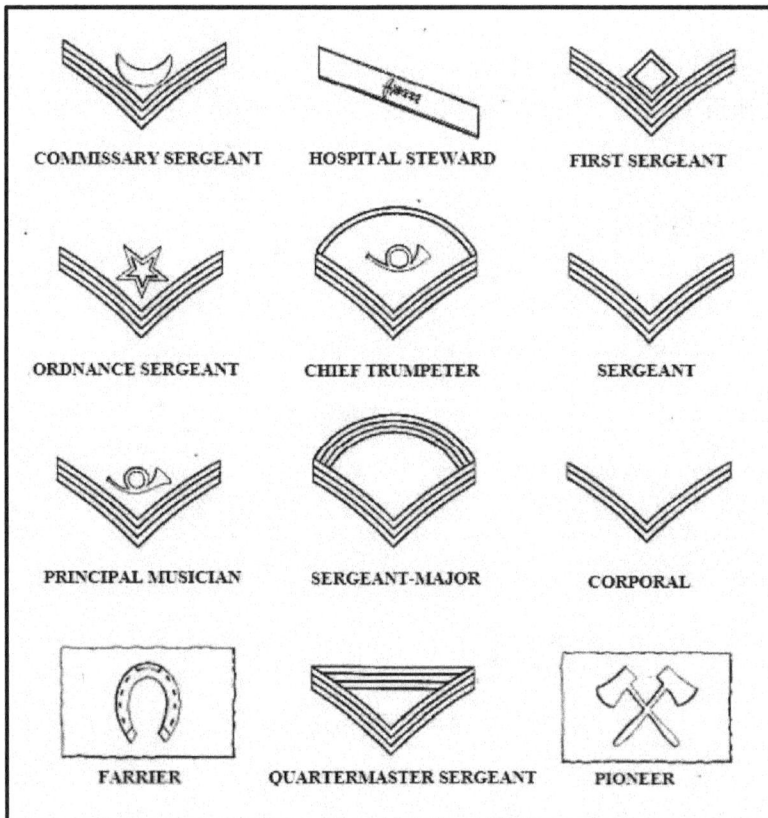

Figure 112: Courtesy of the Uniform of the Army of the United States, 1882.

The image to the left shows the enlisted rank chevrons used by the United States Army from 1872 to 1902, with small changes in the regulations.

The chevrons or ranks of the non-commissioned officers was to be worn on the uniform and blouse above the elbow, with the points down. Insignia was designed of cloth of the same color as the uniform in dark blue (with the exception of Hospital Steward of emerald green).

There have been few changes in the chevron style and ranks in the U.S. Army. Consult each of the aforementioned regulations from 1882, 1889, and 1908.[200]

---

[200] William K. Emerson, *Chevrons: Illustrated History and Catalog of U.S. Army Insignia* (Washington, DD: Smithsonian, 1983), 57-109.

The person at left is Elmer E. Lambert, who enlisted in the United States Army on April 19, 1898, in Concord, New Hampshire. He was assigned to Company F of the 22nd United States Infantry and later transferred to Company I of the 23rd United States Infantry. He was discharged with an excellent record on November 18, 1901, at Fort Logan, CO.

Figure 113: Courtesy of Michael L. Strauss

Lambert's kepi has displayed on top the emblem of crossed rifles (for infantry), above the number "22" for the 22nd United States Infantry, and below the letter "F" for Company F as this comes directly from the Army regulations.[201]

United States Navy

The uniforms and rank structure for the United States Navy was published in 1897 in the year before the start of the Spanish-American War and updated again in 1905. The later edition included several changes in the uniforms and ranks in the Navy.[202]

United States Navy Officer Ranks

Rear Admiral
Commodore
Captain
Commander
Lieutenant Commander

---

[201] *Regulations and Decisions Pertaining to the Uniform of the Army of the United States*, (Washington, DC: Government Printing Office, 897), 33.

[202] *Regulations Governing the Uniform of Commissioned Officers, Warrant Officers, and Enlisted Men of the Navy of the United States, 1897*, (Washington, DC: Government Printing Office, 1897). *Regulations Governing the Uniform of Commissioned Officers, Warrant Officers, and Enlisted Men of the Navy of the United States, 1905*, (Washington, DC: Government Printing Office, 1905), 13-178.

Lieutenant
Lieutenant Junior Grade
Ensign
Naval Cadet
Mate

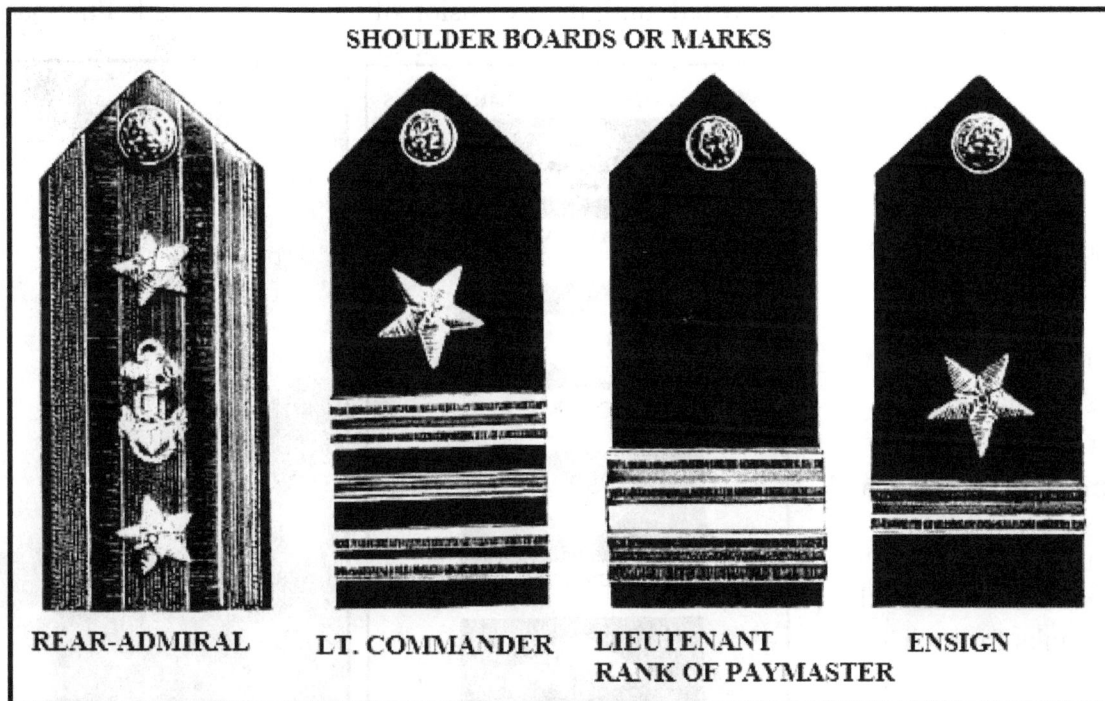

Figure 114: Navy Regulations of 1905.

The above examples of shoulder boards show four different ranks of commissioned officers in the United States Navy at this time. The Navy Paymaster held the equivalent rank of Lieutenant in the service during the time of the Spanish-American War.

United States Navy Officer Specialty Ranks

Surgeon, Assistant Surgeon
Paymaster (Lieutenant), or Assistant Paymaster (Ensign)
Chief Engineer, Engineer, Assistant Engineer
Chaplain
Naval Constructor, Assistant Naval Constructor
Professor of Mathematics, Civil Engineer
Secretary
Clerk, Clark to Paymaster

The history and origins of the ranks of Warrant Officers begin with the Continental Navy in 1775. Non-commissioned officers did not command a ship. Warrant Officers were expert seamen in the operation of the vessel. In recognition of this, the United States Navy issued warrants instead, giving way to the creation of warrant officers. From the end of the Civil War to 1898, four Warrant Officer ranks existed, until the expansion of the rank to include Pharmacist.

Boatswain
Gunner
Carpenter
Sailmaker
Pharmacist (Issued 1899)

The uniform to the right shows a Sailmaker in his Warrant Officer uniform sometime between 1899 and 1901.

The collar devices show the military ranks for each.

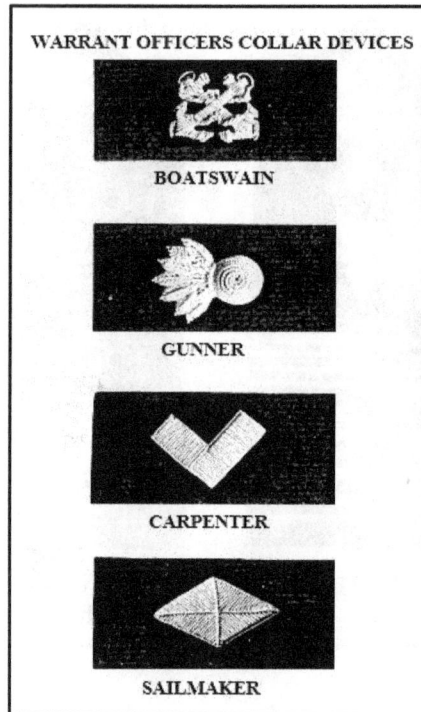

Figure 115: Navy Regulations of 1905.

Figure 116: Courtesy of Library of Congress

United States Navy Enlisted Ranks

The United States Navy in 1885 changed the organizational structure for enlisted military ranks and specialties. Under Navy regulation, three ranks of Petty Officers were created under three different classifications. This was changed in 1893 with the creation of the rank of Chief Petty Officer.[203]

Chief Petty Officers

Seaman Branch	Artificer Branch	Special Branch
Master-at-Arm	Machinists	Yeoman
Boatswains Mate	Carpenter Mate	Apothecaries

---

[203] *U.S. Navy Regulation Circular No. 41* Issued 8 January 1885. Secretary of the Navy; *U.S. Navy Regulation Circular No. 1* Issued 13 March 1893, creating the rank of Chief Petty Officer.

Gunners Mate
Gun Captain
Quartermaster

Bandmaster

Petty Officer First Class

Seaman Branch
Master-at-Arm
Boatswains Mate
Gunners Mate
Gun Captains
Quartermasters
Schoolmaster

Artificer Branch
Machinist
Boilermaker
Coppersmith
Blacksmith
Plumber and Fitters
Sailmakers
Carpenters Mate
Water Tender

Special Branch
Musician
Yeoman

Petty Officer Second Class

Seaman Branch
Master-at-Arm
Boatswains Mate
Gunners Mate
Gun Captains
Quartermasters

Artificer Branch
Machinist
Oiler
Carpenters Mates
Printers

Special Branch
Yeoman

Petty Officer Third Class

Seaman Branch
Master-at-Arm
Coxswains
Gunners Mate
Quartermasters

Artificer Branch
Carpenters Mate
Painters

Special Branch
Yeoman

Seamen First Class

Seaman Branch
Seamen Gunner
Seaman
Apprentice

Artificer Branch
Fireman

Special Branch
Musician

Seamen Second Class

Seaman Branch

Artificer Branch

Special Branch

Ordinary Seamen Apprentice	Fireman Shipwright Sailmaker	Musician Bugler

Seaman Third Class

Seaman Branch	Artificer Branch	Special Branch
Landsmen Apprentice	Coal Passer	Baymen

Messmen Branch

Stewards	Cooks	Cabin Stewards
Wardroom Stewards	Wardroom Cooks	Steerage Stewards
Steerage Cooks	Warrant Officer Stewards	Warrant Officer Cook
Ship Cook First Class	Ship Cook Second Class	Ship Cook 3rd Class
Mess Attendants		

Figure 117: Navy Regulations of 1905

Figure 118: Navy Regulations of 1905.

The above drawing on the left shows Master-at-Arms Chief Petty Officer with Petty Officer First Class Boatswain Mate (circa 1905) in the United States Navy. Above on the right are the chevrons of insignia for Navy Petty Officers, pointing down and sewn above the elbow on the right arm.[204] The specialty marks (or rating badges) are represented and sewn on the inside of the chevron to indicate the job performed in the United States Navy.[205]

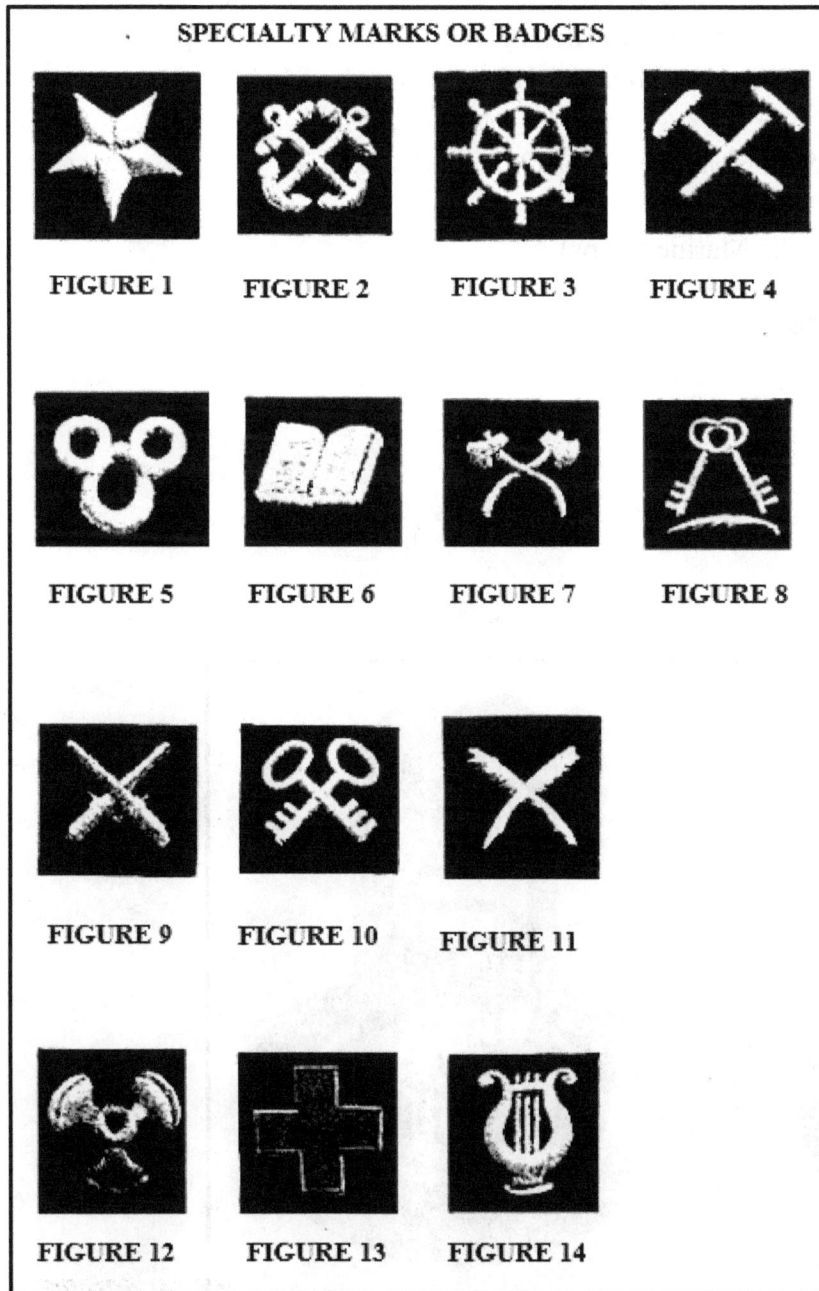

SPECIALTY MARKS OR BADGES

FIGURE 1 FIGURE 2 FIGURE 3 FIGURE 4

FIGURE 5 FIGURE 6 FIGURE 7 FIGURE 8

FIGURE 9 FIGURE 10 FIGURE 11

FIGURE 12 FIGURE 13 FIGURE 14

Figure 1 Master-at-Arms
Figure 2 Boatswain Mate
Figure 3 Quartermaster
Figure 4-Blacksmith or Fitter

Figure 5 Sailmaker Mate
Figure 6 Printer
Figure 7 Carpenter Mate
Figure 8 Turret Captain

Figure 9 Gunner Mate
Figure 10 Chief Yeoman
Figure 11 Yeomen

Figure 12 Electrician
Figure 13 Hospital Steward
Figure 14 Bandmaster

Figure 119: Navy Regulations of 1905

---

[204] *Regulations Governing the Uniform of Commissioned Officers, Warrant Officers, and Enlisted Men of the Navy of the United States, 1905*, (Washington, DC: Government Printing Office, 1905), 48-50.
[205] *Regulations Governing the Uniform of Commissioned Officers, Warrant Officers, and Enlisted Men of the Navy of the United States, 1905*, (Washington, DC: Government Printing Office, 1905, 167.

The uniforms and rank structure for the United States Marine Corps was published in 1892 in the years preceding the Spanish-American War and updated again in 1900. This latest publication was effective until 1904, 1908 and 1913 when additional changes were made in regulations.[206]

United States Marine Corps Officers Ranks

Brigadier General (Commandant of the Marine Corps)
Colonel (Commandant of the Marine Corps)
Colonel
Lieutenant Colonel
Major
Assistant Quartermaster
Captain
1st Lieutenant
2nd Lieutenant

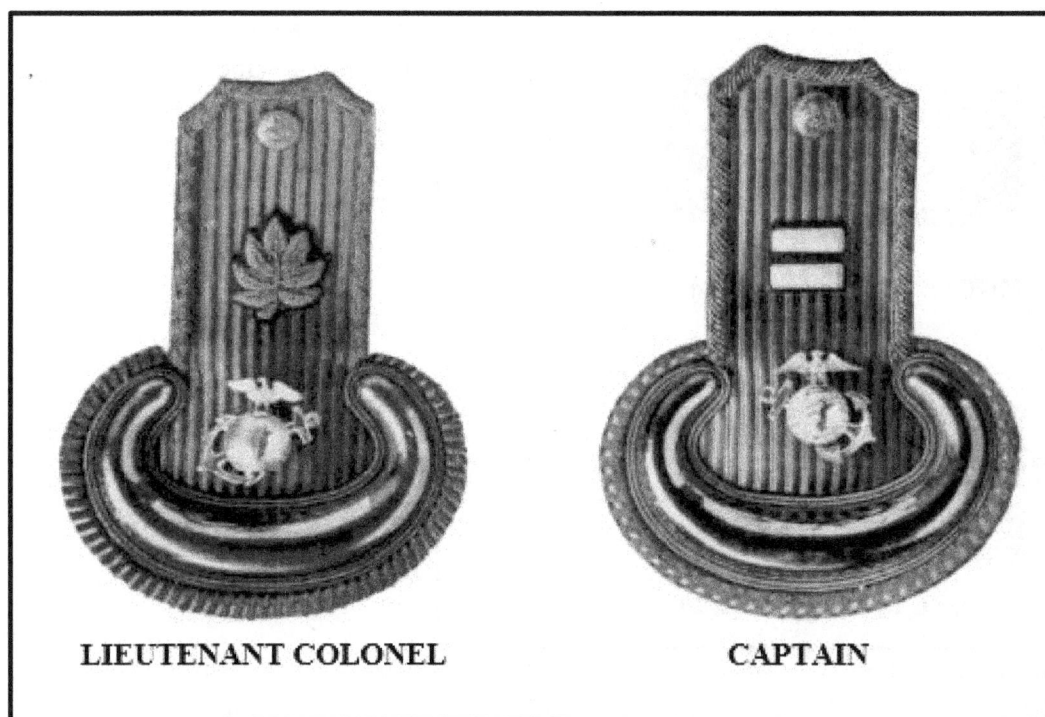

Figure 120: Courtesy of Uniform Regulations United States Marine Corps-1912.

---

[206] *Regulations for the Uniform of the United States Marine Corps*, (Washington, DC: Government Printing Office, 1892), 1-60; and *Regulations for the Uniform of the United States Marine Corps*, (Washington, DC: Government Printing Office, 1900), 1-50; Colonel John A. Driscoll, *The Eagle, Globe, and Anchor, 1868-1968*, (Washington, DC: United States Marine Corps, 1971), 19-31; and Preston B. Perrenot, *United States Marine Corps Grade Insignia Since 1775*, (Lexington, KY: Preston Perrenot, 2011), 1-35.

The rank insignia of enlisted personnel chevrons were to be borne on the uniform coat of yellow silk lace, with scarlet cloth to be worn on the sleeve above each of elbow. The chevrons are pointed up and the same design as the 1912 regulations.[207]

Sergeant-Major
Quartermaster Sergeant
Drum Major
First Sergeant
Gunnery Sergeant (After 1898)
Sergeant
Corporal
Drummer, Fifer
Private
Leader of the Band
Musician 1st Class
Musician 2nd Class
Musician 3rd Class

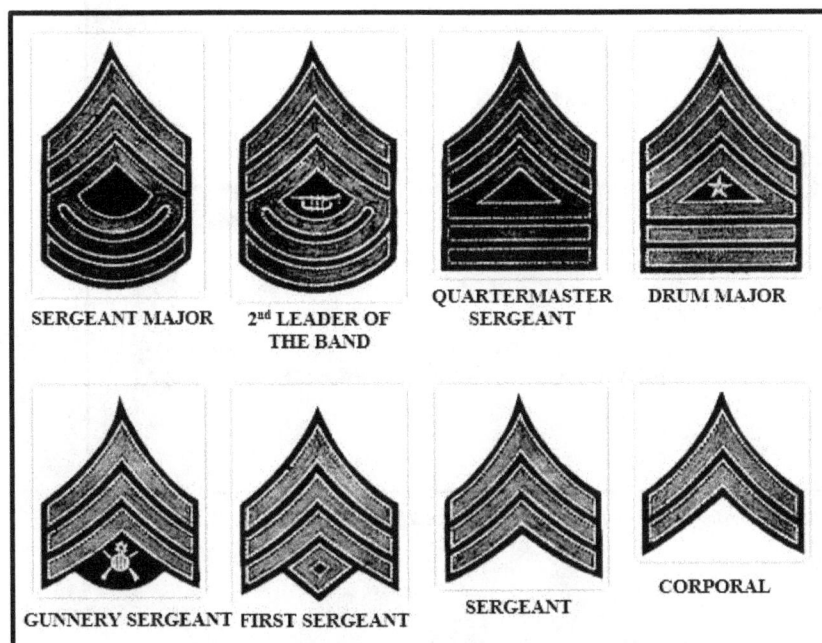

Figure 121: Courtesy of Uniform Regulations United States Marine Corps-1912.

---

[207] *Uniform Regulations United States Marine Corps: Together with Uniform Regulations Common to Both U.S. Navy and Marine Corps*, (Washington, DC: Government Printing Office, 1913), 204-210. Accessed on 3 October 2020 at: https://babel.hathitrust.org/cgi/pt?id=hvd.hnfj6m&view=1up&seq=4. Another excellent source comes from http://www.germandaggers.com/Gallery/USMk.php. Accessed on 7 October 1898 for reference sources.

The uniforms and rank structure were published in the years immediately preceding the Spanish-American War in 1891 and effective until 1908 when the regulations were changed reflecting the last changes before the formation of the United States Coast Guard in 1915.[208]

United States Revenue Cutter Service Officer Ranks

Captain
1st Lieutenant
2nd Lieutenant
3rd Lieutenant
Engineer

The shoulder ornaments of officers were worn as epaulets for all commissioned officers of two gold bullion for full dress. With overcoats the epaulets are not worn, while shoulder straps are worn on the shoulder with the appropriate corps and rank.

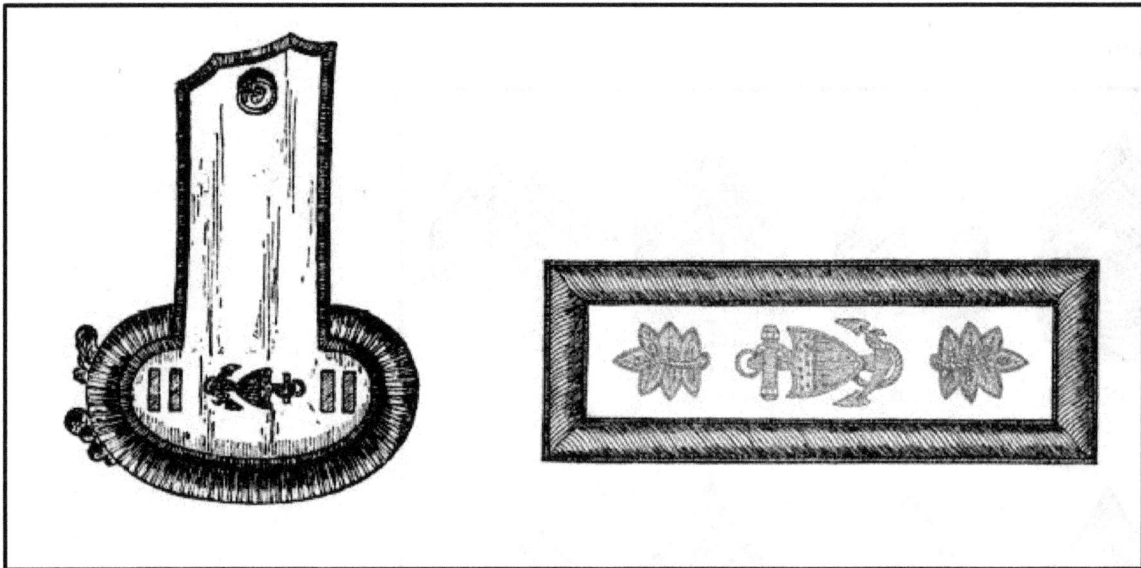

Figure 122: Regulations of Officers and Enlisted Men of the Revenue Cutter Service 1891

---

[208] *Regulations Governing the Uniforms of Officers and Enlisted Men of the United States Revenue Marine*, (Washington, DC: Government Printing Office, 1891), 1-30. Accessed on 29 September 2020 at: https://babel.hathitrust.org/cgi/pt?id=uiug.30112087939580&view=1up&seq=5; and *Regulations governing the Uniforms for Commissioned Officers, Warrant Officers, and Enlisted Men of the Revenue Cutter Service of the United States*, (Washington, DC: Government Printing Office, 1908), 5-27. Accessed on 29 September 2020 at: https://babel.hathitrust.org/cgi/pt?id=hvd.hx4n94&view=1up&seq=4.

The sleeve ornaments of officers are worn on each sleeve to represent each of the commissioned officer ranks for either the dress or overcoat uniform.

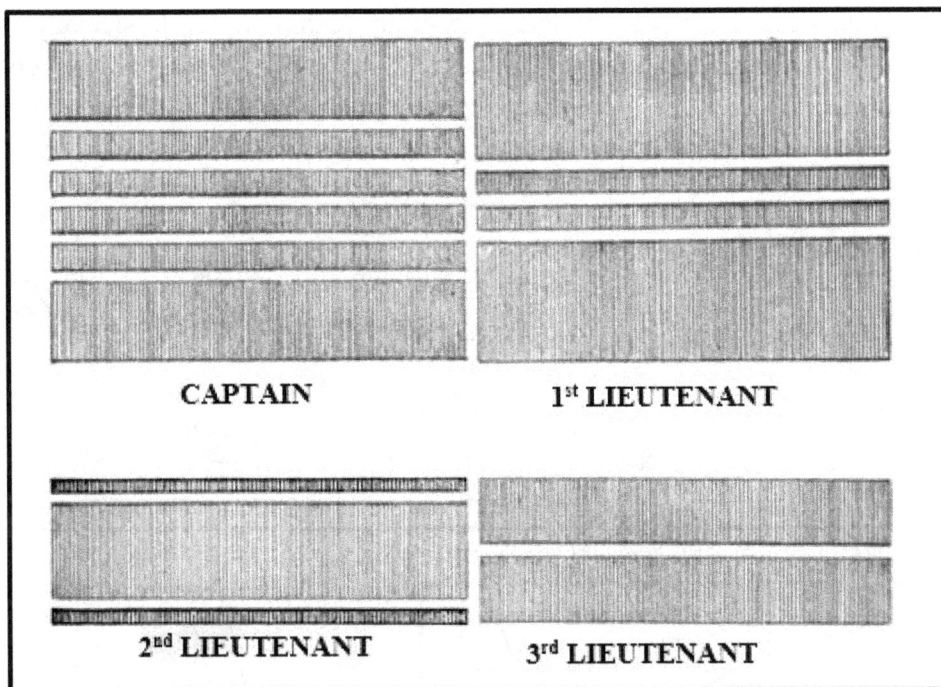

CAPTAIN   1st LIEUTENANT

2nd LIEUTENANT   3rd LIEUTENANT

Figure 123: Regulations of Officers and Enlisted Men of the Revenue Cutter Service 1891

United States Revenue Cutter Service Enlisted Ranks

First Class Petty Officers

Master-at-Arms (See figure 25)
Carpenter (See figure 24)
Gunner (See figure 23)
Boatswain (See figure 22)

Second Class Petty Officers

Quartermaster (See figure 32)
Coxswain (See figure 33)
Oiler (See figure 34)

Non-Petty Officer Status (No rating badges worn)

Seaman
Fireman
Coal Passers
Boys

The ratings badges of petty officers were worn on the outer garment. Different patterns were embroidered for 1st Class Petty Officers in gold on dark navy-blue cloth on the right sleeve between the shoulder and elbow. For 2nd Class Petty Officers, it was white silk on blue jackets or reversed with blue silk on white jackets, with the pattern worn around the cuffs of the overshirt (see drawings below).

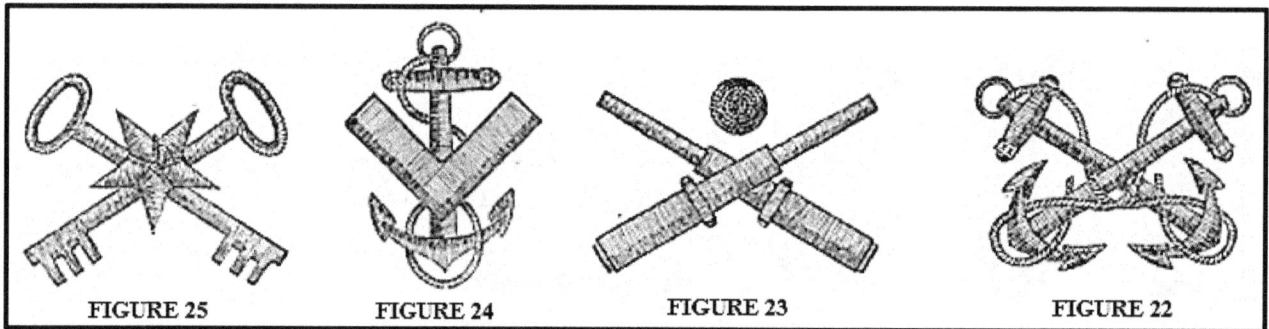

FIGURE 25   FIGURE 24   FIGURE 23   FIGURE 22

Figure 124: Regulations of Officers and Enlisted Men of the Revenue Cutter Service 1891

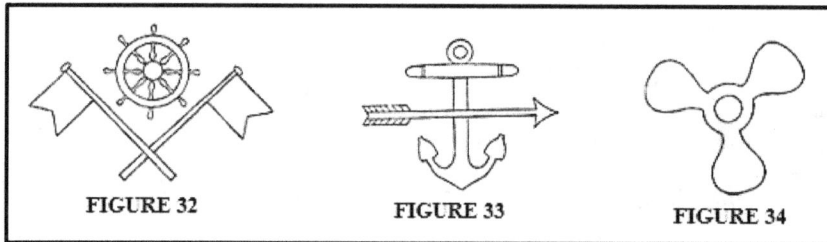

FIGURE 32   FIGURE 33   FIGURE 34

Figure 125: Regulations of Officers and Enlisted Men of the Revenue Cutter Service

Figure to the right is Petty Officer 1st Class Gunner.

DID YOU KNOW the 1st U.S. Volunteer Cavalry referred to as the "*Rough Riders*" and commanded by Lieutenant Colonel Theodore Roosevelt during the battle of San Juan Hill, were used as dismounted cavalry during the Cuba campaign and forced to leave their mounts behind in Florida?

Order of Battle and Losses

This military term dates back to medieval times and means the proximity of troops near their respective battlefield commanders. Later, Prussian general Carl von Clausewitz defined the "Order of Battle" as the drawing up of troops both before and during a battle campaign and the strengths and compositions of the units of command. This then evolved in the United States to include the breakdown of the command structure of corps, divisions, brigades, and regiments both on the field and campaigning including names of the commanders.[209]

First Army Corp-Commanded by Major General John R. Brooke[210]

First Division

First Brigade	Second Brigade	Third Brigade
1st OH Volunteer Infantry	4th OH Volunteer Infantry	16th PA Volunteer Infantry
3rd WI Volunteer Infantry	3rd IL Volunteer Infantry	2nd WI Volunteer Infantry
5th IL Volunteer Infantry	4th PA Volunteer Infantry	157th IN Volunteer Infantry

Second Division

First Brigade	Second Brigade	Third Brigade
31st MI Volunteer Infantry	158th IN Volunteer Infantry	2nd OH Volunteer Infantry
3rd PA Volunteer Infantry	1st WV Volunteer Infantry	14th MN Volunteer Infantry
160th IN Volunteer Infantry	6th OH Volunteer Infantry	1st PA Volunteer Infantry

Third Division

First Brigade	Second Brigade	Third Brigade
1st IL Volunteer Infantry	8th MA Volunteer Infantry	9th PA Volunteer Infantry
12th MN Volunteer Infantry	12th NY Volunteer Infantry	1st NH Volunteer Infantry
5th PA Volunteer Infantry	21st KS Volunteer Infantry	2nd MO Volunteer Infantry

---

[209] Colonel J.J. Graham Translator of *On War by General Carl Von Clausewitz* Volume 3, (London: K. Paul, Trench, Trubner & Co., 1908), 197, 240. Accessed 6 October 2022 at https://catalog.hathitrust.org/Record/007475596.

[210] *Correspondence relating to the War with Spain: Including the Insurrection in the Philippine Island and the China Relief Expedition* Volume 1. (Washington, DC: United States Government Printing Office, 1902), 509-519. The First Corps was headquartered at Camp George H. Thomas in Chickamauga Park, GA, under the command of Major General John R. Brooke, who was replaced by Major General James F. Wade on July 23, 1898, later commanded by Brigadier General Royal T. Frank, and finally Major General Joseph C. Breckinridge on 2 August 1898. Other regiments were replaced from 1898 to 1899, but the corps structure remained relatively unchanged.

Cavalry Brigade-Commanded by Colonel Melvin Grigsby[211]

3rd U.S. Volunteer Cavalry
1st IL Volunteer Cavalry
1st OH Volunteer Cavalry
Troops A and B, Kentucky Volunteer Cavalry

Second Army Corp-Commanded by Major General William M. Graham[212]

First Division

First Brigade	Second Brigade	Third Brigade
1st NJ Volunteer Infantry	6th IL Volunteer Infantry	13th PA Volunteer Infantry
7th OH Volunteer Infantry	6th MA Volunteer Infantry	12th PA Volunteer Infantry
65th NY Volunteer Infantry	8th OH Volunteer Infantry	8th PA Volunteer Infantry
9th OH Volunteer Infantry		

Second Division

First Brigade	Second Brigade	Third Brigade
159th IN Volunteer Infantry	6th PA Volunteer Infantry	1st RI Volunteer Infantry
22nd KS Volunteer Infantry	4th MO Volunteer Infantry	3rd MO Volunteer Infantry
3rd NY Volunteer Infantry	9th OH Volunteer Infantry	2nd TN Volunteer Infantry

Third Division[213]

First Brigade	Second Brigade
9th MA Volunteer Infantry	1st CT Volunteer Infantry
33rd MI Volunteer Infantry	3rd VA Volunteer Infantry
34th MI Volunteer Infantry	

---

[211] Ibid., 512-513. The cavalry brigade under the command of Colonel Melvin Grigsby was attached to the first army corps from June 30, 1898, to July 31, 1898, until reassigned.

[212] Ibid., 519-529. The Second Corps was organized at Camp Russell A. Alger near Falls Church, Virginia. Major General William M. Graham was placed in command and replaced by Major General Samuel B.M. Young on November 2, 1898. Military units were moved inside the divisional structure of the corps.

[213] Ibid., 519. The Third Division of the Second Army Corps was never fully constituted. On June 7, 1898, Brigadier General Francis L. Guenther was given command. No more than two brigades were added.

Third Army Corp-Commanded by Major General James F. Wade[214]

First Division

First Brigade	Second Brigade	Third Brigade
14th NY Volunteer Infantry	2nd NY Volunteer Infantry	1st VT Volunteer Infantry
1st MO Volunteer Infantry	2nd NE Volunteer Infantry	3rd TN Volunteer Infantry
5th MD Volunteer Infantry	1st DC Volunteer Infantry	8th NY Volunteer Infantry

Second Division

First Brigade	Second Brigade	Third Brigade
1st AR Volunteer Infantry	5th MO Volunteer Infantry	1st ME Volunteer Infantry
2nd KY Volunteer Infantry	2nd AR Volunteer Infantry	52nd IA Volunteer Infantry
9th NY Volunteer Infantry	69th NY Volunteer Infantry	1st MS Volunteer Infantry

Fourth Army Corp-Commanded by Major General John J. Coppinger[215]

First Division[216]

First Brigade	Second Brigade	Cavalry Brigade
1st U.S. Infantry	15th U.S. Infantry	2nd U.S. Cavalry
8th U.S. Infantry	16th U.S. Infantry	5th U.S. Cavalry
10th U.S. Infantry	69th NY Volunteer Infantry	
3rd U.S. Infantry	5th U.S. Cavalry	
20th U.S. Infantry	19th U.S. Infantry	
1st FL Volunteer Infantry		

---

[214] Ibid., 530-534. The Third Corps was organized at Camp George H. Thomas in Chickamauga Park, GA, on May 16, 1898, under the command of Major General James F. Wade. The corps consisted of only two divisions in strength, with Wade replaced by Brigadier General Royal T. Frank and later by Major General Joseph C. Breckinridge on August 2, 1898. Orders were made on August 28, 1898, and the corps was moved to Anniston, AL. It was reduced in size to one division strength. The Third Corps was discontinued on October 7, 1898, with some units mustering into the Fourth Corps.

[215] Ibid., 534-539. The Fourth Corps was organized at Mobile, AL, on April 15, 1898, under the command of Major General John J. Coppinger. After his retirement, Major General Joseph Wheeler was placed in command. Part of the corps was moved to Huntsville, AL, with other sections to Tampa, FL, and Miami, FL (due to transfer) to the seventh corps. In November 1898, Brigadier General Abraham K. Arnold relieved Wheeler, and Major General Henry W. Lawton replaced him. The corps was moved back to Anniston, AL, when the senior officer Brigadier General Royal T. Frank was in command, where on January 16, 1899, the corps was discontinued.

[216] Ibid., 535. Several of the regiments of the first division of the Fourth Corps were transferred to the Seventh Corps on June 27, 1898. The independent cavalry brigade under the command of Lt. Colonel Henry E. Noyes of the 2nd U.S. Cavalry was attached from May 31, 1898, to June 30, 1898.

Second Division

First Brigade	Second Brigade	Third Brigade
11th U.S. Infantry	2nd NY Volunteer Infantry	1st OH Volunteer Infantry
9th U.S. Infantry	1st DC Volunteer Infantry	3rd PA Volunteer Infantry
19th U.S. Infantry	5th MD Volunteer Infantry	157th IN Volunteer Infantry
		1st IL Volunteer Infantry

Third Division

First Brigade	Second Brigade
1st FL Volunteer Infantry	2nd GA Volunteer Infantry
5th OH Volunteer Infantry	3rd OH Volunteer Infantry
32nd MI Volunteer Infantry	69th NY Volunteer Infantry

Fifth Army Corp-Commanded by Major General William M. Shafter[217]

First Division

First Brigade	Second Brigade	Third Brigade
6th U.S. Infantry	10th U.S. Infantry	13th U.S. Infantry
16th U.S. Infantry	21st U.S. Infantry	9th U.S. Infantry
71st NY Volunteer Infantry	3rd U.S. Infantry	24th U.S. Infantry

Second Division

First Brigade	Second Brigade	Third Brigade
8th U.S. Infantry	4th U.S. Infantry	12th U.S. Infantry
22nd U.S. Infantry	1st U.S. Infantry	7th U.S. Infantry
2nd MA Volunteer Infantry	25th U.S. Infantry	17th U.S. Infantry

---

[217] Ibid., 539-547. The Fifth Corps was organized on April 15, 1898, with Brigadier General James F. Wade placed in command with several of regiments ordered to Tampa, FL. Major General William M. Shafter replaced Wade on April 29, 1898, to assume overall command. After some training and equipping, more troops were added to the command, and orders were received by telegraph on May 31, 1898, to proceed to Cuba. On June 8, 1898, the United States Army Transport Service arrived and started loading regiments of the corps totaling 815 officers, and 16,072 enlisted men sail to Cuba. The men arrived off Daiquiri, Cuba, on June 22, 1898, and continued to disembark over the next two days. The Fifth Corps was actively involved with the fighting on the island of Cuba and participated in several land engagements at Las Guasimas on 24 June 1898, El Caney on July 1, 1898, San Juan on July 1-3, 1898, and Santiago on July 3, 1898, which surrendered on July 17, 1898. This formally called for the ceasing of hostilities in Cuba and the withdrawal of troops to the United States. Between August 7-24, 1898, the troops were ferried back to the United States and Montauk Point, New York, with the corps being discontinued on October 7, 1898.

Cavalry Division

First Brigade	Second Brigade	Squadron
3rd U.S. Cavalry	1st U.S. Cavalry	Tr. A, C, D, F 2nd U.S. Cav.
6th U.S. Cavalry	10th U.S. Cavalry	
9th U.S. Cavalry		

Detached Troops[218]

Light Artillery Brigade	Engineers	Siege Artillery
1st U.S. Art. Batteries K&E	Co. C. Battalion	4th U.S. Art. Batteries G&H
2nd U.S. Art. Batteries F&A	Co. E. Battalion	5th U.S. Art. Batteries M&K
3rd U.S. Art. Batteries F&C		
4th U.S. Art. Batteries B&F		
5th U.S. Art. Batteries F&D		

Miscellaneous Troops
Balloon Detachment-U.S. Volunteers
Signal Corps 15th Company U.S. Volunteers
2nd U.S. Volunteer Engineers

Third Division

First Brigade	Second Brigade
3rd U.S. Infantry	1st IL Volunteer Infantry
20 U.S. Infantry	1st DC Volunteer Infantry
33rd MI Volunteer Infantry	9th MA Volunteer Infantry
	34th MI Volunteer Infantry
	8th OH Volunteer Infantry

Sixth Army Corp-Commanded by Major General James H. Wilson[219]

Officially organized with the issuing of General Order No. 36 on 7 May 1898 with Major General James H. Wilson directed to take command with headquarters to be located at Camp George H. Thomas in Chickamauga Park, GA. The corps was officially never constituted and discontinued with the issuing of General Order No. 163 on 7 October 1898.

---

[218] Ibid., 539-547. Several units divided into light artillery, engineers, siege artillery, along with a balloon detachment and signal corps unit were all sent to Cuba to fight with the Fifth Corps as support elements.
[219] *Report of the Commission Appointed by the President to Investigate the Conduct of the War Department in the War with Spain*, (Washington, DC: Government Printing Office, 1900), 256-257; and *General Orders and Circulars: Adjutant General Office, 1896* (Washington, DC: Government Printing Office, 1897), 388-391.

Seventh Army Corp-Commanded by Major General Fitzhugh Lee[220]

First Division

First Brigade	Second Brigade	Third Brigade
3rd OH Volunteer Infantry	1st FL Volunteer Infantry	
5th OH Volunteer Infantry	32nd MI Volunteer Infantry	
1st TX Volunteer Infantry	2nd AL Volunteer Infantry	
1st LA Volunteer Infantry	1st OH Volunteer Infantry	
1st AL Volunteer Infantry	2nd TX Volunteer Infantry	
	2nd LA Volunteer Infantry	
	4th U.S. Volunteer Infantry	

Second Division

First Brigade	Second Brigade	Third Brigade
1st NC Volunteer Infantry	1st WI Volunteer Infantry	2nd VA Volunteer Infantry
2nd IL Volunteer Infantry	50th IA Volunteer Infantry	4th VA Volunteer Infantry
2nd NJ Volunteer Infantry	4th IL Volunteer Infantry	49th IA Volunteer Infantry

Third Division

First Brigade	Second Brigade	Detached Command
2nd MS Volunteer Infantry	4th IL Volunteer Infantry	2nd U.S. Volunteer Engineers
2nd U.S. Volunteer Cavalry	6th MO Volunteer Infantry	1st ME Artillery Battalion
3rd NE Volunteer Infantry	2nd SC Volunteer Infantry	2nd U.S. Volunteer Engineers
1st SD Volunteer Infantry		

Detached Command

1st ME Artillery Battalion	Hospital Corps Battalion
1st U.S. Signal Corps Volunteers	2nd U.S. Artillery Battalion
2nd U.S. Volunteer Engineers	7th U.S. Cavalry (First Squadron)

---

[220] *Correspondence relating to the War with Spain: Including the Insurrection in the Philippine Island and the China Relief Expedition* Volume 1. (Washington, DC: United States Government Printing Office, 1902), 547-555. On May 16, 1898, the Seventh Corps assigned commanding officers and officially was organized on May 27, 1898, with Major General Fitzhugh Lee placed in command in Tampa, FL. After training the corps was ordered to Savannah, GA on October 8, 1898. The United States War Department issued General Order No. 184 on December 13, 1898, which ordered the Seventh Corps to Havana, Cuba, for occupation duty. The corps stayed in Cuba through February 1899, when it was ordered back to the United States to be discontinued on May 1, 1899.

Eighth Army Corp-Commanded by Major General Wesley Merritt[221]

Second Division

First Brigade	Second Brigade	Third Brigade
23rd U.S. Infantry	18th U.S. Infantry	4th U.S. Cavalry Troop F&H
14th U.S. Infantry	4th U.S. Cavalry	22nd U.S. Infantry
6th U.S. Artillery	Company A. Engineers	24th U.S. Infantry (8 Cos.)
9th U.S. Infantry	1st CO Volunteer Infantry	21st U.S. Infantry
12th U.S. Infantry	1st NE Volunteer Infantry	
Astor Battery	2nd OR Volunteer Infantry	
	6th U.S. Artillery Batteries D&G	
	10th PA Volunteer Infantry	
	1st CA Volunteer Infantry	
	13th MN Volunteer Infantry	
	1st WY Volunteer Infantry	
	3rd U.S. Artillery Batteries G, H, K, and L	
	Utah Volunteer Artillery-Batteries A&B	

Visayan Military District

6th U.S. Artillery Battery G.
18th U.S. Infantry
6th U.S. Infantry
23rd U.S. Infantry Companies A, I, K, and M
19th U.S. Infantry Companies A, C, E, H, I, K, L, and M

Post of Jolo, Jolo, Philippines

23rd U.S. Infantry

District of Cavite, Luzon Philippines

6th U.S. Artillery Battery B
13th U.S. Infantry Company I.

Not Assigned

24th U.S. Infantry C, E, G, L
Company A. Engineers
Companies E&F Signal Corp

---

[221] Ibid., 556-579. The Eighth Corps was organized as forces comprising the Philippine expedition and constituted on June 21, 1898, with the issuing of General Order No 73 with command given to Major General Wesley Merritt. The Corps has only one division when organized. Major General Elwell S. Otis was then ordered to assume command from General Merritt once the troops arrived in Manilla, Philippines, on July 25, 1898. The Corps participated in the battle of Manilla on August 14, 1898, defeating the Spanish. With their defeat and surrender, the United States turned to occupational duty in the Philippines by forming military districts on the islands. Afterward, they began fighting with the local Tagalog inhabitants in what became known as the Philippine Insurrection from 1899-1902. Although officially discontinued on April 13, 1900, with the issuing of General Order No. 49, the Eight Corps no longer operated but continued units served until 1902 before being withdrawn.

Genealogical interest is growing about events that unfolded in 1898 and, along with it, a desire to learn more about the 280,000 soldiers, sailors, and marines who served (of which 2,061 died from various causes). The United States Government recorded the number of participants and the losses that were suffered during both the Spanish-American War, Boxer Rebellion, and the Philippine Insurrection. One of the most reliable sources comes from *Francis B. Heitman's Historical register and dictionary of the United States Army, from its organization, September 29, 1789, to March 2, 1903.* [222] Losses are recorded in Volume 2 and available digitized online at *Hathi Trust*: https://catalog.hathitrust.org/Record/000334097.

The total losses of men killed or wounded during the Spanish-American War are recorded. Numbers are kept for volunteer units in the United States Army and separated by officers and enlisted. The title of the booklet is "*Statistical Exhibit of Strength of Volunteer Forces Called into Service During the War with Spain; with Losses from all Causes*" digitized and available online at the Connecticut State Library at:

Figure 126: Courtesy of Google Books

Sherd, Rinaldo K	Pvt. Co. H 34 Mich Inf	Died	7-29-98	Cuba
Sheridan, John R	Pvt. Co. G 1 Ill V Inf	Died	9-1-98	NY
Sherman, William D	Capt. Co. K 22 Kan V Inf	Died	8-9-98	Va.
Sherman, William H	Pvt. Co. E 34 Inf	Died	4-12-00	PI
Stultz, Sherman	Pvt. Co. B 159 Ind Inf	Died	8-28-98	
Sherrer, John	Pvt. Co. G 20 Kan Inf	Killed	3-27-99	
Shetleroe, Slonions	Pvt. Co. L 6 O V Inf	Died	9-14-98	O
Sherman, William H	Art Co. E 34 V Inf	Died	4-12-00	PI
Shields, George	Pvt. Co. H 7 US V Inf	Died	7-1-98	Cuba
Shipp, William E	1st Lt. - 10 US Cav	Died	7-1-98	Cuba
Shipman, Carl E	Pvt. Co. B 2 Wis Inf	Died	7-30-98	SC
Shinn, John A	Pvt. Co. H 3 Va Inf	Died	11-16-98	Va
Shilling, Geo F	Cpl. Co. G 1 DC Inf	Died	9-22-98	NY
Shields, Thomas C	2nd Lt. Co. C 1 Miss Inf	Died	10-27-98	Miss
Shields, Edward A	Sgt. Co. C 32 Mich Inf	Died	9-16-98	Fla
Shilling, Fred	Pvt. Co. D 8 NY Inf	Died	8-23-98	Ga

Figure 127: Courtesy of Connecticut State

https://cslib.contentdm.oclc.org/digital/collection/p4005coll11/id/819.

Another sources for casualties during the Spanish-American War and the Philippine Insurrection was published in 1958 by Clarence S. Peterson from Baltimore, MD. He compiled a listing of all known deaths for both wars which is titled *Known military dead during the Spanish-American War and the Philippine Insurrection 1898-1901.* The book is digitized online at the Connecticut State Library: https://cdm16007.contentdm.oclc.org/digital/collection/p267401ccp2/id/3306 and also available on Ohio Memory: https://ohiomemory.org/digital/collection/p267401ccp2/id/3306.

---

[222] Francis B. Heitman, *Historical Register and Dictionary of the United States Army from its Organization, September 29, 1789 to March 2, 1903* Volume 2, (Washington, DC: Government Printing Office, 1903), 287-297.

The above photograph and entry show 1st Lieutenant William E. Shipp of the 10th United States Cavalry, who was killed at the battle of San Juan Hill on July 1, 1898.

The United States Navy had casualty reports covering 1776-1941, including deaths due to enemy action, drownings, wrecked ship casualties, and deaths caused by accidents. These reports are available on Fold3 at https://www.fold3.com/title/808 and are broken down by subseries and are browsable.

GENEALOGY TIP When researching your military ancestor, consider illustrating a timeline of what important historical events happened during their time while in the service. Adding historical facts, dates, and places will make it easier to see the holes.

End of Chapter Extras

At the end of each chapter, listed randomly is one of four ending chapter extras that offer clues, tools, tips, and fun facts on the period of the Spanish-American War.

GENEALOGY CLUE

Clues to specific record sets or sources for research.

GENEALOGY TOOL

Programs, databases, or other useful sources of information.

GENEALOGY TIP

Special tips to help you find your ancestors more effectively.

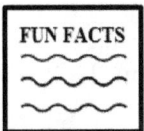

DID YOU KNOW

Interesting facts surrounding the Spanish-American War time period.

Selected Bibliography

Published Primary Sources

Annual Report of the Adjutant General of the State of New York for the Year 1897. Albany: New York State Printer, 1897.

Annual Reports, War Department. Report of the Secretary of War to the President 1922. Washington, DC: Government Printing Office, 1920.

Annual Reports, War Department. Report of the Secretary of War to the President 1922. Washington, DC: Government Printing Office, 1922.

Baugh, Virgil E. *Preliminary Inventories of the National Archives of the United States*. Records of the Bureau of Naval Personnel. No. 123. In Record Group 24. Washington, DC: National Archives and Records Administration, 1960.

Caemmerer, H.P. *Washington the National Capital*. Washington, DC: Government Printing Office, 1932.

CIS Index to Presidential Executive Orders & Proclamations. Washington, DC: Congressional Information Services, Inc., 1987.

Compilations of General Orders Circulars and Bulletins of the War Department Issued between February 15, 1881, and December 31, 1915. Washington, DC: Government Printing Office, 1916.

Fifteenth Census: Instructions to Enumerators, Population and Agriculture. Washington, DC: U.S. Government Printing Office, 1930.

General Orders and Circulars, War Department, 1909. Washington, DC: United States Government Printing Office, 1910.

Johnson, Maizie. *Preliminary Inventory NM-81, Preliminary Inventory of the Records of the Office of the Quartermaster General*. Washington, DC: National Archives and Records Administration, 1967.

_____. *Records of the United States Marine Corps*. National Archives Inventory, RG127. Washington DC: National Archives and Records Administration, 1970.

Laws of the States of New York passed at the one hundred and fortieth session of the Legislature. Albany: J.B. Lyon Company, 1917.

Record of Movements: Vessels of the United States Coast Guard 1790-December 31, 1933. Washington DC: U.S. Coast Guard Headquarters, 1989.

Regulations and Decisions Pertaining to the Uniform of the Army of the United States. Washington, DC: Government Printing Office, 1897.

Report of the Commission Appointed by the President to Investigate the Conduct of the War Department in the War with Spain. Washington, DC: Government Printing Office, 1899.

Report of the Commission Appointed by the President to Investigate the Conduct of the War Department in the War with Spain. Washington, DC: Government Printing Office, 1900.

Roster and Record of Iowa Soldiers of the Mexican War, Indian Campaigns, War of the Rebellion, and the Spanish-American and Philippine Wars. Des Moines: Emory H. English State Printer, 1911.

Sixteenth Decennial Census of the United States: Instructions to Enumerators. Washington, DC: Department of Commerce-Bureau of the Census, 1940.

The Statutes at Large of the United States of America, 1897-1899, 55th Congress, Session II, Resolutions Washington, DC: Government Printing Office, 1899.

Twelfth Census of the United States: Instructions to Enumerators. Washington, DC: U.S. Government Printing Office, 1900.

The United States Revenue Cutter Service in the War with Spain, 1898. Washington, DC; Government Printing Office, 1899.

Two Hundred Years of U.S. Census Taking: Population and Housing Questions, 1790-1990. Washington, DC: U.S. Government Printing Office, 1989.

Published Secondary Sources

Alger, Russell Alexander. *The Spanish-American War.* New York, New York: Harper Brothers, 1901.

Allen R. Millett and Peter Maslowski. For the Common Defense: A Military History of the United States of America. New York: Free Press, 1994.

Astor, Gerald. *The Right to Fight: A History of African Americans in the Military.* Cambridge, Massachusetts: Perseus Books, 1998.

Bain, David H. *Sitting in Darkness: Americans in The Philippines.* Boston, Massachusetts: Houghton Mifflin, 1984.

Barnes, Mark R. *The Spanish-American War and the Philippine Insurrection, 1898-1902: An Annotated Bibliography.* New York, New York: Routledge Press, 2011.

Bartlett, Ichabod S. Ed. *History of Wyoming*. Chicago, Illinois: S.J. Clarke Publishing Company, 1918.

Barton C. Hacker and Margaret Vining. *A Companion to Women's Military History*. Boston: Brill, 2002.

Brewster, Claire. "Women and the Spanish-American Wars of Independence: An Overview". *Feminist Review: Latin America: History, War and Independence* 79 (2005): 20-35.

Brown, Jerold E. *Historical Dictionary of the U.S. Army*. Westport: Greenwood Press, 2001.

Callahan, Edward W. *List of Officers of the Navy of the United States and the Marine Corps from 1775-1900*. New York, New York: L.R. Hamersly & Company, 1901.

Christine Compston and Rachel F. Seidman Editors, *Our Documents: 100 Milestone Documents from the National Archives*. New York: Oxford University Press, 2003.

CIS Index to Presidential Executive Orders & Proclamations. Washington, DC: Congressional Information Services, Inc., 1987

Clodfelter, Michael. *Warfare and Armed Conflicts: A Statistical Encyclopedia of Casualty and Other Figures, 1492-2015*. Jefferson: McFarland & Company, 2017.

Coats, Stephen D. *Gathering at the Golden Gate: Mobilizing for the War in the Philippines, 1898*. Ft. Leavenworth: Combat Studies Institute Press, 2006.

Coffman, Edward M. *The Old Army: A Portrait of the American Army in Peacetime, 1784-1898*. New York, New York: Oxford University Press, 1986.

_____. *Regulars: The American Army, 1898-1941*. Cambridge, Massachusetts: Harvard University Press, 2007.

Cohen, Paul A. Cohen. *History in Three Keys: The Boxers as Event, Experience and Myth*. New York: Columbia University Press, 1997.

Cohen, Stan. *Images of the Spanish-American War, April-August 1898*. Missoula: Pictorial Histories Publishing Company, 1997.

Cosmas, Graham A. *An Army for Empire: The United States in the Spanish-American War*. Shippensburg, Pennsylvania: White Mane Publishing, 1994.

Emerson, William K. *Chevrons: Illustrated History and Catalog of U.S. Army Insignia*. Washington, DC: Smithsonian, 1983.

_____. *Encyclopedia of United States Army Insignia and Uniforms*. Norman, Oklahoma: University of Oklahoma Press, 1996.

Dyal, Donald H. *Historical Dictionary of the Spanish-American War*. Westport, Connecticut: Greenwood Press, 1996.

Field, Ron. *The Spanish-American War, 1898*. Washington DC: Brassey's, 1998.

Foster, Frank. *United States Army Medals, Badges, and Insignia*. Fountain Inn: MOA Press, 2011.

Funston, Frederick. *Memories of Two Wars: Cuban and Philippine Experiences*. Lincoln, Nebraska: University of Nebraska Press, 2009.

Glasson, William. *Federal Military Pensions in the United States*. New York, New York: Oxford University Press, 1918.

Greene, Jerome A. *U.S. Army Uniforms and Equipment, 1889*. Lincoln, Nebraska: University of Nebraska Press, 1986.

Hael D. Doubler and John W. Listman Jr. *The National Guard: An Illustrated History of America's Citizen Soldiers*. Washington, DC: Brassey's Inc., 2003.

Hamersly, Lewis R. *The Records of Living Officers of the U.S. Navy and Marine Corps*. New York: L.R. Hamersly and Company, 1898.

Heitman, Francis B. *Historical register and dictionary of the United States Army, from its organization, September 29, 1789, to March 2, 1903*. vol 2. Washington DC: Government Printing Office, 1903.

Holbrook, Franklin F. *Minnesota in the Spanish-American War and the Philippine Insurrection*. St. Paul: Minnesota War Records Commission, 1923.

Janney, Caroline E. *Remembering the Civil War: Reunion and the Limits of Reconciliation*. Chapel Hill, North Carolina: University of North Carolina Press, 2013.

Johnson, Edward A. *History of Negro Soldiers in the Spanish-American War and other Items of Interest*. Raleigh: Capital Printing Company, 1899.

Kelley, Thomas E. *The U.S. Army and the Spanish-American War era, 1895-1910*. Carlisle, Pennsylvania: U.S. Army Military Research Collection, 1974.

Kerrigan, Evans E. *American War Medals and Decorations*. New York, New York: The Viking Press, 1971.

Klingenberg, Mitchell G. *Lessons in Coalition Warfighting from the Boxer Uprising*. Carlisle: War College Press, 2023.

Lainhart, Ann S. *State Census Records*. Baltimore: Genealogical Publishing Company, 1992.

Langellier, John. *U.S. Armed Forces in China, 1856-1941*. New York: Osprey Publishing, 2012.

Larry B. Maier and Joseph W. Stahl. *Identification Discs of Union Soldiers in the Civil War: A Complete Classification Guide and Illustrated History*. Jefferson: McFarland and Company, 2008.

Leroy, James A. *The Americans in the Philippines: A History of the Conquest and the First Years of Occupation*. New York, New York: AMS Press, 1970.

Lerwill, Leonard L. *The Personnel Replacement System in the United States Army (Washington, DC: United States Army Center for Military History*, 1988.

Linn, Brian McAllister. *The Philippine War, 1899-1902*. Lawrence: University Press of Kansas, 2000.

_____. *The U.S. Army and Counterinsurgency in the Philippines War, 1899-1902*. Chapel Hill, North Carolina: University of North Carolina Press, 1989.

Mabey, Charles R. *The Utah Batteries: A History*. Salt Lake City: Daily Reporter Company, 1900.

Marines in the Spanish-American War, 1895-1899: Anthology and Annotated Bibliography. Washington, DC: History and Museums Division, U.S. Marine Corps, 1998.

Marvin A. Kreidberg and Merton G. Henry. *History of Military Mobilization in the United States Army, 1775-1945*. Washington DC: U.S. Government Printing Office, 1955.

Maslowski, Peter. *For the Common Defense: A Military History of the United States of America*. New York, New York: Free Press, 1994.

McConnell, Stuart C. *Glorious Contentment: The Grand Army of the Republic, 1865-1900*. Chapel Hill, North Carolina: University of North Carolina Press, 1992.

Miller, Nathan. *The U.S. Navy a History*. Annapolis: Naval Institute Press, 1997.

Miller, Stuart Creighton. *Benevolent Assimilation: The American Conquest of the Philippines, 1899-1903*. Westford: Yale University Press, 1982.

Millett, Allan R. *Semper Fidelis: The History of the United States Marine Corps*. New York, New York: The Free Press, 1991.

Mills, Karen M. *Americans Overseas in U.S. Censuses*. Washington, DC: U.S. Government Printing Office, 1993.

Musicant, Ivan. *Empire by Default: The Spanish-American War and the Dawn of the American Century*. New York: Henry Holt and Company, 1998.

Neagles, James C. *U.S. Military Records: A Guide to Federal & State Sources, Colonial America to the Present*. Provo, Utah: Ancestry Publishing, 1994.

Noble, Dennis L. *Historical Register: U.S. Revenue Cutter Service Officers, 1790-1914*. Washington, DC: Coast Guard Historians Office, 1990.

Ostrom, Thomas P. *The United States Coast Guard and National Defense*. Jefferson: McFarland and Company, 2012.

_____. *United States Revenue and Coast Guard Cutters in Naval Warfare, 1790-1918*. Jefferson: McFarland and Company, 2018.

Patricia Taylor and Garry Ryan, *Preliminary Inventory of the Textual Records of the Office of the Surgeon General Army. RG112. Reprint*. Westminster: Heritage Books, 2001

Parsons, Henry. *Parsons Family: Descendants of Cornet Joseph Parson, 1626-1655*. New York: Frank Allaben Genealogical Company, 1912.

Peck, H.T. PhD. *The International Cyclopedia*. New York: Dodd, Mead and Company, 1899.

Peterson, Clarence S. *Known Military Dead during the Spanish-American War and the Philippine Insurrection, 1898-1901*. Baltimore, Maryland: C.S. Peterson, 1958.

Plante, Trevor K. *Military Service Records at the National Archives. Reference Information Paper 109*. Washington, DC: National Archives and Records Administration, 2007.

Polk, Ralph L. Lancaster City and County Directory for 1898. Philadelphia: R.L. Polk & Company Publishers, 1898.

Prego, Louis G. *The Battles of San Juan and El Caney or the Siege of Santiago*. Santiago: Heredia Alta, 1911.

Preston, Diana. *The Boxer Rebellion: The Dramatic Story of China's War on Foreigners that Shook the World in the Summer of 1900*. New York: Berkley Books, 2000.

Quesada, Alejandro de. *Roosevelt's Rough Riders*. New York: Osprey Publishing, 2012.

_____. *Spanish-American War and Philippine Insurrection, 1898-1902*. London, England: Osprey Publishing, 2012.

Risch, Erna. *Quartermaster Support of the Army: A History of the Corps, 1775-1939*. Washington, DC: Quartermaster Historian Office, 1962.

Robinson, Doane. *A Brief History of South Dakota*. New York: American Book Company, 1905.

_____. *History of South Dakota, vol 1*. Indianapolis: B.F. Bowen & Company, 1904.

Sexton, William T. *Soldiers in the Sun: An Adventure in Imperialism.* Harrisburg, Pennsylvania: Military Service Publishing Co. 1939.

Shearer, Benjamin F. *Home Front Heroes: A Biographical Dictionary of Americans During Wartime*, vol 2. Westport: Greenwood Press, 2007.

Shellum, Brian G. *Black Officer in a Buffalo Soldier Regiment: The Military Career of Charles Young.* Lincoln: University of Nebraska Press, 2010.

Silverstone, Paul H. *The New Navy, 1883-1922.* New York: Routledge, 2006.

Sledge, Michael. *Soldier Dead: How We Recover, Identify, Bury, and Honor our Military Fallen.* New York: Columbia University Press, 2005.

Spector, Ronald H. *Admiral of the New Empire: The Life and Career of George Dewey.* Baton Rouge: Louisiana State University Press, 1974.

Stathis, Stephen W. *Congressional Gold Medals, 1776-2002.* New York: Nova Science Publishers, 2003.

Steere, Edward. *The Graves Registration Service in World War II No. 21.* Washington, DC: United States Government Printing Office, 1951.

Sterner, Doris M. *In and Out of Harm's Way: A History of the Navy Nurse Corps.* Seattle: Navy Nurse Corps Association, 1997.

Steward, T.G. *Buffalo Soldiers: The Colored Regulars in the United States Army.* Mineola, New York: Dover Publications, Inc., 2014.

Stewart, Thomas J. *Record of Pennsylvania Volunteers in the Spanish-American War, 1898.* Harrisburg: William Stanley Ray, 1901.

Strait, Newton A. *Alphabetical List of Battles, 1754-1900: War of the Rebellion, Spanish-American War, Philippine Insurrection and all Old Wars with Dates.* Washington DC: Newton A. Strait, 1900.

Strecker, Mark. *Smedley D. Butler, USMC A Biography.* Jefferson: McFarland and Company, 2011.

Szucs, Loretto Dennis. *The Source: A Guidebook to American Genealogy.* Salt Lake City: Ancestry, 2006.

The Official Roster of Ohio Soldiers in the War with Spain. Columbus: Edward T. Miller, 1916.

The United States Revenue Cutter Service in the War with Spain, 1898. Washington, DC: Government Printing Office, 1899.

Trask, David F. *The War with Spain in 1898*. New York: MacMillan, 1981.

Tuccille, Jerome. *The Roughest Riders: The Untold Story of the Black Soldiers in the Spanish-American War*. Chicago: Chicago Review Press, 2015

Tucker, Spencer. *The Encyclopedia of the Spanish-American and Philippine Insurrection: A Political, Social, and Military History*. Denver, Colorado: ABC-CLIO, 2009.

Varney, George J. *A Gazetteer of the State of Maine*. Boston: B.B. Russell, 1881.

Venzon, Anne C. *The Spanish-American War: An Annotated Bibliography*. Volume 11 of Wars of the United States. New York: Garland Publishing, 1990.

Waddell, Steve R. *United States Army Logistics: From the American Revolution to 9/11*. Denver: Greenwood Publishing Group, 2011.

Warren, Michael S. *The National Guard in the Spanish-American War and Philippine Insurrection, 1898-1899*. Fort Leavenworth, Kansas: United States Army Command and General Staff College, 2012.

Werstein, Irving. *Turning Point for America: The Story of the Spanish-American War*. New York, New York: J. Messner, 1964.

Articles

Cunningham, Roger D. "An Experiment which may or may not turn out Well," *Journal of American History*, 10:4 (2005): 9-17.

Collins, Ross F. *Decorations and Medals of the U.S. Bureau of Naval Personnel Information Bulletin*, No. 318 (September 1943): 22-23.

Dautrich, Mabel E. "Fred C. Ainsworth: The Story of a Vermont Archivist". *Vermont History* 27 (January 1959): 22-23.

Gates, John Morgan "The Nature of the Anti-American Resistance Movement in the Philippines, 1899-1901." *The Journal of Asian Studies* 59:3 (2000): 619–640.

Graf, Mercedes. "Sister Nurses in the Spanish-American War". *Prologue: Quarterly of the National Archives* 34:3 (Fall 2002): 197-209.

_____. "Women Physicians in the Spanish-American War" *Army History* 56:1 (Fall 2002): 5-14.

Hirrel, Leo P. "The Beginnings of the Quartermaster Graves Registration Service" *Army Sustainment* 46:4 (July-August 2014): 64-67.

Hurt, James. "Sandburg's Lincoln within History" *Journal of the Abraham Lincoln Association* 20:1 (Winter 1999): 55-65.

Livingston, Rebecca. "Soldiers, Sailors, and Marines of the Spanish-American War: The Legacy of the USS Maine". *Prologue: Quarterly of the National Archives* 30:1 (Spring, 1998): 62-72.

Michael C. Robinson and Frank N. Schubert, "David Fagen: An Afro-American Rebel in the Philippines, 1899-1901" *Pacific Historical Review* 44:1 (February 1975): 68-83.

Mollan, Mark C. "The Army Medal of Honor: The First Fifty-Five Years" *Prologue: Quarterly of the National Archives.* 33:2 (Summer 2001): 128-139.

Peuser, Richard. "Documenting United States Naval Activities during the Spanish-American War". *Prologue: Quarterly of the National Archives.* 30:1 (Spring, 1998): 33-45.

Plante, Trevor K. "The National Home for Disabled Volunteer Soldiers" *Prologue: Quarterly of the National Archives* 36:1 (Spring 2004): 56-61.

_____. "New Glory to Its Already Gallant Record: The First Marine Battalion in the Spanish-American War" *Prologue: Quarterly of the National Archives* 30:1 (Spring 1998): 21-31.

_____. "Researching Service in the U.S. Army During the Philippine Insurrection". *Prologue: Quarterly of the National Archives* 32:2 (Summer 2000): 124-129.

_____. "The National Home for Disabled Volunteer Soldiers" *Prologue: Quarterly of the National Archives* 36:1 (Spring 2004): 56-61.

_____. "U.S. Marines in the Boxer Rebellion". *Prologue: Quarterly of the National Archives* 31:4 (Winter 1999): 284-289.

Prechtel-Kluskens, Claire. "Compiled Military Service Records Part I: The Records Inside the CMSR Jacket". *NGS Magazine* 38:1 (January-March 2012): 36-40.

_____. "Compiled Military Service Records Part II: The Records Outside the CMSR Jacket". *NGS Magazine* 38:2 (April-June 2012): 32-38.

_____. "Compiled Military Service Records Part III: The Record of Events" NGS Magazine 38:3 (July-September 2021): 32-35.

_____. "Compiled Military Service Records Part V: The Bookmark" *NGS Magazine* 41:1 (January-March 2015): 41-44.

_____. "Records for U.S. Military Veterans, Part I: Headstone Design" *NGS Magazine* 39:1 (January-March 2013): 28-31.

_____. "Thank You, General Fred C. Ainsworth," *NGS Magazine* 37:4 (October-December 2011): 54-57.

Ridgely, Randolph Jr. "The Coast Guard Cutter McCulloch at Manilla." *United States Naval Institute Proceedings*. 55 (May 1929): 417-426.

Wooley, Richard W. "A Short History of Identification Badges" *Quartermaster Professional Bulletin* (December 1988): 16.

Yockelson, Mitchell. "I Am Entitled to the Medal of Honor, and I Want It: Theodore Roosevelt and his Quest for Glory" *Prologue: Quarterly of the National Archives* 30 (Summer 1998): 7-19.

Newspapers

Abilene, KS: *Abilene Week Chronicle*

Abilene, KS: *Dickinson County News*

Austin, TX: *The Austin Daily Herald*

Baltimore, MD: *Baltimore Sun*

Bangor, ME: *The Bangor Times*

Boston, MA: *The Boston Globe*

Boston, MA: *The Boston Post*

Bridgeport, CT: *The Bridgeport Telegram*

Brooklyn, NY: *Brooklyn Daily Eagle*

Brooklyn, NY: *Brooklyn Times Union*

Buffalo, NY: *Buffalo Times*

Cumberland, MD: *Cumberland Evening Times*

Detroit, MI: *Detroit Free Press*

Harford, CT: *Hartford Courant*

Indianapolis, IN: *Indianapolis News*

Lancaster, PA: *Lancaster Examiner*

Lancaster, PA: *Lancaster New Era*

Lima, OH: *Lima News*

Los Angeles, CA: *Evening Express*

Memphis, TN: *The Commercial Appeal*

Newport News, VA: *The Daily Press*

New York, NY: *Army and Navy Journal*

New York, NY: *Harpers Weekly*

Oshkosh, WI: *Oshkosh Northwestern*

Owosso, MI: *Owosso Times*

Pittsburgh, PA: *Pittsburgh Post-Gazette*

Pittsburgh, PA: *Pittsburgh Press*

Poughkeepsie, NY: *Poughkeepsie Eagle-News*

Reading, PA: *Reading Times*

Salt Lake City, UT: *Salt Lake Herald*

San Francisco, CA: *San Francisco Call*

Springfield, MO: *Springfield Leader and Press*

Phoenix, AZ: *Arizona Republic*

Washington, DC: *The Evening Star*

www.ingramcontent.com/pod-product-compliance
Lightning Source LLC
Chambersburg PA
CBHW080239270326
41926CB00020B/4299